Essays on Modern Irish Literature

Edited by
John Strachan and Alison O'Malley-Younger

University of
Sunderland Press

© Pilar Villar Argáiz, Brian Burton, Ulf Dantanus, Peter Dempsey, Monica Facchinello, Eóin Flannery, Wei H. Kao, Paddy Lyons, Eamon Maher, Willy Maley, Alison O'Malley-Younger, Gareth Reeves, Daniel W. Ross, John Strachan

ISBN 978-1-873757-86-4

First Published 2007

Cover Design Lucas Swann
Copy edited by Felicity Hepburn

Published in Great Britain by
The University of Sunderland Press
in association with Business Education Publishers Limited
evolve Business Centre
Cygnet Way
Rainton Bridge Business Park
Houghton-le-Spring
Tyne & Wear
DH4 5QY

Tel: 0191 3055165
Fax: 0191 3055506

All rights reserved. No part of this publication may be reproduced, stored in a retrieval system, or transmitted, in any form or by any means, electronic, mechanical, photocopying, recording or otherwise, without the prior permission of the University of Sunderland Press.

British Cataloguing-in-Publications Data
A catalogue record for this book is available from the British Library

Printed in Great Britain by The Alden Group, Oxford.

To Bernard O'Donoghue and Flavia Swann

Contents

Acknowledgements

Foreword
   Andrew Carpenter

Introduction
   John Strachan and Alison O'Malley-Younger

Better Dead, Then Read:
Joyce, Yeats, and the Tolling of Parnell's Death Knell
   Willy Maley   1

'Ah, Poor James!': Death in Joyce's 'The Sisters'
   Peter Dempsey   11

A Belfast the Poets have Imagined:
Louis MacNeice and Derek Mahon
   Brian Burton   25

The Parabolic Structure of William Trevor's
The Story of Lucy Gault
   Daniel W. Ross   39

'Gallous Stories and Dirtier Deeds':
Brian Friel's *The Gentle Island*
   Alison O'Malley-Younger   49

Brian Friel's Love Scenes
   Paddy Lyons   59

Revolution and Revelation:
Brian Friel and the Postcolonial Subject
   Ulf Dantanus   77

'Fearful equivocal words': Virgil, Dante, and the Hells of Heaney
Gareth Reeves 93

Eavan Boland's Revisionary Stance on Nationalism:
A 'Post-nationalist' or a 'Post-colonial' Writer?
Pilar Villar Argáiz 107

Inimitable Ordinariness:
Writing Ireland in John Banville's *The Newton Letter*
Monica Facchinello 121

Tom Paulin: Writing from the Edges
Gareth Reeves 135

The Healing of Trauma in Anne Devlin's *After Easter*:
Female Experience and Nationalistic Historiography
Wei H. Kao 143

Social and Cultural Change in Ireland as seen in
Roddy Doyle's Paula Spencer Novels
Eamon Maher 157

Terrorised Youths – Colum McCann's *Everything in this Country Must* and the Northern Irish Troubles
Eóin Flannery 169

Notes on the Contributors 185

Index 189

Acknowledgements

The co-editors would like to thank the contributors to this volume both for the excellence of their contributions and for the skill and efficiency which they demonstrated in the preparation of this book. We are also grateful to colleagues at the University of Sunderland for their support of the North East Irish Culture Network (NEICN), notably Dr Peter Durrans, Associate Dean of School, Professor Richard Terry and Professor Stuart Sim of English Studies, Professor Tony Hepburn of the University Press, and Professor Andrew Slade and Simon Kerridge of the Graduate Research School, which provided the editors with Research Fellowships to complete this volume. We are also indebted to the colleagues outwith Sunderland who have supported NEICN, amongst them Professor Luke Gibbons, Dr Paddy Lyons, Professor Willy Maley, Dr John Nash, Professor Michael O'Neill, Professor James Stirling and Professor Pat Waugh. Thanks also go to Dr Brian Burton for compiling the index to this volume and to Lucas Swann for the cover design and art work. Our most notable debts are to the dedicatees of this volume: Professor Flavia Swann, Dean of the School of Arts, Design, Media and Culture, who has tirelessly supported our work over the years and been pivotal in the development of Irish Studies at Sunderland and Dr Bernard O'Donoghue, a constant friend and supporter of NEICN, English Studies at Sunderland, and the University as a whole.

Foreword

In their introduction to *Representing Ireland, Past Present and Future*, (2005) Frank Beardow and Alison O'Malley-Younger drew attention to Edna Longley's comment in the *Times Literary Supplement* in 1985, that what Ireland needed was more (rather than less) literary criticism. *Representing Ireland* was not the only book to try and address that 'lack' in the last few years. But literary criticism, particularly textual criticism, is going through a hard time at present, as publishers commission books on cultural rather than literary matters. The trend away from traditional literary criticism was discussed at the International Forum on Irish Studies, held in Florence in October 2005 where one of the 'gaps' identified by the panel on 'Trends and Gaps in Research', was none other than 'Literary Analysis'.

The problem seems to be that some cultural critics are inclined to generalise about literary texts without sufficient investigation of how they actually work – without close reading, in fact. However, this volume, *Essays on Modern Irish Literature,* shows clearly how valuable close reading can be, presenting, as it does, several fine examples of the analysis of modern Irish texts and also (and this is particularly welcome) printing passages of primary material – poems, plays and prose – to illustrate points. The result is some fascinating readings of Irish writing – of the work of MacNeice and Mahon, of Trevor, Friel and Heaney, of Anne Devlin and Roddy Doyle – to pick just a few. Critical approaches based on formal literary analysis may be unfashionable in Irish Studies (struggling as it is to define itself in a world where universities demand 'interdisciplinarity' and yet fund teaching and research through tightly defined disciplinary boundaries) but they are an essential part of the way forward for this multi-disciplined enterprise. In addition to explaining the intellectual, cultural and political contexts of Irish writing, we should be teaching university students how to read and how to enjoy Irish texts.

However, I believe that the time has come for us to move to the next stage in the critical assessment of Irish writing; and extend our gaze to encompass not only the more neglected writers of twentieth-century Ireland (those of Colum McCann's generation in particular) but also some of the currently neglected areas of Irish writing – self-published fiction, autobiographical, community and life writing, for instance. Much interesting material is slipping through our grasp, as scholars keep going back to tease out the significance of the work of a select group of highly literate and often intellectual observers of Irish life – the holy trinity of the Revival, and those deemed worthy to succeed them in the pantheon. Perhaps, for Irish Studies, the word 'literature' has had its day and we should replace it with the less exclusive and judgmental word 'writing'; if we did so, then we would find ourselves widening the lens through which we read and comment on Irish writing. This would not only expose our students to a broader range of material but, in time, lead to a reappraisal of the writers of the pantheon. For the moment, however, I warmly welcome the appearance of this provocative, stimulating and original collection of essays on modern Irish writing – writing which is here often shown to be 'as fully flavoured as a nut or apple'.

Andrew Carpenter,
University College Dublin

Introduction

John Strachan and Alison O'Malley-Younger
University of Sunderland

> Every nation begins with poetry and ends with algebra, and passion has always refused to express itself in algebraical terms
> W. B. Yeats, *Plays and Controversies* (1927)

In order to understand modern Ireland, it is necessary to know modern Irish literature. One would search hard to find a country where literature has so deeply informed a sense of national identity as it evolved over the last century, as it has in Ireland. Perhaps this is unsurprising, given the cultural riches manifest in the island during that period. Few authorities would dispute the notion that W. B. Yeats, James Joyce and Samuel Beckett were amongst the most significant authors of the twentieth century, and, indeed, in Seamus Heaney and Brian Friel Ireland has a fair claim to possess the most notable of contemporary Western European poets and dramatists. Since the Literary Revival of the 1880s, which is generally - and this a conviction shared by the present volume - seen as the start of modern Irish literature, the complex cultural and political history of Ireland resounds through its poetry, drama and prose. This book addresses that rich literary culture, from its nineteenth-century foundation in Yeats, child of the mid-1860s, and Joyce, born in the 1880s, through to the contemporary work of Anne Devlin and Roddy Doyle, born in the 1950s, and Colum McCann, child of the mid-1960s. It examines the warp and weft of the political, personal and philosophical as they intertwine in Irish literary culture, attending to both the formal organization and the ideological nuance of the texts with which it engages. Yeats once famously declared that 'Art is but a vision of reality' (Yeats, 2001, p. 74), and this collection addresses Irish visions of reality over the last one hundred and twenty-five years.

I

This book begins in the contemplation of death and its resonance, and closes with the possibility of hope and new life. In the first of its essays, Willy Maley addresses the literary manifestations of a defining moment in modern Irish history in his account of the way in which the disgrace and death of Charles Stewart Parnell was received and represented by the founding fathers of modern Irish literature, W. B. Yeats and James Joyce. Arguing that 'The fall of Parnell was a pivotal moment for both writers', Maley traces the powerful afterlife which the lost leader possessed in their writing and the manner in which both men imagined Parnell returning to 'haunt' contemporary Ireland, simultaneously both inspiration and rebuke. For Maley, this is part of a much wider tendency, and one which can be read in national terms: in his account 'the dead - haunting, hidden, historic - appear to have a vice-like grip on Irish culture, where the compulsion to grieve, mandatory mourning, runs deep'. In Ireland, even more than in other cultures, the dead are ineluctable, simultaneously absent and yet all too present. As Maley's absorbing essay demonstrates, the departed resound, less than silently, through the early work of the country's greatest novelist. Indeed, 'The Dead' is, of course, the very title of the most famous of Joyce's short stories, and it brings his first book, *Dubliners*, to a conclusion of appropriately Joycean circularity, given that that great work begins with 'The Sisters', an ambiguous treatment of the implications of death and the impact of the dead on the living which is examined here in a subtle and nuanced essay by Peter Dempsey. 'Joyce's fiction', as Dempsey points out, 'is suffused with death'. Furthermore, as Dempsey's piece also reminds us, the subject of death informs both the narrative and the oratorical strategies of Joyce's work, specifically through the rhetorical figures of ellipsis and metalepsis; the former encouraging us to look 'inwards' at the psychology of the characters, the latter inviting us to look 'outwards' at the story as an artistic construction. Dempsey demonstrates how, through a complex process of figurative play, this enigmatic story has drawn generations of readers into its uncomfortable and forbidding orbit, unsettling many long-held beliefs about the nature of narrative and, indeed, setting out the terms in which its author's subsequent work would be read.

Claire Connolly has written that 'as the subject of theory, postcolonial or otherwise, "Ireland" must be understood as both the twenty-six counties and the six-county statelet' (Connolly, 2001, p. 312), and certainly the 'statelet' echoes through this volume: five of the thirteen authors discussed here were born there and another, Tom Paulin, though born in Leeds, is indubitably a Northern Irish writer. Furthermore, the province echoes through this collection in thematic terms, from Brian Burton's fine essay on the importance of Belfast in the work of Louis MacNeice and Derek Mahon through to Eóin Flannery's compelling account of the sociopolitical impact of the Troubles in Colum McCann's short fiction. Burton offers a detailed account of MacNeice and Mahon as they engage with Belfast and its socioeconomic cultures, addressing themes and motifs common to the work of the two poets: home and alienation, belonging and isolation, and the ambiguity of identity associated with being an 'Anglo-Irish Protestant in Ireland [and] an Irishman in England'. MacNeice's thematic legacy for Mahon is an unwillingness to conform to what the former unenthusiastically called Belfast's 'fickle norms'; both poets 'enact the refusal to conform to the demands of a tribe that knows the cost of everything and the value of nothing'. Burton's essay attends to form closely, arguing that MacNeice's poetic legacy for Mahon was 'an elegant virtuosity of verse form and construction'. Studying literary form divorced from the sociohistorical contexts from which it springs is an arid discipline, especially with reference to Ireland, a land with rather too much in the way of politics. However, form remains a crucial part of the study of poetry, fiction and drama, and the contributors to this volume successfully fuse formal analysis with consideration of the ideological significance of the works under discussion. Another fine example is Daniel W. Ross's account of William Trevor's *The Story of Lucy Gault* (2002). Set in County Cork in 1921 at the height of civil unrest, Trevor's novel thematises a number of issues which recur in modern Irish writing: loss, violence, and exile, and tragedy both personal and political. Ross's essay locates his work as part of a parabolic tradition initiated in scripture and employed by writers as diverse as Wordsworth and Kafka which resonates through contemporary writing from Calvino to Heaney. Linking the parable to Freud's descriptions of the manifest and latent content of dreams, Ross highlights the mystery and elusiveness of a form which uses sustained metaphor 'to speak the heretofore unspoken or unspeakable'. He suggests that the novel is a 'parable for Ireland', an allegory which comments on the country's past, present and future and concludes by suggesting that, despite the dark tone of much of the book, it points towards a reconciliation which can offer a 'proper corrective to a bitter history of things left unsaid and undone'.

Joyce and Yeats notwithstanding, Brian Friel looms large in these pages, not only as the most important Irish dramatist since Beckett but also because his work is the site of much theoretically informed recent debate within Irish Studies. A troika of essays here attend to Friel: two deal with particular aspects of the dramatist's work; one uses contemporary criticism of his *oeuvre* to comment upon the state of Irish Studies as a whole. The first, by Alison O'Malley-Younger, is concerned with the manner in which Brian Friel subverts the romantic notion of the Irish *duine uasal*, or noble peasant, in his 1971 play *The Gentle Island*, a work which she defines as an 'ironic Antipastoral'. Concentrating on representations of violence and scapegoating in the play, she suggests that 'Friel draws an oblique parallel with varieties of romantic nationalism to explore the dynamics of a culture shaped by persistent and pervasive violence'. This, O'Malley-Younger argues, offers an implicit critique of monologic nationalist discourse. Underpinning her discussion is the suggestion that Friel, in the postmodern manner, disavows the idea that there can be empirical, incontrovertible and irrefutable truth and that a myopic fidelity to any given 'truth' can lead to self-deception and ultimately result in stasis and ossification. Paddy Lyons's complementary essay on Friel's drama is a highly accomplished account of his love scenes. One does not necessarily associate the dramatist with the amatory, but Lyons convincingly demonstrates the importance of such moments in Friel's work. Deploying theoretical trajectories from Althusser, Badiou, Lacan and Lyotard, Lyons contends that Friel's drama 'amounts to a radical departure from the practices of early modernism'. Friel breaks the theatrical frame to produce a drama which is performative in a cumulative effect made possible only through the interaction of the playwright, the actors and the audience. Discussing the issues of time, talk and tenderness in Friel's key dramas with great insight, and focusing on the absences and disidentifications in his complex art, Lyons argues that here the love scene can become not a site of abandonment, as demanded by the modernist poetic, but a creative and to some extent a hopeful space.

As Lyons and O'Malley-Younger's essays demonstrate, this book closely engages with matters of theory and its role in contemporary inquiry into Irish literature. In the third of its essays on Friel, Ulf Dantanus engages with the most notable manner in which Ireland has been theorised over the last fifteen years, postcolonial theory. The field of Irish Studies is not noted for a total unanimity of voice, and not all of the contributors here sing from the same hymn sheet, particularly with respect to this vexed question of the relevance of postcolonial theory to Ireland. Whereas several essayists in this volume testify to the continuing centrality of the postcolonial method in the discipline, Ulf Dantanus sounds a powerful counterblast, wondering aloud 'how Irish is postcolonialism and how postcolonial is Ireland?' The answer for him is that Ireland is *different*, and there are dangers in 'a globalised postcolonial theoretical model [being] imposed as a critical paradigm' which 'somehow include[s] Ireland at the expense of Irish specificity'. The sheer dominance of the theoretical method also troubles Dantanus; 'a potentially unhealthy relationship' has grown up between Irish Studies and postcolonial theory and there is now a danger of 'a form of sycophantic dependence associated with the bandwagon syndrome'. For him there is actually a 'chiasma between postcolonial studies and Brian Friel's work'. In place of the uniform certainties of Bhabha and Spivak's theoretical juggernaut, Dantanus commends the continuing relevance of close reading techniques to Friel's complex and multivocal work. Instead of the uniform application of voguish theory, sometimes we must be content to acknowledge that Friel, and Ireland, are more opaque than a one-size-fits-all theory would suggest. In conclusion, Dantanus suggests that losing the interpretive comfort zone can be liberating and that we must sometimes address Friel's drama through the lenses of the intangible, the transcendent and the revelatory. Whether or not the reader sees Dantanus's important essay as a useful corrective to the *bien pensant* pieties of modern criticism of Irish culture or as a backward-looking wishing away of the most important trend within Irish Studies over the last fifteen years, it is part of a healthy and important debate within the discipline. As Stuart Sim has written, in an earlier volume in this series, 'It is not a dry academic concern to debate whether postcolonial theory applies to Ireland ... but one with implications and repercussions as to how Ireland presents itself to the world' (Sim, 2005, p. xiii).

A brace of essays by Gareth Reeves address the work of Seamus Heaney and Tom Paulin. Though much critical ink has been spilt on Dante's influence on Heaney, rather less has been written on his debt to the Italian writer's own master and guide, Virgil. Reeves's first essay redresses the balance, whilst simultaneously demonstrating how 'the convergence of Virgil and Dante takes a symbolic significance in the development of [Heaney's] poetics'. Reeves finds in Heaney's fine elegy 'The Strand at Lough Beg' 'a linguistic mingling of the aureate and the quotidian' and argues that this has a wider application, informing Heaney's 'un-Eliotic version of the Dante-Virgil relationship'. Whereas Eliot, reflecting conventional opinion, sees Dante as a 'universal poet of Western Christendom', Heaney, with Osip Mandelstam, counter-intuitively but insightfully, has a rather more 'local and vernacular poet'. Reeves' rich essay traces Virgil's ineluctable presence in Heaney's translation of Dante, in the 'Virgilian echoes' of poems such as 'Trail of Tears' and, finally, in his direct adaptations, notably of the *Eclogues*, where, far from the 'Latinate-classical-canonical' poetry of Eliot's imagination, Virgil is described as 'my hedge-school master' who 'gives instruction to the poet in Ireland's nascent peace process'. In his second essay, Reeves examines the belligerent genius of Tom Paulin, portraying him as a self-proclaimed outsider who 'writes intelligently, and frequently courting the dangerous, from the edges'. Reeves addresses Paulin in his combative mode, 'Desertmartin' with its condemnation of religious certainty, whether Paisleyite or Islamic, and at his more gnomic, 'The Book of Juniper', simultaneously oracular and 'hedged about with comic and tonal antics'. Engaging closely with recent critical notice of Paulin by Edna Longley and Peter Macdonald, Reeves's essay is a valuable contribution to the study of a controversial, 'clownish' (at least in his own account), and yet never inconsequential figure.

Unlike Ulf Dantanus, Pilar Villar Argáiz is confident of the applicability of the term 'postcolonial' to Ireland, and by extension to Irish literature. Using Elleke Boehmer's definition of the term postcolonial as literature 'that sets out in one way or another to resist colonialist perspectives' (Boehmer, 1995, p. 3), Villar Argáiz thoughtfully examines Boland's position as a woman writer in Ireland, arguing that she presents herself as positioned on the margins of a fundamentally male tradition and a patriarchal canon wherein men are writers and women are written: not poets but the subject of poetry. She concludes that Boland adopts a 'liminal' stance between postcolonialism and postnationalism, one which allows her to celebrate 'a cross-cultural form of Irishness' between and beyond 'inherited definitions of nationality and femininity'. Wei H. Kao's essay on Anne Devlin's *After Easter* (1994), a welcome piece on a drama comparatively neglected in critical terms, is similarly concerned with the relationship between representations of Ireland and the fluid nature of cultural identity. Kao focuses on female identity, arguing that Devlin's stance is pluralist and revisionist in contradistinction to the monologic and patriarchal approach of conventional historical narratives. Focusing upon the psychological trauma experienced by women in the Troubles, Kao uses theories of postcolonialism to argue that Devlin's characters, marginalised by gender, politics and sexuality, exemplify those areas of Irish society that have been excluded from traditional historical writing and political discourse.

The notion of Ireland as an invention or fictive concept has been central to a number of critical works on Irish texts, sub-texts and contexts. This, and the related idea of 'writing Ireland', underpins Monica Facchinello's careful and nuanced analysis of John Banville's 1982 novella *The Newton Letter*. Addressing what she sees as Banville's revisionary and intertextual approach to myth and history, Facchinello suggests that the writer's essentially poetic technique - his obliqueness and vagueness - challenges conventional mimetic representations and offers 'unexpected alternatives and new possibilities' to the question of writing Ireland. Eamon Maher offers readings of Trevor's fellow Man Booker prize-winner Roddy Doyle's *The Woman Who Walked into Doors* (1996), a powerful account of long-suffering alcoholic Paula as she recalls her malevolent, abusive, charming - and thankfully now dead - husband Charlo, and what Anne Devlin has insightfully called its 'condition-of-Ireland' sequel, *Paula Spencer* (2006) [1]. Maher makes a persuasive case for the literary significance of Doyle's work. The fact that his books are publishing blockbusters (at least in terms of literary fiction) should not blind us from seeing their skill, artistry and importance. Contextualising his work in contemporary, working class Dublin, Maher probes Doyle's indictment of a 'certain Catholic mindset that was opposed to change'. Throughout the essay Maher highlights the novelist's unflinching treatment of contentious and often unpalatable issues such as religion, gender, domestic violence, mental illness, infidelity and alcoholism. Brian Donnelly, with reference to Doyle's earlier fiction, praised his willingness to address issues 'outside the horizons of Irish literature, ways of life hidden from the concerns of people who typically buy and read literary fiction in Ireland'; Eamon Maher shows how the Paula Spencer novels are an important development of Doyle's willingness to confront an Ireland not often articulated in the country's fiction. Maher concludes, convincingly, that Doyle's contribution to Irish literature resides in his ability and willingness to address the occluded, ordinary lives of those 'who have been failed by the political, religious and educational systems and yet who survive'.

The final essay in this book, by Eóin Flannery, addresses the manner in which the spectre of the Northern Irish Troubles is manifested in fictional form. Whilst most critical attention has fastened upon their treatment in the novel, Flannery instead focuses his argument on the short stories of Colum McCann. He maintains that McCann offers 'an illumination of basic human truths' set against the 'debilitating shadow of the Troubles'. Examining McCann's decision to employ magic realism in these stories, Flannery highlights how narratives of violence permeate individual and communal rituals 'not as pessimistic absolutes but with the narrative contingency of myth, magic and folklore'. His analysis is both theoretically and contextually precise, skillfully veering between the twin vectors of the actual and the abstract, and demonstrating how the personal and the political are symbolically interwoven in the notion of the corporeal body (that of an adolescent girl, that of a hunger striker) metaphorically inscribed by the violence endemic in the body politic. Flannery argues that this recurring motif of the somatic foregrounds the manner in which the political extremities of the Troubles were thus 'scripted onto the carceral'. However, in the midst of this wretched immediacy there is a glimpse of hope; even in the darkest hour of Ireland's recent history the reader is able to 'divine moments of hope or of imagination ... beyond the foreshortened mindscapes of sectarianism'. It remains to be seen if the renewal hinted at in McCann's fiction and evident in recent political life in Northern Ireland will prove permanent or but a chimera. It is to be hoped that McCann's proleptic fictional vision of a new Irish *status quo*, and of a nascent equanimity, is, indeed, prophetic.

Notes

[1] From Anne Devlin's review of *Paula Spencer*, *The Guardian*, 9 September 2006.

References

Boehmer, E. (1995), *Colonial and Postcolonial Literature*, Oxford University Press, Oxford.

Connolly, C. (2001), 'Theorising Ireland', *Irish Studies Review*, 9 (3), December 2001, pp. 301-315.

Sim, S. (2005), foreword to *Representing Ireland: Past, Present and Future*, ed. A. O'Malley-Younger and F. Beardow, Sunderland University Press, Sunderland, p. xiii.

Yeats, W. B. (2001), *The Major Works*, ed. E. Larissy, Oxford University Press, Oxford.

Essays on Modern Irish Literature

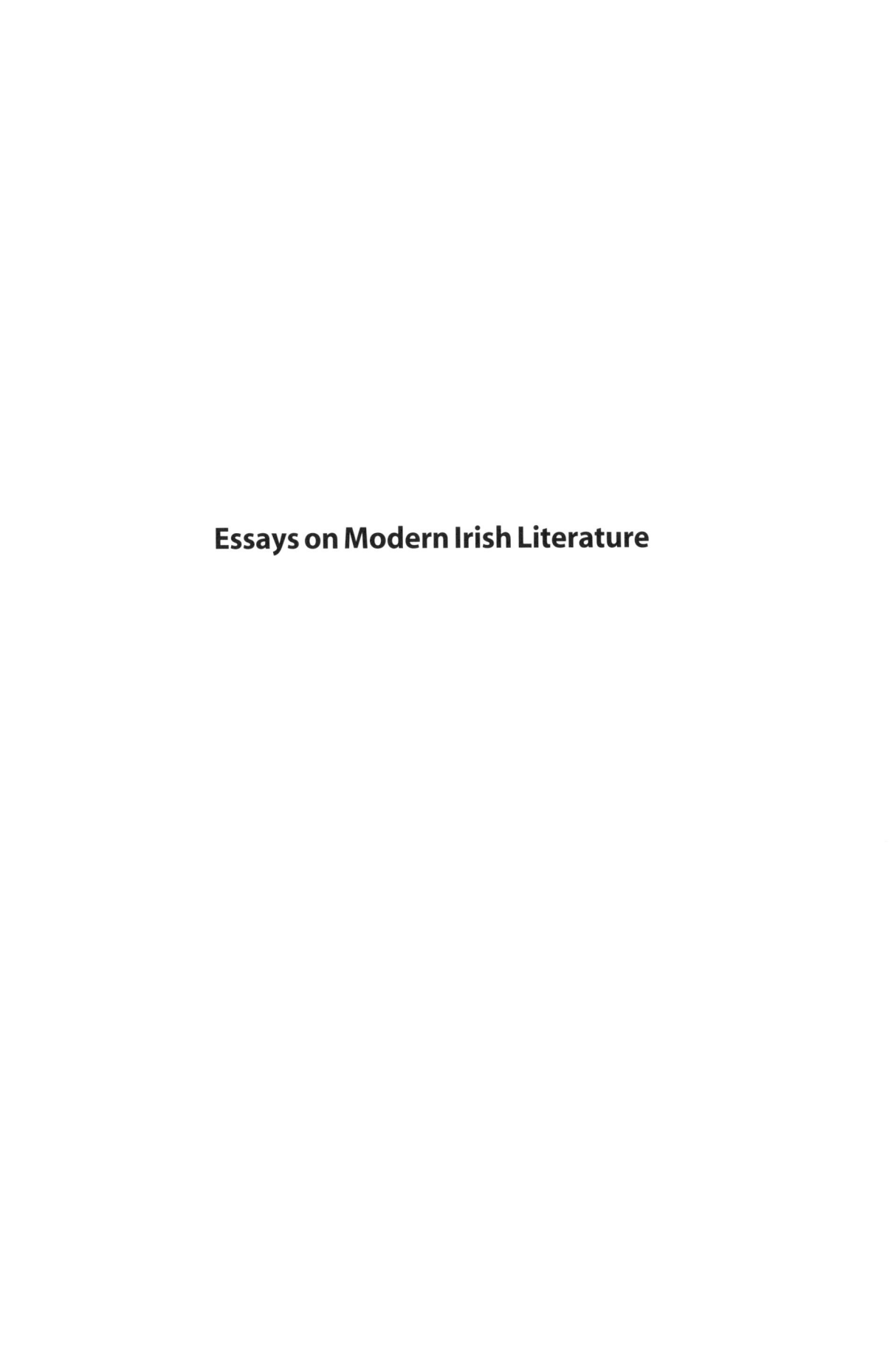

Better Dead, Then Read: Joyce, Yeats, and the Tolling of Parnell's Death Knell

Willy Maley
University of Glasgow

In a short work entitled *Aporias*, Jacques Derrida begins by stating that death means something different across borders, between nations, throughout history, and that there are 'cultures of death', before going on to say that 'culture itself, culture in general, is essentially ... the culture of death ... a *history of death*' (Derrida, 1993, p. 43; emphasis in original). I can't speak for culture in general, if such a thing exists, but the dead - haunting, hidden, historic - appear to have a vice-like grip on Irish culture, where the compulsion to grieve, mandatory mourning, runs deep. Derrida insists, dependably unconventional as ever, that 'every culture entails a treatise or treatment of death, each of them treats the end according to a different partition' (Derrida, 1993, p. 43). In Ireland, culture and partition go hand-in-glove, and within the culture(s) there are different takes on death, different means of disposing of the dead. In this essay, I plan to referee some stiff competition between Joyce and Yeats over the burial rights to Charles Stewart Parnell, the Irish Protestant parliamentary leader laid low by scandal.

The Irish, the story goes, are especially prone to a worshipful culture of death. As Joyce observed after the death of the Fenian leader John O'Leary, 'the Irish, even though they break the hearts of those who sacrifice their lives for their native land, never fail to show great respect for the dead' (Mason, 1956, p. 121). This responsiveness to the dead can scar, and scare, the living. In Ireland, at least in Joyce's account, you have to be dead to get any respect, which is why he was livid on hearing that his brother admired Swift, retorting with satirical swiftness: 'I prefer people who are alive'. Yeats, on the other hand, regarded Swift as a precursor, of himself and of Parnell, and he differed from Joyce in his attitude to both. Yeats said of the dead dean: 'Swift haunts me: he is always just round the next corner'. An obsession with the dead brings in its wake ghosts and the Gothic. Ireland is a hostage to phantom. The fact that Ian Paisley found it necessary to stand on a platform after a recent election and declare himself still to be in the land of the living - 'We are not dead!' -

suggests that the wake and the work of mourning goes on into the wee small hours. A wake is a long time in politics.

In *Ulysses*, punning on the age-old adage 'An Englishman's home is his castle', Leopold Bloom reflects that 'The Irishman's house is his coffin', and speculates that fear of death is crucial to Catholicism's hold on the Irish people (Joyce, 1969, p. 111). Death in Joyce is bound up with piety, sacrifice, martyrdom and heroism, all of which he considered to be rotten to the core. But what is the proper response to the dead? Paralysis? Catharsis? Something in-between? Stephen Dedalus remarks bitterly in his diary fragment at the end of *A Portrait of the Artist as a Young Man*: 'Let the dead bury the dead. Ay. And let the dead marry the dead'. 'Let the dead bury the dead'; otherwise, the implication is clear, they will bury the living (Levin, 1977, p. 362). But as Derrida reminds us, stating the obvious for once, the dead can't bury the dead, not literally, and the living can't bury the dead either, not completely, certainly not permanently. The dead and buried never go to ground for good, but resurface as ghosts and memories, spectres and spurs to action.

The rich vein of obligatory bereavement in Irish culture is evident in the literary reaction to the death of the Irish political leader Charles Stewart Parnell in 1891. A parliamentary leader dies. The nation mourns a political leader sanctified in death, even by the conservatives, a familiar refrain. Parnell, whose forenames ring a bell that spells doom and whose surname is resonant of the passing-bell, is a figure in whom many of the tensions and contradictions of Irish nationalism crystallized, the leader whose relationship with the Irish actress 'Kitty' O'Shea led to condemnation from Catholic Ireland and, as his supporters would have it, an early grave. Parnell had been living with O'Shea for a decade, but the 'scandal' broke when her husband, Captain O'Shea, sued for divorce, naming Parnell.

Parnell's death impinged upon the work and worlds of Joyce and Yeats in different but related ways. The fall of Parnell was a formative influence for both writers. Its importance cannot be exaggerated - but I'll do my best. And in this haunting hyperbole I will be aided and abetted by a number of writers and critics, but chiefly by Joyce and Yeats. Parnell's fall from grace raised many issues, issues of sexuality, religion, martyrdom, sacrifice, censorship, divorce, morality, the media, betrayal, and death, both as paralysis and catharsis. It inspired a number of literary responses, and it is instructive I think to look at the lessons that Joyce and Yeats learned from what was an ambivalent experience of object loss and subject liberation, the wisdom they drew from what was essentially an experience of defeat, denial, and division. If, for Yeats, Parnell's death left an Ireland that was 'soft wax', then for Joyce that malleable material could only take the imprint of fresh stereotypes (Flanagan, 1975, p. 45). What for Yeats was an opportunity to be lauded was for Joyce an impasse to be lamented.

Yet there are tensions and twists along the way. In Stephen's diary at the end of *A Portrait of the Artist*, Joyce has him quote from Yeats's *The Wind Among the Reeds*

(1899) but with his own inflexion. Under the heading 'He Remembers Forgotten Beauty' Yeats had written thus:

> When my arms wrap you round I press
> My heart upon the loveliness
> That has long faded from the world. (Yeats, 1982, pp. 69-70)

In Joyce's version, this becomes:

> Michael Robartes remembers forgotten beauty and, when his arms wrap her round, he presses in his arms the loveliness which has long faded from the world. Not this. Not at all. I desire to press in my arms the loveliness which has not yet come into the world. (Levin, 1977, p. 364)

As Richard Ellmann has pointed out, here Joyce represents Yeats as caught in the past, 'static', while Joyce looks to the future (Ellmann, 1975, p. 464). But in both authors' early responses to the death of Parnell it was Yeats who looked to the future. In 1923 he declared that:

> The modern literature of Ireland, and indeed all that stir of thought which prepared for the Anglo-Irish war, began when Parnell fell from power in 1891. A disillusioned and embittered Ireland turned from parliamentary politics; an event was conceived and the race began, as I think, to be troubled by that event's long gestation. (Cited in O'Brien, 1965, p. 219)

The loss to politics was the gain of culture. Parnell's fall paved the way for Yeats to claim to be the country's spiritual guide. Henceforth, the theatre and the book would be the public forum in which the fate of the nation was determined. In *Explorations*, Yeats wrote:

> The fall of Parnell had freed the imagination from practical politics, from agrarian grievance and political enmity, and turned it to imaginative nationalism, to Gaelic, to the ancient stories, and at last to lyrical poetry and drama ... What shall occupy our imagination? We must, I think, decide among these three ideas of national life; that of Swift; that of a great Italian of his day [Mazzini]; that of modern England. (Cited in Deane, 1985, p. 45)

For Joyce the fall of Parnell had not 'freed the imagination' so much as it had exposed the lack of it. In 'The Shade of Parnell', an essay written in 1912, Joyce maintained that:

> The influence exerted on the Irish people by Parnell defies critical analysis. He had a speech defect and a delicate physique; he was ignorant of the history of his native land; his short and fragmentary speeches lacked eloquence, poetry and humour; his cold and formal bearing separated

him from his own colleagues; he was a Protestant, a descendant of an aristocratic family, and, as a crowning disgrace, he spoke with a distinct English accent. (Mason, 1956, pp. 134-5)

Joyce describes Parnell's meteoric rise to the point where 'he held in his hands the fate of the government' and, in the minds of many, the destiny of the nation. The first Home Rule Bill was read at Westminster in 1886. Ireland stood on the verge of an historic moment. Then came the fall, with one fall following another, as they do if you read your Milton. In Joyce's words:

Parnell's fall came in the midst of these events like lightning from a clear sky. He fell hopelessly in love with a married woman, and when her husband, Captain O'Shea, asked for a divorce, the ministers Gladstone and Morley openly refused to legislate in favour of Ireland if the sinner remained as head of the Nationalist Party ... He was deposed in obedience to Gladstone's orders ... The high and low clergy entered the lists to finish him off. The Irish press emptied on him and the woman he loved the vials of their envy. The citizens of Castlecomer threw quicklime in his eyes. He went from county to county, from city to city, 'like a hunted deer', a spectral figure with the signs of death on his forehead. Within a year he died of a broken heart at the age of 45.

The ghost of the 'uncrowned king' will weigh on the hearts of those who remember him ... but it will not be a vindictive ghost. The melancholy which invaded his mind was perhaps the profound conviction that, in his hour of need, one of the disciples who dipped his hand in the same bowl with him would betray him. That he fought to the very end with this desolate certainty in mind is his greatest claim to nobility. (Mason, 1956, p. 136)

The betrayal of Parnell, the uncrowned king of Ireland, is compared with that of Christ. Despite Joyce's apparent repudiation of Catholicism - and for him this meant a repudiation of Christianity - he cast Parnell in the role of redeemer, renounced by his own people and thrown to the Romans. Joyce closes with words of intense bitterness and irony:

In his final desperate appeal to his countrymen, [Parnell] begged them not to throw him as a sop to the English wolves howling around them. It redounds to their honour that they did not fail this appeal. They did not throw him to the English wolves; they tore him to pieces themselves. (Mason, 1956, pp. 136-7)

Joyce's image of Parnell as a 'hunted deer' was a dominant one at the time. Yeats, in an essay on 'The Tragic Generation' in his *Autobiographies* noted that 'a quotation from Goethe ran through the papers, describing Irish jealousy. "The Irish seem to me like a pack of hounds, always dragging down some noble stag"' (Yeats, 1953, p. 190). Yeats's verse 'To a Shade', published in 1914, echoes Joyce's thoughts on Parnell's passing:

If you have revisited the town, thin Shade,
Whether to look upon your monument
(I wonder if the builder has been paid)
Or happier-thoughted when the day is spent
To drink of that salt breath out of the sea
When grey gulls flit about instead of men,
And the gaunt houses put on majesty:
Let these content you and be gone again;
For they are at their old tricks yet. (Yeats, 1982, p. 123)

By coincidence, the very same year - 1914 - Joyce returned to the spectral figure of Parnell in what he later acknowledged as his favourite story in *Dubliners*, 'Ivy-Day in the Committee Room', a dark tale of time-serving and despondency, lit up at the end with the recitation of a poem entitled 'The Death of Parnell'. Critics and readers have argued about the status of the poem, in the same way they have debated the ending of 'The Dead' (Hodgart, 1969; O'Grady, 1988; Stern, 1979). Is it ironic? Is it to be opposed to, or juxtaposed with, the preceding narrative? Do corrupt politics and hyperbole about the dignity of dead leaders go hand-in-hand? Is there a fatal complicity between the rehearsal of this heavy verse and the hopelessness from which it arises, like a phoenix from the ashes?

He is dead. Our Uncrowned King is dead.
O, Erin, mourn with grief and woe
For he lies dead whom the fell gang
Of modern hypocrites laid low.

He lies slain by the coward hounds
He raised to glory from the mire;
And Erin's hopes and Erin's dreams
Perish upon her monarch's pyre.

... Shame on the coward, caitiff hands
That smote their Lord or with a kiss
Betrayed him to the rabble-rout
Of fawning priests - no friends of his. (Levin, 1977, pp. 108-9)

Thomas O'Grady, in '"Ivy Day in the Committee Room": The Use and Abuse of Parnell' (1988), sees the story as a carefully constructed attack on antiquarian and monumental history, a critique of an obsession with the past for its own sake, and of a glorification of a past peopled with heroes. Both of these approaches to history - a dry history of documents and a thunderous history of heroes - lend themselves to paralysis, stifling political action. Evoking the dead can be a call to arms or an appeal for calm. It can pacify or prompt, placate or provoke. The poem recited by Hynes is said to have been written by Joyce's brother, 'and sung by him in 1896'. It has been described as 'a masterpiece of bathos .... a deadly parody of the sentimental patriotic rubbish typical of the Irish popular music of the previous century' (Hodgart, 1969, pp. 118, 120, 121). However, in the light of Joyce's essay on Parnell it is harder to see this as mere parody. Parnell is dead. But the dead are the very life stuff of history, more real than the living. To echo Stephen Dedalus, history is a nightmare from which we are trying to awake. Waking from the nightmare of history - or sleeping through it (taking up Joyce's baton Saul Bellow once quipped that history was a nightmare during which he was trying to get some sleep) - is a question of coming to terms with the dead, with, as Marx put it, 'the tradition of all the dead generations [that] weigh[s] like a nightmare on the brain of the living'. For Joyce, the only reasonable response if one is aware of the cyclical nature of history, and its repetition of heroism and betrayal, is to debunk it, to break out of the depressing tradition of martyrdom and fallen angels.

Parnell occupies the same position in 'Ivy Day' as Michael Furey in 'The Dead'. It is the Hamlet Effect, the phenomenon of betrayal and death leading in turn to the excessive power of the dead, who return to haunt the living. Two years after *Dubliners*, Joyce returned to Parnell in *A Portrait of the Artist as A Young Man*. Young Stephen Dedalus has a geography lesson that is also a lesson in history and politics, as he places himself in relation to the world:

> There was a picture of the earth on the first page of his geography: a big ball in the middle of clouds. Fleming had a box of crayons and one night during free study he had coloured the earth green and the clouds maroon. That was like the two brushes in Dante's press, the brush with the green velvet back for Parnell and the brush with the maroon velvet back for Michael Davitt. But he had not told Fleming to colour them those colours. Fleming had done it himself ... He turned over the flyleaf and looked wearily at the green round earth in the middle of the maroon clouds. He wondered which was right, to be for the green or for the maroon, because Dante had ripped the green velvet back off the brush that was for Parnell one day with her scissors and had told him that Parnell was a bad man. He wondered if they were arguing at home about that. That was called politics. There were two sides in it: Dante was on one side and his father and Mr Casey were on the other side but his mother and Uncle Charles were on no side. Every day there was something in the paper about it. (Levin, 1977, pp. 183-4)

Are there two sides to every story, only two? 'That was called politics. There were two sides in it'. Remember that Joyce saw a fatal complicity between the Roman and British tyranny in Ireland. Two sides: same difference. Later, in the famous Christmas dinner scene, Stephen's first Christmas dinner with the adults, the figure of Parnell is again invoked. When Dante says indignantly that Stephen will 'remember all this when he grows up ... the language he heard against God and religion and priests in his own home', Mr Casey replies 'Let him remember too ... the language with which the priests and the priests' pawns broke Parnell's heart and hounded him into his grave. Let him remember that too when he grows up':

> Sons of bitches! cried Mr Dedalus. When he was down they turned on him to betray him and rend him like rats in a sewer. Low-lived dogs! And they look it! By Christ, they look it! (Levin, 1977, p. 197)

Dante calls them 'renegade Catholics', and to Mr Casey's protest that he, too, is a Roman Catholic, she says: 'Catholic indeed! ... The blackest protestant in the land would not speak the language I have heard this evening'. The scene ends with Casey crying out:

> - Poor Parnell! ... My dead king!
> He sobbed loudly and bitterly.
> Stephen, raising his terror-stricken face, saw that his father's eyes were full of tears. (Levin, 1977, p. 202)

Afterwards, Stephen considers writing a poem on Parnell. Stuck for words, instead he writes out the names of his classmates. Like the closing verse of Yeats's 'Easter 1916', this act of naming is a ritual that wards off the spectre of death, except that Joyce is making a litany of the living. Ireland's national figures tend to be either beatified or demonized. In 'Ivy Day', the truth of Parnell lies somewhere between Lyons's moralizing condemnation and Hynes's mawkish canonizing, just as in *A Portrait* it lies between Mrs O'Riordan's sanctimonious vituperation and Mr Casey's vehement sanctification.

Towards the end of *A Portrait*, in an exchange with Davin, the Irish nationalist, Stephen says: 'No honourable and sincere man ... has given up to you his life and his youth and his affections from the days of Tone to those of Parnell, but you sold him to the enemy or failed him in need or reviled him and left him for another' (Levin, 1977, p. 327). Having acknowledged that he is a product of his country, Stephen now says: 'You talk to me of nationality, language, religion. I shall try to fly by those nets' (Levin, 1977, p. 327). The nets Joyce has in mind are those of necrophilia as well as nationality, both nets forming a fine mesh that constrains the living. Yeats spoke with equal passion of the impact of 'the Parnell controversy':

> There were reasons to justify a man's joining either party, but there were none to justify, on one side or on the other, lying accusations forgetful of past service, a frenzy of detraction. (Yeats, 1982, p. 529)

Again, two parties. That's politics for you. But the death of Parnell was both a tragedy and an opportunity for Yeats: what he lost in terms of political prospects he gained in terms of artistic inspiration. The line pursued in one of his poems on Parnell - 'Mourn, and then Onward' - is self-explanatory. The death of Parnell closed one door - or coffin lid - and opened another.

In 1935 Yeats returned to the lament for Parnell in a poem entitled 'Parnell's Funeral':

> An age is the reversal of an age:
> When strangers murdered Emmet, Fitzgerald, Tone,
> We lived like men who watched a painted stage.
> What matter for the scene, the scene once gone:
> It had not touched our lives. But popular rage,
> *Hysterica passio* dragged this quarry down.
> None shared our guilt; nor did we play a part
> Upon a painted stage when we devoured his heart. (Yeats, 1982, p. 319)

This is an important poem, a poem of jealousy and guilt. Yeats insists on 'our guilt', making Parnell part of an inclusive nation, where it could be argued that it was precisely Parnell's status as a stranger, at least in the eyes of a certain nationalist discourse, that led to his downfall. In other words the guilt lies not with Yeats and his fellow Protestants but with the fawning priests, no friends of his. Compare Joyce's insistence that it was the Roman tyranny that did for Parnell, that and the British one, in the shape of Gladstone. Think of the kind of biographical detail that Joyce provided, and his perennial preoccupation with the double yoke of British and Roman imperialism. Yeats's poem continues:

> Had de Valéra eaten Parnell's heart,
> No loose-lipped demagogue had won the day,
> No civil rancour torn the land apart.
>
> Had Cosgrave eaten Parnell's heart, the land's
> Imagination had been satisfied,
> Or lacking that, government in such hands,
> O'Higgins its sole statesman had not died.
>
> Had even O'Duffy - but I name no more -
> Their school a crowd, his master solitude;
> Through Jonathan Swift's dark grove he passed, and there
> Plucked bitter wisdom that enriched his blood. (Yeats, 1982, p. 320)

Swift again, haunting Yeats and Parnell. Edna Longley says of this poem that it 'suggests, in the wake of Yeats's disillusionment over divorce, censorship and other matters, that Parnell's real funeral, the funeral of free cross-cultural discussion, is now taking place: "Had de Valera eaten Parnell's heart", "Had Cosgrave eaten Parnell's heart ..." Neither of the Civil War parties has absorbed the values which, for Yeats, link the eighteenth-century Protestant nation, Parnell and his own art. The poem's "bitter wisdom" is contemporary' (Longley, 1994, p. 133). Yeats's first thought, that Parnell's death had freed the imagination from practical politics was tempered as practical politics came back with a vengeance and the imagination was fettered once more. In *Last Poems* (1936-39), Yeats returned to Parnell again, first in a ballad entitled 'Come Gather Round me Parnellites', once more bitterly ironic:

Come gather round me, Parnellites,
And praise our chosen man;
Stand upright on your legs awhile,
Stand upright while you can,
For soon we lie where he is laid,
And he is underground;
Come fill up all those glasses
And pass the bottle round.

...
The Bishops and the Party
That tragic story made,
A husband that had sold his wife
And after that betrayed;
But stories that live longest
Are sung above the glass,
And Parnell loved his country,
And Parnell loved his lass. (Yeats, 1982, pp. 355-6)

And then again, in a poem called simply 'Parnell', running to two lines:

Parnell came down the road, he said to a cheering man:
'Ireland shall get her freedom and you still break stone'.
(Yeats, 1982, p. 359)

Memorializing Parnell, his place in Irish culture, politics, and history, was a complicated process. For Joyce, the fall of Parnell was a failure of imagination as much as of politics, nothing but the same old story of hypocrisy and betrayal. Like the Mayo peasants turning on Synge's eponymous Playboy of the Western World, Christy Mahon, when the gallus story becomes a dirty deed the people are ready to bury their heroes. Ironically, in death, Parnell became a martyr, added to the roll call of dead heroes, reinforcing the common conclusion of colonial ideology and nationalist mythology, that the only good Irishman is a dead Irishman. For Yeats, Parnell's fall meant something different, initially a freeing up of the imagination in the wake of the effective collapse of constitutional politics, later an instance of the unimaginative nature of practical politics. Yeats is closer to Joyce, perhaps, than he at first appears. Granted, Joyce did not draw the distinction between politics and literature that Yeats assumes and insists upon. Either way the posthumous part played by Parnell in Irish history tells us something about the larger place of the dead, and the differing attitudes of Joyce and Yeats - both of whom lamented Parnell's loss, albeit Yeats as an end of politics, and Joyce as yet another episode in a lengthy narrative of betrayal. In each case there is a compulsion to write it out, to bring Parnell back to life in a kind of 'funereality', to imagine the dead leader as a shade or ghost returned to haunt Ireland, to remind it of work-in-progress, the unfinished business of mourning and the business - 'as usual', if Derrida is to be believed - of culture.

References

Deane, S. (1985), *Celtic Revivals: Essays in Modern Irish Literature, 1880-1980*, Faber, London.

Derrida, J. (1993), *Aporias: Dying - Awaiting (one another at) the Limits of Truth*, trans. T. Dutoit, Stanford University Press, Stanford.

Ellmann, R. (1967), *Yeats and Joyce*, Dolmen Press, Dublin.

Flanagan, T. (1975), 'Yeats, Joyce, and the Matter of Ireland', *Critical Inquiry* 2 (1), pp. 43-67.

Hodgart, M. J. C. (1969), 'Ivy Day in the Committee Room', in *James Joyce's 'Dubliners': Critical Essays*, ed. C. Hart, London, pp. 115-121.

Joyce, J. (1969), *Ulysses*, Penguin, Harmondsworth.

Levin, H. (ed.) (1977), *The Essential James Joyce*, Granada, St Albans, Herts.

Longley, E. (1994), *The Living Stream: Literature and Revisionism in Ireland*, Bloodaxe, Newcastle upon Tyne.

Mason, E. (1956), 'James Joyce's Shrill Note – The *Piccolo Della Sera* Articles', *Twentieth-Century Literature* 2 (3), pp. 115-39.

O'Brien, C. C. (1965), 'Passion and Cunning: An Essay on the Politics of W. B. Yeats', in *In Excited Reverie: A Centenary Tribute to William Butler Yeats 1865-1939*, ed. A. N. Jeffares and K. G. W. Cross, Macmillan, New York, pp. 208-75.

O'Grady, T. B. (1988), '"Ivy Day in the Committee Room": The Use and Abuse of Parnell', in *'Dubliners'*, ed. H. Bloom, Chelsea House, New York, pp. 131-142.

Stern, F. C. (1973), '"Parnell is Dead": "Ivy Day in the Committee Room"', *James Joyce Quarterly* 10, pp. 228-239.

Yeats, W. B. (1953), *Autobiographies*, Macmillan, New York.

Yeats, W. B. (1982) *Collected Poems*, Macmillan, London and Basingstoke.

'Ah, poor James!': Death in Joyce's 'The Sisters'

Peter Dempsey
University of Sunderland

In Joyce's 'The Sisters', death and the responses to it form the subject-matter of the story. However, the topic also enters the rhetorical and the narrative strategies of the piece, specifically through the figures of ellipsis and metalepsis. Through these figures, the story encourages kinds of interpretations that have us, its readers, in a parallel fashion to the characters, reflect on the 'immanent' quality of human existence, on our fantasies of the possibility of escaping death and on our worldly understanding of its impossibility. Let us begin at the ending of the story: 'Wide-awake and laughing-like to himself …. So then, of course, when they saw that, that made them think that there was something gone wrong with him ….' (Joyce, 1992a, p. 10). It may seem a little otiose to begin our consideration by insisting on the importance of a mere three dots in a short story that deals with the weighty enigma of death. However, this form of ellipsis, what the narrator of Gilbert Adair's *pastiche* crime novel *The Act of Roger Murgatroyd* calls 'a trio of tantalising suspension points' (Adair, 2006, p. 59) is the very emblem of the enigma in Joyce's famously enigmatic story. 'The Sisters' is the first tale in the writer's first book of fiction and had first appeared ten years earlier in a shorter version, his first published story. So, at the beginning of the twentieth century, we have one of the most enigmatic stories of the century launching a literary career of one of the most profoundly enigmatic of novelists. Joyce's second novel, let it not be forgotten, is named after an Homeric hero who - in a work of over a quarter of a million words we should remember to be shocked to contemplate - is mentioned only *once* (Joyce, 2000, p. 250), yet whose deeds apparently shape the text at every level.

Declan Kiberd, in his introduction to that novel, suggests that 'it could be argued that the entire structure of *Ulysses* might take as its paradigm the unfinished sentence' ending with the 'bleak inconclusiveness of a dot–dot–dot' (Joyce, 2000, p. xliii), and of course 'The Sisters' ends in a tantalisingly inconclusive way with just such an ellipsis, thus offering the reader a curiously porous border with the rest of the collection, but also with a disturbing lack of conventional narrative closure. The story is of course no anomaly in Joyce's fiction. 'The Sisters' contains, *in ovo*, many of the techniques to be found in the rest of *Dubliners* (1914) and in Joyce's multiparous fiction generally. They were to become part of the literary DNA of modernism and of what followed. As his biographer Richard Ellmann says of 'The Sisters', 'He cradles here the technique which has now become a commonplace of contemporary fiction' (Ellmann, 1982, p. 84). In a letter of 1906, the young Joyce announced the style in which he would couch *Dubliners*: 'I have written it for the most part in a style of scrupulous meanness' (Joyce, 1975b, p. 83). It is this 'scrupulous meanness' which, in large part, gives 'The Sisters' its unsettling power.

How did such an enigmatic story come into being? In 1904 the poet and literary editor of *The Irish Homestead* George Russell ('AE'), wrote to the 22 year-old Joyce asking him to provide a 'simple', 'rural' story for his paper, commenting 'It is easily earned money if you can write fluently and don't mind playing to the common understanding' (Joyce, 1975a, p. 43). A story of the period less fitting this description than 'The Sisters' would be hard to find. Given Russell's advice, the most remarkable thing to the present-day reader is that it was ever published at all. So in Dublin in 1904, a weekly journal dismissed by Stephen Dedalus in *Ulysses* (1922) as 'the pig's paper' (Joyce, 2000, p. 247) published probably the most avant-garde short story yet written in English.

'The Sisters' tells, in what seems a cool and rather cold-blooded way, of a death and its immediate aftermath for those closest to the deceased. It begins with the young, unnamed narrator of the story considering the impending death of Father Flynn, a priest with whom he had formed a close bond and who we are led to think entertained hopes that the boy would one day enter the priesthood. Father Flynn had already suffered a number of paralysing strokes and the boy dwells on the word 'paralysis' when thinking of the priest's inevitable fate. On the boy's return to his aunt and uncle's house, he is told that Father Flynn is dead. His uncle and Old Cotter, a family friend, discuss the boy's relationship with the priest and it is clear that Old Cotter disapproved of it, though he is unwilling to spell out the nature of his disapproval. The boy recalls his visits to the priest and their discussions of theology and history. That night he has an unsettling dream about the priest. Later, the child visits the priest's house with his aunt. Father Flynn's two elderly sisters, Nannie and Eliza, show their guests upstairs and all pray around the coffin, except the boy who regards the scene dispassionately. Over sherry and crackers the adults discuss Father Flynn and Eliza recalls her brother's progressively bizarre behaviour in the period leading up to his death, which began with the breaking of a chalice during Mass and ended with the discovery of her brother shut in a confessional box, laughing to himself. With this curious and troubling speech, the story comes to an abrupt end.

Popular theories about the cause of the mysterious paralysis of the priest run from his illness as representative of a moribund Catholic church, or of the state of a whole city and by extension a nation, to the quite plausible argument that its source was syphilis, known in Ireland at the time as 'general paresis of the insane' [1]. With this interpretation comes a slew of possibilities, all centring on forms of sexual corruption, some of them involving the young narrator, others not. Old Cotter's hesitations and verbal ellipses, his refusal to say what his objections were to the boy's relationship with the priest hints, at the very least, at some form of possibly corrupt knowledge the boy has in advance of his years, and as we shall see, questions of knowing and being in relation to death are at the heart of the story.

Dubliners induces in the reader a desire for knowledge which the stories, as we read on, will never fully provide. Hesitations, mysteries of motivation and the very lightest touches of allusiveness abound. For example, it is clear that the penultimate story of the collection, 'Grace' is divided, like Caesar's Gaul, into three. Tom Kernan is found drunk and injured in a pub's basement lavatory. Later he convalesces with friends and finally he attends a religious retreat with these same friends. Reading Ellmann's biography, it comes as something of a surprise to discover that the story's tripartite structure nods to Dante's *Divine Comedy*; rather a formidable weight for a short story to bear, even if the parallel is a light-hearted one (Ellmann, 1982, p. 229). The benighted reader finds that Joyce, as Chandler hoped to do in 'A Little Cloud', has 'put in allusions' (Joyce, 1992a, p. 69) [2], but we certainly don't have the forehead-slapping moment of recognition the discovery of such allusions usually brings – though once we are in this fallen state of knowledge and read again the first line of 'The Sisters', 'There was no hope for him this time' (p. 1), it now seems to echo the famous admonition over the gates of hell in the *Inferno* and begins the much-discussed theme of thwarted dreams of escape to be found throughout the collection.

It is easy to conclude then, along with the author that 'the spirit directing my pen seems to me so plainly mischievous' (Joyce, 1975a, p. 99). Reading the original version of 'The Sisters' published in *The Irish Homestead* reveals how thoroughly Joyce revised it for publication in *Dubliners*, and revised it in a way that shows the young writer's natural bent towards thematic patterning and artful allusion which would be found everywhere in his later work. Even so, who would have thought that Joyce's half-joking but prophetic statement to one of his translators defending the immense complexity of *Ulysses* would apply to what many regard as his relatively straightforward apprentice work?: 'I've put in so many enigmas and puzzles that it will keep the professors busy for centuries arguing over what I meant' (Ellmann, 1982, p. 521).

When discussing drama in a lecture he gave as a young graduate in 1900, Joyce talks of 'reading it for ourselves, piecing the various parts, and going closer to see wherever the writing on the parchment is fainter or less legible' (Joyce, 1959, p. 50). For seventy years or more, critics have taken Joyce's advice and have been vigorously holding the textual feet of 'The Sisters' to the fire in an attempt to get it to yield up its enigmas. Analyses of the story are a tribute to human ingenuity, but while it might appear that the critical commentary on it is something of a mare's nest for any reader hoping to find any broad consistency in interpretation, over the years there has developed a broadly consistent agreement on the story's very resistance to interpretation. A few examples: Robert N. Adams calls 'The Sisters' 'chronically recalcitrant to analysis'; Mitzi Brunsdale that it is 'one of his most difficult and enigmatic of short stories'; for R. B. Kershner it is 'the first and strangest of the stories', while for Donald Torchiana it's 'the most controversial piece in *Dubliners*'. Much earlier, William York Tindall's influential 1959 reading of the piece calls it 'one of the most complex and disturbing in the sequence ... Nothing comes quite clear'. Finally, Warren Beck quotes the short story writer Frank O'Connor's assessment, which sums up the general response to the story until recent times: 'the point still eludes me' [3].

Towards the end of the story Nannie, one of the late priest's sisters, 'pointed ... interrogatively' (p. 6) and over the years the interrogative form has been the mainstay of critical commentary on the story, an echolalia of questions: what was the nature of the relationship between the boy and the priest? Why did Father Flynn seem to lose his mind? What does Mr Cotter imply he knows about the boy's and priest's relationship? What does the boy's strange dream tell us about that relationship? These are all questions concerning the significance of the facts as laid before us by the narrator, but while the story initially appears to be a piece of disinterested literary realism, by its end certain elements also seem to take on a subtle but insistent symbolic resonance. Because 'The Sisters' seems radically unresolved within the conventions of European story-telling of its time, the reader is driven back into the story to find its possible meaning at another level. In what Edward Brandabur calls 'more sophisticated interpretations' (Brandabur, 1971, p. 48), the questions become ones such as these: what then is the significance of the broken chalice? Are the priest's devoted sisters emblematic of Catholic Ireland? Is the Priest? And finally, do we read any great significance into the triad of strange words the boy says to himself on hearing of the priest's death; 'paralysis', 'gnomon', and 'simony'? 'The Sisters' is, as Father Purdon says of a Biblical passage in 'Grace', 'one of the most difficult texts...to interpret' (p. 173). There is also a sort of mirroring between the story and the criticism it has generated. There is 'something uncanny' (p. 1) about the way the latter takes the shape of the former inasmuch as the interrogative style of the story is mimed by the cascade of questions the story provokes from the criticism. We will find much of this kind of repetition and circularity at work in this rather disquieting story, but more importantly, the disquiet is directly related to the disconcerting rhetorical and narrative devices used to trouble the reader's attempts at making a coherent narrative of the text.

If 'The Sisters' has been seen as a difficult piece of early modernism, more recently, critics of a post-structuralist kidney such as Margot Norris and Garry M. Leonard have trumped or possibly short-circuited the commentary on the story and on *Dubliners* more generally. Like Mrs Mooney, the landlady in 'The Boarding House' who deals with moral problems 'as a cleaver deals with meat' (p. 58), they argue with Jesuitical cleverness that the goal of adequate interpretation or complete understanding is a chimera and that this is the very point of the story. We have travelled a long way from Frank O'Connor's admission of incomprehension; not getting the point is now the point of the story. As Leonard has it, 'It is the experience of incomprehension that is the lesson of *Dubliners*' (Leonard, 1993, p. 17). Of course, incomprehension alone would not make much of a tale; 'The Sisters' engenders a readerly desire for knowledge, even if it is ultimately thwarted. Here again there is a consonance between the kinds of epistemological concerns the characters in the story have and the kinds of questions the reader initially wishes to have answered and it is in the characters' use of ellipses that this can be seen most forcibly.

The story's ellipses provoke questions about what the characters know and how, when enough epistemological torque is applied, the reader is encouraged to traduce the conventional narrative boundaries to ask it questions which can be seen as ontological, that is, about the very nature of the story as a story, about its identity or form. These latter kinds of questions can be addressed by looking at what narratologists call metalepses. Through the use of ellipses, which are narrative gaps, and one type of metalepsis, which is the shifting of narrative levels, Joyce's tale has something to say about our understanding of death. To make explicit the spatial metaphor that is being used here, ellipses take us more deeply 'into' the story, while metalepsis take us 'out', allows us to stand back from it. The narrative asks its readers both to identify with its characters and to distance ourselves from them; to engage with their epistemological endeavours and to view the piece as a literary work, that is, to address its ontological status. Though for now we may keep these movements into and out of the text separate, by the story's conclusion, we will see how 'The Sisters' oscillates between epistemological and ontological concerns.

Unlikely though it might at first appear, both the ellipses and the readerly possibility of breaking the conventions of narrative levels in the story point us towards a meditation on death. How is this so? Firstly, ellipses evoke questions of the unknowable. These are epistemological questions. Secondly, the crossing of a narrative boundary will ultimately call to mind the crossing of the most profound boundary of all; that between life and death. Epistemology is the philosophy of knowledge, and asks questions such as 'What do we know and how do we know it?', while ontology is the study of being or existence itself, and asks questions such as 'What is existence?; What is the nature of an object? What constitutes its identity?' [4].

Firstly, ellipses and the epistemological questions they bring to the reader's mind. What exactly is an ellipsis? Richard Lanham's useful *Handlist of Rhetorical Terms* tells us that ellipsis means 'to fall short, to leave out' (Lanham, 1968, p. 39). This is close to the rhetorical figure of aposiopesis, which Lanham describes as 'becoming silent' and as 'an idea, though unexpressed, is clearly perceived' (Lanham, 1968, p. 15). An example of this kind of ellipsis in the story would be the boy's aunt's question about Father Flynn: 'Did he … peacefully? She asked' (p. 7). This ellipsis is a classic aposiopesis, for the missing word 'die' is avoided by the aunt out of her sense of social delicacy, but in terms of the story is foregrounded through its very absence. The word is central to the story and easily retrieved. The rest of the ellipses, however, cannot be so easily interpreted.

In this characterisation, the other ellipses in 'The Sisters' are a kind of anti-aposiopesis, for as any reader will verify, very little in the story is very clearly perceived. Take the following comments by Old Cotter to the boy's Uncle Jack, on the boy's and the priest's relationship: 'there was something queer…something uncanny about him. I'll tell you my opinion…' (p. 1); 'I think it was one of those…peculiar cases…But it's hard to say….He began to puff again at his pipe without giving us his theory' (pp. 1-2); 'let a young lad run about and play with young lads of his own age and not be … Am I right, Jack?' (p. 2); 'When children see things like that, you know, it has an effect …' (p. 3). In all these cases the three dots that mark an ellipsis cannot, in the world of the story, be meaningfully filled. As the boy himself says of Old Cotter, 'I puzzled my head to extract meaning from his unfinished sentences' (p. 3). To a large degree, these ellipses give the story its enigmatic quality.

In his book on sixteenth-century rhetoric, Lee Sonnino offers a more useful definition of aposiopesis for our purposes. Sonnino quotes Quintilian writing on aposiopesis thus: 'what is suppressed is uncertain' and Scaliger in a similar vein: 'When we stop without a word of explanation … we simply break off' (Sonnino, 1968, p. 142). This form of ellipsis occurs throughout the story and reaches its apotheosis in the story's very last line. Eliza tells of her brother being found in the confessional laughing to himself and comments, 'So then, of course, when they saw that, that made them think that there was something gone wrong with him …. ' This falling silent, this aporetic 'breaking off', as Scaliger has it, has come to have about it the flavour of death, at least since the work of the most-discussed author in *Ulysses*. As Brian Vickers writes in his *In Defence of Rhetoric*, 'The broken-off sentence, Shakespeare observed, is also a peculiarly appropriate way of symbolising death' (Vickers, 1998, p. 336).

So, in a story about death, death is at work in the rhetorical strategies of the story. In the first instance, it is in the ellipses that litter the text, but not just there. To go back to the material from which stories are made, it might be said that language itself carries within it an intimation of our mortality. We are after all mortals, 'the dying ones' according to *The Iliad*'s Achilles. The idea that language and therefore our very identity is inhabited by death is put surprisingly boldly by Jacques Derrida in *Speech and Phenomena*, where the usually gnomic philosopher states that 'My death is structurally necessary to the pronouncing of the *I*' (Derrida, 1973, pp. 96-7) and this is so because '*I am* originally means *I am mortal. I am immortal* is an impossible proposition' (Derrida, 1973, p. 54). Later, in *Writing and Difference,* Derrida tells us (admittedly rather more opaquely) 'Life is death' (Derrida, 1989, p. 202). This formulation, broadly similar to Temple's in Joyce's *Portrait* 'Reproduction is the beginning of death' (Joyce, 1992b, p. 208), is a type of metalepsis, meaning here 'a distance cause', a form of 'extreme compression' (Holman and Harmon, 1980, p. 297). Metalepsis has a more familiar meaning taken from narratology and it is with this use in mind that I would like to look again at death in 'The Sisters' and consider once more those ellipses which seem to cause such epistemological anxiety in both the story's characters and its readers.

First of all it is worth remembering Joyce's fiction is suffused with death. The two leading male characters in *Ulysses* are in mourning clothes, Bloom for Paddy Dignam's funeral and Stephen for his mother, while of course the title of Joyce's last novel evokes a pre-funeral rite. As Nietzsche writes in *The Gay Science* (1882), first published in the year of Joyce's birth and a book Mr Duffy of 'A Painful Case' has on his shelf (p. 108), 'Let us beware of saying that death is opposed to life. The living is merely a type of what is dead, and a very rare type' (Nietzsche, 1973, p. 168), a point reinforced by a sententious comment of Robert Hand's in Joyce's play *Exiles*: 'There was an eternity before we were born; another will come after we are dead' (Joyce, 1976, p. 585). But it is at a more profound level that death features in the structure of 'The Sisters'.

Twenty years ago, Brian McHale suggested that 'death is the one ontological boundary that we are all certain to experience, the only one we shall all inevitably have to cross. In a sense, every ontological boundary is an analogue or metaphor of death' (McHale, 1987, p. 231). How does this work in narrative discourse? McHale quotes Walter J. Ong in support of his thesis: 'The ... work which deals with life and death honestly – often turns out to be in some way about itself ...that is to say, a work about death often modulates readily if eerily, into a work about literature' (McHale p. 231). We can see such a process at work in 'The Sisters' in the following fashion. Gerard Genette explains the concept of narrative levels as the 'shifting but sacred frontier between two worlds, the world in which one tells, the world of which one tells' (Genette, 1980, p. 236). Genette calls any shift in narrative levels, or frame-breaking 'metalepsis'. For McHale, metalepses are 'the violations of ontological boundaries' (McHale, p. 227). To be sure, all the characters and events in 'The Sisters' remain in the same narrative plane. The narrative frame is not broken as it is in, say, Flann O'Brien's *At Swim-Two-Birds* (1939), where at one point characters invented by a novelist plot their revenge upon him and enter into his world in pursuit of it. This kind of 'infection' of one narrative level by the other is somewhat disturbing for a reader's understanding of the nature of reality in the text. The largely dour and grim *Dubliners* seems as far as possible removed from the flagrantly metafictional hi-jinks to be found in the likes of *At Swim–Two-Birds*.

Nevertheless, 'The Sisters' is a disturbing story; but rather than the characters shifting narrative levels and breaking the fictional frame, what happens is that in our attempt to make sense of the story as readers, we are driven beyond the fictional universe of the characters through the rhetorical trope of metalepsis. In Joyce's story though, it is a reading technique, one into which the text manoeuvres us. It taps into our dread of death and offers us a fantastical resolution to the problem of the 'immanence' of life. At the same time, because metalepsis is a rhetorical device that cannot really manifest itself in the material world, the implication must be that such 'transcendence' is taking place only in a fiction, or to put it more boldly, that transcendence itself is a comforting fiction, merely a figurative dream of escape conjured up by the story, paralleling the more material hopes of escape desired by many of the characters in *Dubliners*.

The quiet allusion to the *Inferno* in the story's first line and the contemplation of the word 'paralysis' hints at the impossibility of escape for the characters in the stories. Many have dreams of escape that are then frustrated, from the eponymous Eveline's failed attempt to run away to Bob Doran's weary decision to marry Polly the landlady's daughter in 'The Boarding House'. Others feel trapped by the routine of work and the responsibilities of family life, such as Chandler in 'A Little Cloud' and Farringdon in 'Counterparts'. When Joyce began it in 1904, he himself described his collection in a letter in terms of entrapment and stasis: 'I shall call the series *Dubliners* to betray the soul of that hemiplegia or paralysis which many consider a city' (Joyce, 1975b, p. 22). Years later, defending his work to his publisher, he was still using the same terms. But Joyce could also elide the moral and the aesthetic. When he wrote about 'the struggle against conventions in which I am at present involved' (Joyce, 1975a, p. 99), he was thinking not only of *Dubliners*'s candid depiction of sexual, social and political relations in Victorian and Edwardian Dublin and arguing against the censorship of his work, but also of the literary conventions he was about to dramatically overturn. His aesthetic and moral radicalism can be seen in the frank description of the seedier side of Dublin life and his sympathy for even the most reprehensible of his characters whose behaviour he seems to understand. 'Poor Corley' Joyce writes in a letter about the despicable seducer of 'Two Gallants' (Joyce, 1975a, p. 199). These characters are trapped in the circles of hell that are Joyce's Dublin and though some still harbour dreams of escape, we suspect that they have as much chance of achieving them as the souls in the *Inferno*.

John William Corrington picks up this idea in an essay on 'The Sisters'. He quotes sociologist Richard Weaver's concept of 'the dream of escape' we experience as a consequence of 'an intuitive feeling about the immanent nature of reality' (Corrington, 1969, p. 13). Corrington quotes a critic on Chekhov, who says the Russian playwright deals with 'people who find themselves in a trap or in a box' (Corrington, 1969, p. 17). John Donne's tenth 'Meditation' takes this idea more literally and is close to the world of Joyce's story when he writes of '*Nature's nest of Boxes*; The Heavens contain the *Earth*, the *Earth*, *Cities*, *Cities*, *Men*. And all these are *Concentric*; the common centre to them all is *decay, ruin*' (Donne, 2004, p. 35). 'The Sisters' has many images of 'boxes' - enclosed spaces such as kitchens, dead rooms, confessionals, and finally Father Flynn's coffin. Its destination is that paradigmatic enclosed space, the grave, and graves feature in the famous passage that closes the final story of the collection, 'The Dead'. We might also draw a parallel between these Donne-like boxes and levels or layers of narration, which has consequences for a reading of Joyce's first story as a story. To consider these consequences though, we have to look at what we can say with some certainty about the events of the story and discussion for most readers will begin when certainties break down, so first readings of 'The Sisters' will surely concentrate on trying in some way to fill in the ellipses; they will attempt to find some kind of explanation for these breakings-off of dialogue.

These kinds of analyses read Old Cotter's ellipses, for example, as the understandably oblique references to moral corruption of the young and in its worst form, paedophilia: 'Let a young lad run about and play with young lads of his own age and not be … Am I right, Jack?' (p. 2); 'When children see things like that, you know, it has an effect …' (p. 3). But as Edward Brandabur has said, 'a substantial conjecture is needed to explain the priest's mysterious hold on the protagonist' (Brandabur, 1971, p. 40). Substantial indeed; once we have peeled away the layers of comment in the narrative we find that such a conjecture is very hard to substantiate. Like Father Flynn's dropped chalice, ultimately 'it contained nothing' (p. 10). In one sense, because of its very form, 'The Sisters' certainly demands that we do our best to try to read these ellipses in terms of the world that produced them, that is, taking seriously the reality represented by the narrator. At the very least, the literary realism of the story initially requires it. We are encouraged to delve deep into the narrative, to be the 'more subtle inquisitor' Joyce writes of in his letter defending his collection of stories to his publisher (Joyce, 1975a, p. 134), to give an 'immanent' reading in the sense that we remain within the world of the story to understand it. In another sense, the story's enigmatic qualities drive us to read these same epistemologically-loaded ellipses in another way. If we look again at some of the characters' comments, 'The Sisters' certainly appears to be 'one of those … peculiar cases' (pp.1-2).

As the young narrator thinks about Old Cotter's halting comments on the unsuitability of the boy's relationship with the old priest, he says 'I puzzled my head to extract meaning from his unfinished sentences' (p. 3). One way of reading this sentence is metaleptically: to shift it 'up' a narrative level and to see it as a comment of the story's enigmatic qualities. We might apply what William York Tindall once wrote about Joyce's last fiction - '*Finnegans Wake* is about *Finnegans Wake*' (Tindall, 1959, p. 237) - to Joyce's first. 'The Sisters' is about itself inasmuch as it is about enigma. However, what the story deals with is not what may be behind the enigma, but is an example of enigma itself. This baffling story paradoxically generates the simplest form of truth; the tautology. 'The Sisters' is about 'The Sisters'; the enigma of the story is the very symbol of the enigma. It might appear then, that like Wittgenstein's artichoke, there are only layers (Wittgenstein, 2001, p. 110). In 'The Sisters', metalepsis seems to be a reading strategy we may use to deal with the irresolvable enigmas in the story, but it is one that the story has foreseen. The metaleptic move also allows 'The Sisters' a way of gesturing both at the possibility of escaping from the nest of narrative boxes that is our life, and the impossibility of such a flight. The story holds out the possibility by expecting us to make the metaleptic leap to a higher narrative level in our attempt to make sense of the work before us, but of course we cannot do this in our own lives without positing some form of transcendental reality. The story is therefore in some small way thinking through the idea of an afterlife, that ultimate wish-fulfilling escape from our present lives.

All commentators on the collection discuss the ways in which the characters in *Dubliners* seek escape, but the characters sometimes seek escape in a similar fashion to the process of metalepsis outlined above. 'We wouldn't see him want for anything while he was in it' (p. 8), says Eliza of her dead brother, and the metaphor of being 'in' life, being enclosed, encircled by it, is a familiar and pervasive one. A way of attempting a form of transcendence to escape the lethal immanence of human existence is to metaleptically move from the role of character and take on the role of author of your own fate. As Brian McHale observes, 'An author, by definition, occupies an ontological level superior to that of his or her character' (McHale, 1987, p. 222). Mr Duffy in 'A Painful Case' and Chandler of 'A Little Cloud' both refer to themselves in the third person. Mr Duffy composes in his mind 'from time to time a short sentence about himself containing a subject in the third person and a predicate in the past tense' (p. 104). Such attempts will fail, because 'Though you may imagine that you have jumped out of yourself, you never can actually do so' (Douglas Hofstadter, cited in McHale, 1987, p. 232), simply because, no matter what you do to avoid it, like the titular lobster in the Beckett story, you are going to end up in the metaphorical cooking pot.

Joyce went on to organise his next fiction around notions of artistic freedom culminating in what might be called one huge and audacious metalepsis. It is a critical commonplace to point out the images of escape and flight that pervade Joyce's first novel. As *A Portrait of the Artist as a Young Man* concludes, we wonder whether the young artist Stephen Dedalus will succeed in writing a great work – and we cannot know. But if we accept a metaleptic shift of narrative levels in the novel, we could say that Dedalus writes something like the very book we have just finished, and of course the same can be said of the middle-aged proto-*litterateur* Marcel at the end of Proust's novel. As authors occupying an ontological level superior to that of their characters, the trope of metalepsis turns these works into self-generating novels. Hey, presto! Stephen and Marcel seem to escape the confines of the pages of their respective novels as Joyce and Proust. Their artist-figure protagonists are heroic, heavily ironised though they may be. The biggest irony of all however, is that it is only on the page that they escape the iron-clad immanence of existence.

Where we end up in this economy of narrative exchange is with two shades: the ghostly figure of the implied author – 'Ah! Poor James!' (p. 8), and the poor, doomed, implied reader – us – when we open the pages of *Dubliners* to contemplate the dreadful truth of our ultimate absence, figuratively and bitterly brought home through the characters' dreams and fantasies of escaping their various fates. To generalise the first line of 'The Sisters', there's no hope, then, for any of us in the world of Joyce's *Dubliners*. Jorge Luis Borges has suggested that narrative frame-breaking has a disturbing effect on the stability and authority of the reader. In 'Partial Magic in the Quixote', Borges writes 'If the characters of a fictional work can be readers or spectators, we, its readers or spectators, can be fictional' (Borges, 1970, p. 231). This idea, though he doesn't use the term, is a form of metalepsis. Borges's destabilising of the reader presents us with the abysmal possibility that we may be characters in another's narrative. Joyce's story conjures up its own destablising effects through the manner in which we are encouraged to read a number of the exchanges of dialogue at different narrative levels.

To recap: 'The Sisters' asks its readers both to identify with its characters and to distance ourselves from them; to engage in their epistemological endeavours and to view the story as a literary work by addressing its ontological status. This can be seen in the shortest sentences of narrative and in briefest exchanges of dialogue. If the most obvious case is the boy narrator's comment on Old Cotter's elliptical remarks ('I puzzled my head to extract meaning from his unfinished sentences'), where the epistemological drive of the comment can also be read as an ontological observation on the story itself, then the boy's only two instances of direct speech may be less obvious but no less relevant. Unsurprisingly, both these instances of speech are interrogatives. On being told by his uncle that his 'old friend is gone, you'll be sorry to hear', the boy asks 'Who?, Said I' (p. 2). On hearing that it is Father Flynn, he asks 'Is he dead?' (p. 2). We could, at a push, see the two questions asked by the boy as representing the two narrative positions discussed above. The first question is broadly epistemological: 'Who?, Said I'. The second is broadly ontological: 'Is he dead?' The first concerns knowing, the second concerns being. It could quite fairly be objected that the characterisation of these two sentences doesn't hold up very rigorously – if ontology deals with questions of identity, then the first of the boy's questions would do as well as an example as the second. I think the story concedes this, because although they have been separated above, the important thing is not that there are two ways of thinking or reading at work here, or two potential levels of narration in the story – I think there are - but that there is oscillation between them. It is not two moves, but one; it is the oscillation itself at the heart of 'The Sisters'. In a rather sinister story that leads us into a collection concerned with moral, political and emotional paralysis and the hopelessness of escaping from it, 'The Sisters' gets its vibrancy from its dynamic and yet lugubrious narrative style; what can only be called, considering its use of the most baleful of materials, its fundamental playfulness. The tale is constantly playing with notions of what counts as inside the story and what counts as outside.

One last example of how an ellipsis works metaleptically is in the final sentence of the story. The trailing off of Eliza's speech, if we recall what Brian Vickers says about Shakespeare's use of aposiopesis, signifies death, but of course this last sentence is also the last sentence of the story itself, its three dots open out onto the rest of the collection. To use Genette's terminology (though there are others one might adopt) and keeping the story's dizzying potential narratological oscillation in mind, we can read the ellipsis at the end not just as referring to 'the world in which one tells', that is, Eliza's world as reported in direct speech by the boy narrator, but also 'the world of which one tells', the realm of the implied author.

It can be objected that all 'symbolic' readings, treating the events of a narrative as meaning something other than what is stated in the text, are metaleptic, so why not save a great deal of effort and just call the narrative allegorical or symbolic? But of what is it symbolic? According to this reading, of the story itself. If the interpretation is pushed far enough, 'The Sisters' turns back, Moebius-like, on itself. There is also a continuous oscillation above in what is claimed as the effort of the reader and what is seen as the cunning of the story, but the various claims are probably inseparable. Why this is the case is an appropriate instance of Joycean circularity: it is so because of the way the story has taught us to read. So while there may be no genuine hope for any of us in the universe of *Dubliners*, we might take comfort from the fact that after more than one hundred years since its publication, through reading the novelist's later work, we are coming to terms with Joyce's first story. But then again, in all that time no-one has yet come up with a very convincing reason why it is called 'The Sisters'.

Notes

[1] See Waisbren and Walzl (1974).

[2] All references to 'The Sisters' will be from this edition and are henceforth referenced by page number only.

[3] See Adams (p. 170); Brunsdale (p. 7); Kershner (p. 23); Torchiana (p. 19); Tindall (p. 13); Beck (p. 42).

[4] The first chapter of Brian McHale's *Postmodern Fiction* (1987) uses the difference between epistemological and ontological questions to distinguish modern from postmodern fiction. Though McHale is persuasive, I think both kinds of question are at work in Joyce's story.

References

Adair, G. (2006), *The Act of Roger Murgatroyd*, Faber & Faber, London.

Adams, R. N. (1966), *James Joyce: Common Sense and Beyond*, Random House, New York.

Beck, W. (1966), *Joyce's Dubliners: Substance, Vision, Art*, Duke University Press, Durham NC.

Beckett, S. (1972), *More Pricks Than Kicks*, Picador, London.

Beja, M. (ed.) (1973), *Dubliners and A Portrait of the Artist as a Young Man: A Casebook*, Macmillan, Basingstoke.

Borges, J. L. (1970), *Labyrinths*, Penguin, Harmondsworth.

Brandabur, E. (1971), *A Scrupulous Meanness: A Study of Joyce's Early Work*, University of Illinois Press, Urbana, IL.

Brunsdale, M. M. (1993), *James Joyce: A Study of the Short Fiction*, Twayne, New York.

Corrington, J. W. (1969), 'The Sisters' in *James Joyce's Dubliners: Critical Essays*, ed. C. Hart, Faber & Faber, London, pp. 12-24.

Derrida, J. (1973), *Speech and Phenomena*, Northwestern University Press, Evanston.

Derrida, J. (1989), *Writing and Difference*, Routledge and Kegan Paul, London.

Donne, J. (2004), *Devotions Upon Emergent Occasions,* Kessinger, New York.

Ellmann, R. (1982), *James Joyce*, Oxford University Press, Oxford.

Genette G. (1980), *Narrative Discourse: An Essay in Method*, Blackwell, Oxford.

Hart, C. (ed.) (1969), *James Joyce's Dubliners: Critical Essays*, Faber & Faber, London.

Holman, C. H. and Harmon, W. (1980), *A Handbook to Literature*, Bobs Merrill, New York.

Joyce, J. (1959), *The Critical Writings of James Joyce*, ed. E. Mason and R. Ellmann, Faber & Faber, London.

Joyce, J. (1975a), *Letters of James Joyce Volume II*, ed. R. Ellmann, Faber & Faber, London.

Joyce, J. (1975b), *Selected Letters of James Joyce*, ed. R. Ellmann, Faber & Faber, London.

Joyce, J. (1976), *The Portable James Joyce*, ed. H. Levin, Penguin, Harmondsworth.

Joyce, J. (1992a), *Dubliners*, ed. T. Brown. Penguin, Harmondsworth.

Joyce, J. (1992b), *A Portrait of the Artist as a Young Man*, ed. S. Deane, Penguin, Harmondsworth.

Joyce, J. (2000), *Ulysses*, ed. D. Kiberd, Penguin, Harmondsworth.

Kenner, H. (1978), *Joyce's Voices*, University of Columbia Press, New York.

Kenner, H. (1987), *Dublin's Joyce*, University of Columbia Press, New York.

Kershner, R. B. (1989), *Joyce, Bakhtin and Popular Literature: Chronicle of Disorder*, University of North Carolina Press, Chapel Hill, NC.

Lanham, R. A. (1968), *A Handlist of Rhetorical Terms*, University of California Press, Berkeley, CA.

Leonard, G. M. (1993), *Reading Dubliners Again: A Lacanian Perspective*, Syracuse University Press, New York.

McHale, B. (1987), *Postmodern Fiction*, Routledge, London.

Nietzsche, F. (1974), *The Gay Science*, trans. W. Kauffmann. Vintage, New York.

Norris, M. (2003), *Suspicious Readings of Joyce's Dubliners*, University of Pennsylvania Press, Philadelphia, PA.

Sonnino, L. A. (1968), *A Handbook to Sixteenth-Century Rhetoric*, Routledge & Kegan Paul, London.

Tindall, W. Y. (1959), *A Reader's Guide to James Joyce*, Noonday, New York.

Torchiana, D. T. (1986), *Backgrounds for Joyce's 'Dubliners'*, Macmillan, Basingstoke.

Vickers, B. (1998), *In Defence of Rhetoric*, Oxford University Press, Oxford.

Waisbren, B. A. and Walzl, F. L. (1974), 'Paresis and the Priest: James Joyce's Symbolic use of Syphilis in "The Sisters"', *Annals of Internal Medicine*, 80, pp. 758-762.

Wittgenstein, L. (2001), *Philosophical Investigations*, trans. G. Anscombe, 3rd ed. Blackwell, Oxford.

A Belfast the Poets have Imagined: Louis MacNeice and Derek Mahon

Brian Burton

University of Sunderland

It is common knowledge that for many years the reputation of Louis MacNeice was overshadowed by the daunting figure of Auden. One of the problems faced by MacNeice was that critics and readers were unable to bracket him convincingly and solely within either of the literary traditions to which he apparently belonged. Despite numerous allusions in his poems to Belfast and a mythologised West of Ireland, he was seen neither as sufficiently Irish for readers of Yeats and Kavanagh, nor as English as Auden and Spender, poets with whom he was bracketed, along with C. Day-Lewis, under the derisory epithet 'MacSpaunday'. However, during the 1960s and 70s a new breed of young Northern Irish poets emerged, hailing MacNeice as a major formative influence on their own writing. Michael Longley and Paul Muldoon have been vociferous in their praise of MacNeice, and each has played his part in the campaign to establish MacNeice within the pantheon of modern Irish poets (see, for example, *The Faber Book of Contemporary Irish Poetry*, edited by Paul Muldoon, which allocates more than 60 pages to MacNeice's work, more than any other anthology). But Derek Mahon was to take MacNeice's example furthest in his poetry. A common religious and social background links the two, certainly, but MacNeice's presence lurks among many of Mahon's poems on several far deeper, and more significant, levels. MacNeice's legacy exerts itself in Mahon's work not only in their respective treatments of similar themes, but also in matters of form and technique. Such features include an abiding tendency towards irony and scepticism, a carefully crafted ambiguity that frequently defies paraphrase, and an elegant virtuosity of verse form and construction. Each of these qualities is present in their writings on home and alienation.

MacNeice felt destined to become something of an outsider from a young age, stating in 'Carrickfergus' (MacNeice, 1979, pp. 69-70), 'I was the rector's son, born to the Anglican order, / Banned for ever from the candles of the Irish poor'. By dint of his Anglo-Irish, Ulster Protestant heritage, MacNeice could not hope to share the thoughts, experiences or feelings of the Catholic minority in Ulster: yet nor is there any suggestion in this poem of true or complete allegiance to 'the Anglican order'. Being born to a social position usually carries the inference of natural or presumptuous acceptance ('to the manor born', for instance), but MacNeice implies an inheritance over which he has absolutely no control, and over which the figure of his father looms large. Hemmed in by the Norman-built city walls, while subjected to a sense of enslavement by soldiers returning from World War II, MacNeice is surrounded by the masculine values that keep him ostracised from his fellow countrymen. Female influence is completely lacking in the poem, the poet being separated from his mother, his governess, 'the mill girls', and, he seems to imply, the feminine, Catholic dimension of 'Mother Ireland'. It is as though he is suggesting that disconnection from home can be equated with the lack of stability produced by the absence of a maternal figure. Yet we find no sentimentality in these lines, just a matter-of-fact resignation towards the recognition that disconnection is, so to speak, the way things are in Belfast and the way they are likely to continue to be. The strongly positioned word 'Banned' reinforces MacNeice's own sense of segregation. The poem's opening gambit – 'I was born in Belfast between the mountain and the gantries' – also establishes his position as a kind of 'nowhere man' incapable of finding any sense of belonging either among the indigenous Gaelic population, for whom ideas of land, home and nationality go hand-in-hand, or among the Protestant community whose unwavering commercialism and industrialisation of the province have continually exacerbated religious and political tensions.

'Carrickfergus' is a deceptively complex poem, and MacNeice is careful not to make explicit his feelings towards either the Protestant or the Catholic inhabitants of Ulster. The Irish Quarter, a liminal home for dispossessed Gaels, is a deprived area ('a slum for the blind and the halt'), while members of the Protestant community, exemplified by the privileged family interred in the crypt of his father's church, are guaranteed 'their portion' in the afterlife. Although speculation may conclude that MacNeice's sympathy lies predominantly with the impoverished Catholics, the poem refuses to draw an entirely clear picture regarding his perspective on and attitude towards his fellow Protestants. Like Beckett and Joyce, MacNeice 'reject[s] political formulations about humanity', endeavouring instead to present a balanced view of humanity stripped of ideological trappings (Johnston, 1997, p. 225). Indeed, one of the defining features of MacNeice's poetry is a stubbornly contained 'evasive honesty' that frequently makes it almost impossible to pin down accurately any firmly held political or religious position (Fraser, 1959, p. 180). This quality may well have been inherited from his Anglican bishop father who preached pacifism while, somewhat paradoxically, expounding Home Rule, but there is no doubt that it was also passed on by MacNeice to Mahon whose work is similarly elusive, often infuriatingly so.

MacNeice's early poem 'Belfast' (MacNeice, 1979, p. 17) takes on a far more sinister aspect than anything found in 'Carrickfergus':

> Down there at the end of the melancholy lough
> Against the lurid sky over the stained water
> Where hammers clang murderously on the girders
> Like crucifixes the gantries stand.

The juxtaposition of violence, religion and industrial commercialism rams home MacNeice's measured, denunciatory response to profit-orientated culture. The northerner's 'hard cold fire' provides neither warmth nor light; it is 'cowled' amid the 'gloom' of an inimically intransigent regime that prefers its religious iconography to be aesthetically primitive artefacts of 'buyable beauty' rather than symbols of authentic worship. Once again MacNeice avoids the reductive oversimplification of ascribing blame for Belfast's condition to any religious faction. Scenes derived from the Protestant-dominated shipyards and the sound of 'Orange drums' are set against traditional Catholic images of 'the garish Virgin' and the Madonna. Edna Longley has claimed that the last line of this stanza 'fuses industrial and religious oppressiveness, to symbolize Protestant rule', but this judgment does not quite ring true, the crucifix being a predominantly – though not exclusively, of course – Catholic image (Longley, 1996, p. 20).

'Belfast' shares with 'Carrickfergus' the harsh, clanging consonance of northern speech that MacNeice remembered from childhood, and this linguistic device is used to heap barely modulated scorn on an increasingly materialistic culture that has scarred the landscape with its technology of mass production. The very fabric of the poem is designed to articulate the character of both the city and its people, its phraseology mirroring the construction of the city walls described in 'Carrickfergus': 'the hard, solid diction is part of the meaning of the poem', writes Terence Brown (Brown, 1975, p. 169). The city's church may take 'the form of a cross' but its walls are designed to isolate it from the countryside, the rest of Ireland proper, and more especially Belfast's Catholic population who had become the Normans' 'slave[s]'. However, 'Carrickfergus', published six years after 'Belfast', shows a more mature MacNeice taking a less antagonistic approach towards the enslaving effects of Belfast's turbulent history. The misogynistic overtones of the earlier poem ('the male kind murders each its woman') regress to a less violent, though no less effective, sense of absence, while its contrived, unpunctuated syntax would eventually make way for the increasingly journalistic style of reportage he came to favour, most famously in *Autumn Journal*. MacNeice was undoubtedly influenced by Eliot's enabling acceptance of the modern city as ripe material for poetry, and in his hands this style proves remarkably productive. Gareth Reeves has observed that this journalistic form 'can accommodate contradictions without sounding contradictory: faithful to the moment, to time passing, to capturing and holding the "ephemeral" on "tangent wings"' (O'Neill and Reeves, 1992, p. 185). Faithfulness and honesty, no matter how evasive, contribute to the poem's finely balanced registering that MacNeice, irrespective of personal feelings towards the city and its inhabitants, has a fundamental responsibility to present his impressions honestly and with sincerity.

These themes of isolation, disjointed religious inheritance, and the sense of being physically attached to a home city (despite feeling spiritually and intellectually divorced from it), provide recurrent motifs in Derek Mahon's poetry. One of his earliest poems is the direct poetic successor to MacNeice's 'Belfast'. 'In Belfast' (Mahon, 1968, p. 6) begins, 'Walking among my own this windy morning / In a tide of sunlight between shower and shower'. While MacNeice's poem opens without direct reference to either the poet or the poem's speaker, Mahon immediately situates himself centrally amidst the community to which he ostensibly belongs, establishing his position from the outset as a means of conferring a more authoritative perspective on the poem than that provided by MacNeice. While MacNeice's speaker retains the position of outsider looking in, Mahon is *in medias res*, walking among his fellow citizens. However, he is quick to dispel any genuine sense of allegiance between himself and 'his' people since the word 'my' still serves to reinforce individuality and independence. His enlightened position as privileged recipient of poetic inspiration ('a tide of sunlight') instantly singles him out from the deluge of humanity he must endure in the course of his travels. Climatic and meteorological diction compounds his isolation: while the poet associates himself with 'sunlight', the uneducated, unsophisticated Belfast populace is afflicted with the darker aspects of stormy weather. It is also interesting to note Mahon's use of the word 'tide', for quite apart from representing his constant ebbing and flowing away from and back to Belfast, an aspect of his cosmopolitan lifestyle that undermines any concrete concept of 'home', Mahon also uses the word in a context completely antithetical to that suggested by MacNeice's 'Belfast'. While MacNeice allegorises the tides of the sea ('the salt carrion water') as the means by which parasitical industrialists make their fortunes, the image is transformed by Mahon into a rather different kind of transport. The escapist potential of the sea here becomes a transcendental, imaginative escape into poetry, a form of beauty unappreciated and misunderstood by the greater part of Belfast's citizenry. Expressions such as 'resume' and 'Once more' help to reinforce Mahon's chosen itinerancy, suggesting repeated rueful returns to the darkness of unreason signified by Belfast. He cannot belong completely without reneging on his principles and ideals, or without abandoning the warm, nourishing light of reason for 'The cold gaze of a sanctimonious God'. 'In Belfast' has, at its heart, a structure of hierarchical allegiances. Although Mahon declares 'we keep sullen silence in light and shade' seemingly out of communal spirit, there are actually two different referents for 'we' here. On one hand it denotes the small, illuminated artistic community to which he truly belongs and who prefer to ironise their relationship with the province rather than engage directly with its politics; on the other, it signifies the brutal society from which he is isolated and is described by MacNeice in 'Belfast' in such damningly violent terms: 'The sun goes down with a banging of Orange drums / While the male kind murders each its woman / To whose prayer for oblivion answers no Madonna'.

MacNeice's view of Belfast is informed by a savagely ironical apprehension of shame and disgust, yet it is precisely the antinomies contained within this ironic stance that foreground the nature of his revulsion. *The Strings Are False*, MacNeice's unfinished autobiography, exposes an honest, unabashed tendency towards snobbery in his inability to understand fully the lives of those for whom intellectual and aesthetic endeavours are not important. He admits his failure to recognise that the northern temperament has been forged, like the steel of Belfast ships, by material necessities beyond its control. He also confesses to his intrinsic ignorance, brought on by detachment, of the macho shipbuilding community whose activities contrast so sharply with those of the almost exclusively female linen workers (the 'shawled factory-wom[e]n'). When 'Belfast' speaks of 'us who walk in the street so buoyantly and glib', 'buoyantly' provides a simple yet effective pun on the efficiency and success of the ship-workers' labours for which he has little real understanding or sympathy, and the line makes a poignant, pointed comment on the lack of either buoyancy or glibness in the northern character. His remarks also constitute a coming to terms, a realisation that, whatever his social circumstances, whether as an Anglo-Irish Protestant in Ireland or as an Irishman in England, he is fated never to feel truly at home. The opening line of 'Carrickfergus' ('I was born between the mountain and the gantries') scrutinises the duality of connection and dislocation, not just in the juxtaposition of Belfast's rural and urban landscapes, but equally importantly in the ambiguous preposition 'between'. Paradoxically, this could suggest both entrapment and the enabling perspective of being able to see the landscape in its entirety, and, indeed, both sides of the political divide. Mahon's poem, however, exhibits no such ambiguity. Mahon similarly positions himself in a position of betweenness, but rather than being allowed a dual perspective he feels hemmed in and stifled by the featureless majority who, as 'shower[s]', take the brunt of his intellectual derogation. He consequently considers himself inexorably set apart from his allotted community and its pernicious, inauthentic influence.

These differences go some way towards explaining Mahon's revision of the final stanza of 'In Belfast' from the version that originally appeared in 1964 in the magazine *Icarus*. MacNeice's presence is particularly strong here:

> Poetry and fluent drivel, know your place –
> Take shape in some more glib environment
> Away from shipyard gantry, bolt and rivet.
> Elsewhere assess existence; ask to what end
> It tends, wherefore and why. In Belfast live it. (in Longley, 1984, p. 66)

The irony-tinged scepticism throws into question the value of art amid a philistine environment, and it is clear that the alliteratively mocking language of 'glib' and 'gantry' emerged from a poetic consciousness that had absorbed MacNeice's imagery and diction almost wholesale. Mahon reinforces MacNeice's observation that the frivolity usually associated with glibness has no place in an environment so oppressively antagonistic towards artistic creativity. The ingenious rhyming of 'rivet' and 'live it' also owes a debt of gratitude to MacNeice who, especially when reflecting on Belfast from elsewhere, could wittily rhyme 'among the buses' with 'sarcophaguses' (MacNeice, 1979, p. 20), and 'Platonic Forms' with 'fickle norms' (p. 18). The scrupulous command 'In Belfast live it' captures precisely the essence of Mahon's – and, indeed, MacNeice's – argument that objective imaginative or intellectual reflection has no place here, that Belfast is a domain of immediate subjective existence purged of all rational thought, and that questioning loyalties via art will not be tolerated.

It may be that this version of the stanza was wholly revised because Mahon realised that it exhibits an excessively angry or even immature attitude towards Belfast, and that with four more years of personal development came an understanding that the city requires compassion rather than derision (hence the subsequent rhyming of 'city' with 'pity', even though pity does tend to infer a somewhat condescending attitude of superiority). If this is indeed the case, then Mahon, rather than moving away from MacNeice's influence by revising the poem so substantially, approaches it yet more closely. Brendan Kennelly has written that MacNeice 'proposes an alternative to prejudice in the North … A humanistic alternative to piosity' (Kennelly, 1994, p. 128). Mahon evidently absorbed this humanism during the period between the poem's two versions, shifting the emphasis away from frustrated denigration towards an attempt to understand more fully the truth of his predicament; hence the later version's assertion, 'One part of my mind must learn to know its place', the implication being that learning will allow Mahon to 'remember not to forget' whence he came.

Memory likewise plays a vital role in MacNeice's feeling of being enslaved. Haunting, haunted images such as 'The yarn-mill called its funeral cry at noon', 'a drowning moon', 'Banned for ever', 'the sentry's challenge echoing all day long', 'the gate-lodge / Barred to civilians', and 'lost sirens' all confer on 'Carrickfergus' an abiding air of loss and regret. Yet even though MacNeice escaped to an English boarding school, the poem contains little in the way of reprieve. The boat that took him to England is, like the soldiers' uniforms on the train from Carlisle, 'camouflaged', an indication that MacNeice's movements must be conducted under a cloak of suspicion, deception and concealment. Moreover, 'the world of parents / Contracted into a puppet world of sons' which he found in provincial Dorset proved to be a further reminder of his own background, his own social estrangement, and his own inheritance. The poem ends almost as it begins, with the military restrictions conveyed by 'the soldiers with their guns' echoing the claustrophobic confinement of 'the bottle-neck harbour collects the mud which jams / The little boats beneath the Norman castle', while the fiscal implications of 'Contracted' recall the economic ramifications of 'Belfast'.

'Glengormley' (Mahon, 1968, p. 5) is to Mahon what 'Carrickfergus' is to MacNeice. Each of these poems is a dramatic indictment of the Belfast suburbs where the poets spent their early lives and which subsequently shaped their respective perceptions of life in the province. MacNeice's dialectic of a fractured identity inhabiting a cold world where past and present collide can be equally located in Mahon's consciousness. The light, satirical rhythms of 'Glengormley' bring to mind another early MacNeice poem, 'Sunday Morning' (MacNeice, 1979, p. 23), which describes the routine banality of a suburban existence that 'deadens and endures'. But Mahon's delicate wit conceals an underlying bitterness that is directed towards a community which, like MacNeice's contracted 'puppet world', suffers from closed mindedness and a displaced collective memory shut off from violent reality, blithely hiding itself in ignorance behind trimmed hedges, manicured lawns, and mundane domestic neutrality. A sense of mythic history has been all but expunged from the Belfast milieu depicted by these poems. While MacNeice relies on tangible historical artefacts – the Norman walls and the tomb of the Chichesters, for example – to provide evidence for the perpetuated barbarism, Mahon invokes the mythical past only to subsequently cast it from memory. His suburban sanctuary is safe from the monsters and giants 'Who tore up sods twelve miles by six / And hurled them out to sea to become islands'; but at the same time there are no longer any saints or heroes who might offer some protection against the new era's 'dangerous tokens'. We find here an ironic allusion to MacNeice's diatribe in *Autumn Journal* against the verbiage propounded by nationalist myth-makers: 'The land of scholars and saints: / Scholars and saints my eye, the land of ambush, / Purblind manifestos, never-ending complaints' (MacNeice, 1979, p. 132). MacNeice paints Ireland as a self-deceiving 'world that never was' that cannot stand alone either culturally or economically, blaming in part 'the sentimental English' who have helped foster false perceptions of Ireland through a combination of historical guilt, romanticised ignorance, and mercantile superiority. Moreover, he regards Ireland as complicit in this spurious identity, trading on its history through the sale of garish Virgins while peddling its sectarian differences as narcotic inducements to its own people:

> I would pray for that island; mob mania in the air,
> I cannot assume their easy bravery
> Drugged with a slogan, chewing the old lie
> That parallel lines will meet at infinity. (MacNeice, 1979, p. 54-58)

This poem was written from the geographically distant perspective of Birmingham, but 'Valediction' (MacNeice, 1979, pp. 52-54) also exhibits its own form of detachment with MacNeice proclaiming his impending departure from the legacy of 'arson and murder' in search of a life more suited to his civilised sensibilities:

> I will acquire an attitude not yours
> And become as one of your holiday visitors,
> And however often I may come
> Farewell, my country, and in perpetuum. (MacNeice, 1979, p. 52)

Yet MacNeice freely admits that he 'cannot deny my past to which my self is wed', and the tone of this section displays an attenuated bitterness that emphasises his resentment towards the way his own identity links inextricably to that of his mother country. He still admires the landscape, Ireland's natural beauty appealing directly to his aesthetic sensibilities, but his choice to become little more than a tourist allows him the freedom to disengage himself from the concealed reality of historical violence and to 'see Sackville Street / Without the sandbags'.

Mahon is certainly far less vehement when ascribing blame, but he too acknowledges the fact that when it comes to sectarian violence in Ireland, English influence is rarely far away. Indeed, Belfast's established order is rooted in the English model of commercial expansion and territorialism, and colonial conquest is mocked in 'Glengormley' through the word 'tamed'. But Mahon differs from MacNeice in his acceptance of Belfast as the proper place in which to do battle against forces hostile to the imagination. In what sounds curiously like a sly dig at MacNeice, Mahon has suggested that responsibility for Ireland's culture is divided equally between political barriers and the way Irish writers have helped perpetuate the artificial myth of Ireland as home of the literary muse:

> The suburbs of Belfast have a peculiar relationship to the Irish cultural situation inasmuch as they're the final anathema for the traditional Irish imagination. A lot of people who are important in Irish poetry cannot accept that the Protestant suburbs in Belfast are a part of Ireland, you know. At an aesthetic level they can't accept that. (Cooke, 1973, p. 10)

'Glengormley' operates on a number of primarily ironic levels, both criticising and accepting contemporary reality and the ostensibly civilising effects of colonialism, while seeming to regret the passing of an ancient, if barbaric, order. But the poem is ultimately characterised by circumspection, and the humorous beginning deflates any possibility of condemning outright the very people who constitute Mahon's tribe. Mahon cannot bring himself to ascribe culpability to those for whom a quiet life equates tentatively with universal peace while the artistic community of 'In Belfast' also retains its own 'sullen silence'. His real anger is therefore directed at the damage caused by nationalist propaganda and a form of language which can be just as debilitating and destructive as guns and bombs: 'Only words hurt us now', he writes, showing moral indignation at the lack of pacifying political action in a place where small dogs and watering cans have come to symbolise a new order of conformity and the dread of collective responsibility.

It is surprising, then, to find that 'In Belfast', the poem succeeding 'Glengormley' in *Night-Crossing*, actually confronts and attempts to define the relationship between Belfast and artistic responsibility. We can discern a rather different Mahon here, a Mahon whose attitude towards Belfast has altered slightly though significantly from the previous poem. Whereas 'Glengormley' links the self with the necessity of spatial and temporal existence, 'In Belfast', despite its continued refusal of direct political engagement, undergoes a shift in attitude. Necessity is associated here with only 'One part of my mind', while responsibility is relegated from outright compulsion to a moral contingency through the word 'Should'. Mahon, like the MacNeice of 'Carrickfergus', chooses to shun the social and historic realms of myth in order to focus on the diurnal realities of Belfast's sectarian divisions. While 'Carrickfergus' carries the narrative of violence through the centuries, from Norman invasion to World War I, Mahon contracts the threat and fear of insurgence into a single line: 'The spurious mystery in the knowing nod'. Mahon is familiar with and, indeed, complicit in this knowledge, the only alternative to which is a reversion to 'sullen silence' and a renunciation of collective responsibility that fails to engage in direct involvement with physical hostilities. (It should be noted that this collected version of 'In Belfast' predates the Troubles by at least a year and therefore cannot be regarded as a direct comment upon them.) Such knowledge is but one aspect of Mahon's 'old conspiracy' with his place of origin and with the Protestant values that constitute 'the unwieldy images of the squinting heart'. If the heart must squint it is because open communication in Belfast is so problematic. The internal rhyme of 'unwieldy' and 'yield' ironises the possibility of a fruitful discourse accessible to all, especially given the extent of sectarianism in the North. This ironic function is cemented by the religious language of the second stanza: 'We could *all* be saved by keeping an eye on the hill / At the top of every street, for there it is, / Eternally, if irrelevantly, visible'. The collective pronoun allies Mahon with the community in a purely ironic way, for if one eye only is open to the possibility of salvation, then it is natural to conclude that the other must be remain closed permanently in blithe ignorance of that possibility. Mahon, in other words, registers what the inhabitants of Belfast are confronted with every day – the struggle between acceptance of abstract, irrelevant religious inheritance and the practical realities of the external world and ordinary life. Although the imagery and iconography of religion are solidly tangible, diurnal necessity renders the spiritual significance of such objects obsolete and ultimately unfelt, while the conditional 'could' ultimately denies the possibility of salvation, at least in MacNeice's conception of it, as a transcendental absolute. The subtlety of Mahon's exposition serves as a reminder of MacNeice's deep impact on his poetry as he attempts to attain a similarly rigorous balance between emotive desires and empirical truth.

Robyn Marsack has claimed that in 'Carrickfergus', 'there is nothing introspective', and given the dominance of sense impressions in the poem it is easy to see why she should make this assertion (Marsack, 1982, p. 14). However it is clear that MacNeice's descriptions of historical events, along with the prominent imagery of death ('crucifixes', 'carrion', 'murders'), mask some deeply personal responses to the events surrounding him. Indeed, the poem's structure serves as a kind of camouflage for the poet's ingrained alienation, and his peripherality is emphasised by his absence from the poem until the 'us' of the penultimate stanza. Nevertheless, both 'Belfast', with its complex, tough, unyielding syntax, and 'Carrickfergus' can be seen not so much as expressions of desire for escape from the pressures and problems life in Belfast brings, but as direct confrontations with those difficulties, confrontations which might afford some entry, no matter how slight or frustrated, into both the collective Belfast psyche and MacNeice's own attitude towards the mechanisms of confinement that conspire to enslave individual minds.

Likewise, the revised final stanza of 'In Belfast' raises the ante on Mahon's gamble to return home by introducing a moral imperative:

> One part of my mind must learn to know its place –
> The things that happen in the kitchen-houses
> And echoing back-streets of this desperate city
> Should engage more than my casual interest,
> Exact more interest than my casual pity.

That 'must' speaks volumes for Mahon's compulsive drive towards authentic behaviour. He has found silence in the Belfast of his childhood, but it is 'sullen' and belongs to the dark ritualism characterised by 'spurious mystery' and 'the knowing nod', thinly-veiled references to sectarian divisions that intimate the perpetuation of fear and intimidation. It is interesting to note Mahon's use of the word 'sullen' here. In 'Once Alien Here' by John Hewitt, another Ulster Protestant, the first two stanzas contrast the 'urgent labour' and commercial interests of English colonisers with 'The sullen Irish limping to the hills' (Hewitt, 1991, pp. 20-21). The indigenous population, having been deprived of their land, still carry with them their enchantments, spells and rich mythic heritage, unlike the populace of Belfast's suburbs where such myths have been extirpated. Hewitt confers dignity on the usurped Irish, while Mahon's colonisers are reduced to fearful, shadowy figures aware of their lack of rootedness. MacNeice, Hewitt and Mahon thus all point in their own individual ways to the problems created by the distancing effects of an unassimilated Protestant consciousness (see Dawe, 1995, pp. 94-95).

Ethical necessity and its concomitant fight for self-preservation denote, in 'In Belfast', a mind divided by the disparity between the rational self-consciousness that contrives to dwell within a cocoon of authentic need and the bad faith of inauthenticity that submits, without question, to 'the unwieldy images of the squinting heart'. Unlike MacNeice, Mahon is intimately familiar with 'the kitchen-houses / And echoing back-streets' of his native environment. Yet while the guilt of being divided between loyalty to self and loyalty to home *should* raise more than casual interest or pity, he holds emotion and sentiment in check for fear of submitting to the external demands of inheritance. The first indication of this inner turmoil is provided by the strongly positioned caesura, which leaves the question hanging in tense irresolution; the second is shown by the equally strongly positioned 'Should' which qualifies both the unstressed moral imperative 'must' and the powerful rhyme of 'city' and 'pity'. Here Mahon acknowledges the responsibility he, as artist and Protestant, feels towards his community by conflating objective reality with subjective emotion. However, his commitment to such a project falters in the face of two things: a personal need to remain authentic, and the self-reproaching knowledge that pity implies superiority in the way it looks down on those it is intended to aid or save. He understands that any 'prayer for oblivion', to borrow MacNeice's phrase from 'Belfast', must invariably fall on deaf ears given the irrelevance of 'a sanctimonious God' (an image that, like pity, implies self-righteous superiority); hence the defiant tone of 'There is a perverse pride in being on the side / Of the fallen angels and refusing to get up'. Yet while Mahon's intimate knowledge of Belfast ought to provoke moral outrage and something more than 'casual interest', it fails implacably to do so. The subtle diminution of the moral imperative from 'must' to 'Should' reflects the choice Mahon has made, and his forthright decision to be loyal to his own consciousness holds sway, favouring an authentic recognition of empirical mortal existence over the contingent 'astute salvations' offered spuriously by history and religion. In order to achieve personal salvation, the poet's mind *must* be divided between the unreason associated with the obfuscatory gloom of place and people, and the ratiocination of enlightened self-knowledge as a means of keeping separate the emotions of subjective feeling and intellectual enlightenment. That is, it is the poet's duty to see clearly by keeping both eyes open in his twin pursuit of truth and an authentic mode of existence, balancing sensory perceptions against an understanding of both external reality and personal requirements.

The whole tone of this final stanza is one of determined, dispassionate detachment – further echoing MacNeice's 'Belfast' – mediated by an air of moral ambiguity which refuses to yield any concrete resolution to the psychological need for self-realisation in a climate hostile to the free-thinking individual. The shift from first person singular in the first stanza, through the collective pronouns of the second and third, and ultimately back to the first person in the final stanza denotes Mahon's stalwart refusal to conform to an imposed form of identity which adheres to what MacNeice terms 'fickle norms' (MacNeice, 1979, p. 18). Mahon is rightly critical of Irish poets who refuse to explore the possibilities offered by such metaphysical issues, blaming their attitude on the persisting influence of Yeats and 'the shadows of the Celtic Twilight cast by [his] own early poems', and he despairs of these poets' 'reverence for a poetry which evaded the metaphysical unease in which all poetry of lasting value has its source' (Mahon, 1972, p. 12). The transition from the uncertainty of 'could' to the moral directive 'Should' addresses Mahon's uneasy refusal to rise to the bait laid down by a Protestant orthodoxy that claims to offer moral certainty and 'astute salvations', but confers only intellectual and emotional paralysis. Abnegating the conscience that would incur such self-destruction, Mahon promises to 'remember not to forget', thus providing himself with a salient reminder that those who forget the past are condemned to repeat it. Yet this unease seems destined to persist, despite his apparent belief in the power of memory to overcome the horrors of the present and provide a means of escape into a more optimistic future, for we are unable to escape completely from any past constituted and defined by subjective memories: as MacNeice states in 'Valediction', 'history never dies'. By the same token, however, the events and experiences we recall through memory are also subject to flux. While the past itself cannot be changed, the individual's view of it can alter significantly when experience is interpreted through the prism of self-reflection. But equally importantly, future choices can only be made in the light of the past. The ethical constituent of the poem's could-must-should structure balances precariously on the knife-edge of memory, continually defying Mahon's self-determining attempt to assert his individuality. He registers the fact that the repeating of history can only be avoided once the search for existential freedom results in the choice to abandon forever the constraints of a society which has itself abandoned the right to choose.

The language and construction of 'In Belfast' expand further on Mahon's discontent, especially with regard to the poem's presentation of temporal movement. In the first stanza, the phrases 'I resume' and 'I remember not to forget' establish a retrospective perspective through their present relation to past events. However, one particular phrase contained in the last stanza – 'One part of my mind must learn to know its place' – alludes to a future event while again being set in the present.

Although the shift from remembering (and the suggestion that something has already been learned) to learning implies a form of regression, the sense of the past contained in 'resume' and 'remember' still vies for dominance with the anticipated futurity of 'learn'. This structural aspect of the poem is remarkably complex, yet it illuminates an essential aspect of Mahon's aesthetic and his ironical attempt to elude historical flux. The poem's structure is itself a form of escape from the limitations forced on him by a society towards which he is reluctant to show either responsibility or sympathy. Mahon has no need to emulate MacNeice's attempt to confront and understand the social forces of Belfast as he is already in possession of that understanding. Nevertheless, Mahon's reluctance is still tempered by an act reminiscent of MacNeice's critique of what Seamus Heaney has called Belfast's 'agnostic world of economic interest' (Heaney, 1984, p. 57). For Mahon, the word 'interest', repeated over the poem's last two lines, reinforces capitalist ideas regarding a contractual obligation to repay a debt, while simultaneously reiterating MacNeice's scornful attack on commercialism in 'Belfast'. But Mahon feels no such obligation towards his people; nor is he prepared to run the risk of ontological bankruptcy and the total loss of self by surrendering personal identity to anonymity and rejection. These poems thus enact the refusal to conform to the demands of a tribe that knows the cost of everything and the value of nothing.

References

Brown, T. (1975), *Louis MacNeice: Sceptical Vision*, Gill and Macmillan, Dublin.

Cooke, H. (1973), 'Harriet Cooke talks to the poet Derek Mahon', *Irish Times*, 17 Jan., p. 10.

Dawe, G. (1995), *Against Piety: Essays in Irish Poetry*, Lagan Press, Belfast.

Fraser, G. S. (1959), *Vision and Rhetoric: Studies in Modern Poetry*, Faber & Faber, London.

Heaney, S. (1984), *Preoccupations: Selected Prose 1968-1978*, Faber & Faber, London.

Hewitt, J. (1991), *The Collected Poems of John Hewitt*, ed. F. Ormsby, Blackstaff Press, Belfast.

Johnston, D. (1997), *Irish Poetry After Joyce*, 2nd ed. Syracuse University Press, New York.

Kennelly, B. (1994), *Journey into Joy: Selected Prose*, ed., Å. Persson, Bloodaxe, Newcastle upon Tyne.

Longley, E. (1984), 'The Writer and Belfast', in *The Irish Writer and the City*, *Irish Literary Studies*, 18, ed. M. Harmon, Colin Smythe, Gerrards Cross, Bucks, pp. 65-89.

Longley, E. (1996), *Louis MacNeice: A Critical Study*, Faber & Faber, London.

MacNeice, L. (1979), *Collected Poems*, ed. E. R. Dodds, Faber & Faber, London.

Mahon, D. (1968), *Night-Crossing*, Oxford University Press, London.

Mahon, D. (ed.) (1972), *The Sphere Book of Modern Irish Poetry*, Sphere Books, London.

Marsack, R. (1982), *The Cave of Making: The Poetry of Louis MacNeice*, Oxford University Press, Oxford.

Muldoon, P. (1986), *The Faber Book of Contemporary Irish Poetry*, Faber & Faber, London.

O'Neill, M., and Reeves, G. (1992), *Auden, MacNeice, Spender: The Thirties Poetry*, Macmillan, Basingstoke.

The Parabolic Structure of William Trevor's *The Story of Lucy Gault*

Daniel W. Ross
Columbus State University

Many readers think of William Trevor as a master of the short story. His brief novel, *The Story of Lucy Gault,* first published in hardback in 2002, draws on his skill as a teller of brief, but powerful tales. In *Lucy Gault,* Trevor has also subtly drawn on the tradition of the parable to create a particularly deft, perhaps elusive, commentary on recent Irish history. As we will see, the novel ultimately recognises Ireland's movement into a more global and prosperous modernity, while glancing back at the kind of paralysis and fear that long delayed Ireland's emergence as a modern nation. For Trevor, the parable was the ideal form for contextualising Ireland's paralysis while dramatising the painful consequences of its past for generations of Irish people.

The parable is an ancient and highly respected literary form, evident in a variety of cultures and literatures. Though it is most readily associated with ancient writing, recent critics have detected elements of the parable in such texts as Wordsworth's 'Michael' (Westbrook, 1997) and Melville's story, 'Bartleby, the Scrivener' (Doloff, 1997). In modern literature the parable has returned with a vengeance—perhaps because modern writers are especially apt to be drawn to the enigmatic quality of the parable as a mysterious 'dark saying' (MacNeice, 1965) - often appearing as a way of demonstrating the paradoxical, confusing, or even inexplicable nature of life. As employed by modern writers like Kafka, Calvino, and Borges, modern parables may stand in stark opposition to their kabbalistic predecessors, focusing on loss and emptiness in contrast to 'the world of plenitude' suggested by the Gnostic tradition (Naveh, 2000). Parables have a close relationship to metaphor, though they often invoke comparisons that are sometimes not evident as comparisons. MacNeice (1965) provides a useful description of the way parables work surreptitiously, often on two levels, which he compares to Freud's distinction between manifest and latent content.

Parable begins in the realm of the familiar and then moves outward into mystery. This is the source of both the richness and the elusiveness of parable, for the inattentive reader or listener remains trapped in the familiar and misses the meaning of the story. In his classic study of the parables of Jesus, William Barclay (1970) captured this quality when he described Jesus' strategy: 'He wanted to persuade men to pass a judgment on things with which they were well acquainted, and then to compel them to transfer that judgment to something to whose significance they had been blind' (Barclay (1970), p. 13). Thus, Barclay calls attention to the dual intent of parable—to change the thinking and the actions of humans. While the subject of many of Jesus' parables was a description of the 'kingdom of heaven,' there is no denying that these pointed stories were meant to alter behavior in this life.

In the modern period the parable has emerged as an important tool of contemporary Irish writers such as Seamus Heaney and William Trevor. The attraction of these writers to parable may be explained by the suggestion of some theorists that parable 'is a language of last resort, language attempting through metaphor pushed into narrative motion to speak the heretofore unspoken or unspeakable' (Westbrook, 1997, p. 111). Parable has the power to signify unobtrusively; this is also the reason its significance can be entirely missed. Robert Frost cleverly captured this aspect of parables when he said that he liked to write poems in the form of parable, so the wrong persons would not understand and be saved. Parable is a language of code, one which openly invites misreading (Westbrook, 1997); as Jesus makes clear in the gospels, he chooses parable as a method of being heard only by those who will hear while withholding meaning from those who are not invited to participate. As such, parable places exceptional emphasis on the reader's willingness to listen, to interpret, and, ultimately, to respond.

Mary Hoyt-Fitzgerald (1995) has stated that Trevor uses a form she refers to as the 'Protestant parable,' though she does not describe this form in any detail. I want to focus on the way Trevor has incorporated the structure and richness of parable into his recent novel, *The Story of Lucy Gault* (2003). This is a remarkably subtle and brief novel which, like parable itself, seems to call attention to itself only to defy interpretation. The novel contains allusions to and hints of several of the parables of Jesus, though the most pervasive influence, I will argue, is the Parable of the Talents.

Timing always seems to be an important factor in Jesus's use of parables. Invariably the parable is a warning, a call to change one's ways or take a new course of action before it is too late. J. Hillis Miller has suggested that parables are directed 'toward last things, toward the mysteries of the kingdom of heaven and how to get there' (Hillis Miller, 1981, p. 181). In this regard, Captain Gault's remark to his solicitor after his return to Lahardane captures the very concern that the parable seeks to prevent: 'How like our domestic tragedy it is that I have come too late' (Trevor, 2003, p. 160). Belatedness is anathema to parabolic wisdom which always seeks to foreclose the feeling that one has acted too late.

Jesus tells his disciples the Parable of the Talents at a particularly critical moment in his history. According to the Gospel of Matthew, the parable is related in the final week of Jesus's life, after the glory of the triumphal entry into Jerusalem has begun to descend into chaos, just before his trial and crucifixion. The parable is timed to represent one of his last, and presumably, most important teachings. Like many other stories Jesus tells, the Parable of the Talents insists on good husbandry, strongly suggesting that the waste of resources, especially human resources, is one of the least forgivable sins.

The parable of the talents has a central if unobtrusive role in William Trevor's *The Story of Lucy Gault*. Trevor's novel, I contend, not only draws on the tradition of the parable, but it actually becomes itself a parable of modern Ireland. Even the title of the novel suggests something of a parable, a story that comes to have a meaning larger than Lucy's life itself. Many such novels simply bear the name of the heroine for its title (e.g., *Jane Eyre* or *Mrs Dalloway*), but Trevor has chosen to draw attention to the *story* of Lucy Gault, emphasizing the 'storiness'. Storiness, as such, is an important theme of the novel. Indeed, as Trevor makes clear, the story of Lucy becomes a legend in her local community, an emblematic tale of loss, waste, and failure.

Trevor's allusion to the Parable of the Talents is subtle but significant. It occurs amid a scene of recognition, when the recently-widowed Captain Everard Gault finally returns to his Irish estate at Lahardane after an absence of almost thirty years. As he approaches his long-abandoned home, the Captain pauses to count 'the cattle he had made over to Henry, twice as many now as he had left behind' (Trevor, 2003, p. 151). The implication is clear: Henry has fulfilled his role as the faithful servant, doubling his master's investment during his absence. Indeed, Henry represents in this version the 'good enough' servant, who is praised by the master in the parable, but not the ideal servant who multiplied his master's bounty fivefold. However, Trevor's principal purpose in alluding to the parable is to comment on the owner who has left the estate, and his child, so long in the hands of others.

In this regard, Trevor has reversed the roles of master and servant in his appropriation of the parable form. In the Parable of the Talents, as in many others that Jesus used, it is a given that the master is beneficent and wise. When the unfaithful servant of the Parable of the Talents rationalizes his behavior by blaming the master for being a 'harsh man' (Matt. 25: 24), he is condemned to the outer darkness. But what happens, Trevor's novel seems to ask, when the servants are faithful but the master himself fails in his duty? Trevor, who often critiques the behavior of the Anglo-Irish, uses the story of Lucy Gault to raise disturbing questions about the failures of this group at a critical juncture in Irish history.

In Matthew's gospel, the motivating force behind the wicked servant's decision to bury the talent is fear, and certainly fear is the reason Everard and Heloise Gault abandon their estate for so long. This is not to suggest that either Matthew's text or Trevor's novel mocks the reasons for fear; Trevor has set the novel in the context of the Irish Civil war, a time of legitimate fear, especially in light of Heloise's English background. Furthermore, Trevor enhances the legitimacy of their fear by indicating that other owners have been burned off their estates and by stating that the local constabulary has been stretched past its capabilities. Fear is a reasonable response to this situation: what Trevor critiques is the waste that results when fear almost wholly governs one's response to such a crisis. And yet, as the faithful servant Henry's meditations years later indicate, the fear of the Gaults exceeds the bounds of reason:

> Cutting a new sole, [Henry] found himself reflecting, as he often did, on how it would be now if this remote house had been forgotten in the vengeance of 1921, if a threat in the night had not engendered such fear and such distress. Another man, different in nature and temperament from the Captain, might not have heeded the nervous premonitions of his wife, might have dismissed them as unwarranted and foolish, might not have considered it a wife's place to be upset. That three callow youths, hardly knowing what they were doing in their excitement, had exercised such power still seemed to Henry to be extraordinary. (Trevor, 2003, p. 128)

Trevor, thus, uses his narrative voice to counter the rationalizations of the Gaults. Clearly, it is the servant, not the master, whose thinking is balanced and rational.

The setting of the Irish War of Independence, filled as it is with suggestions of danger, transition, and uncertainty, is almost an ideal one for the use of a parable. In her study of the form Gila Safran Naveh notes that parables often 'arise out of a practical crisis of some sort' (Naveh, 2000, p. 10) and offer a way to engage an audience to explore new meanings for the context. Naveh believes the parable applies especially well to the historical dilemma faced by the Jews: 'in a world where Jewish people were constantly threatened with extinction and cast off their land, the only way they could survive was by adhering stubbornly to the Torah and the law. Parabolic discourse, with legions of tropes and rhetoric, seemed uniquely appropriate to teach them the way how' (p. 32). This analysis suggests that the user of a parable presupposes the existence of a moral order and a set of principles which can help restore stability, if only the audience will take heed and listen. Trevor fits this description. Furthermore, Ireland in the 1920s has similarities to ancient Israel. Delivered at last as an independent nation after more than 700 years of foreign domination, Ireland was threatening to destroy itself through internal strife.

It is important to remember that Trevor's novel is an historical one, originally published in 2002 (references in the present essay are in the 2003 Penguin edition). Consequently, it is designed to speak both to Ireland's past and its present condition. Such a strategy is consistent with the 'doubleness' often displayed in parables. As Naveh puts it, the parable often contains 'a double meaning related to the symbolic representation of a past conflict and a (symbolic) present conflict' (Naveh, 2000, p. 28). While I agree with that assessment, I would add, with Miller (1991) that it also looks to the future. I will offer some speculation about that present and future aspects of the conflict later; first, however, I will explore further Trevor's use of parable to expose the failings of Everard and Heloise Gault as poor stewards of their resources.

The parabolic theme of waste is emphasized by repeated instances in the novel of missed opportunities, unwritten or unmailed letters, things left unsaid, questions never asked, and so forth. In truth, most of the major actions of the novel are failures to act. Thus, Trevor offers a picture of a paralysed family, an all-too-familiar portrayal of the Protestant 'Big House' family at the outbreak of the War for Independence. Despite his reputation as a realist, Trevor stretches credulity by portraying a couple who totally abandon the home of their lost daughter even though there is no irrefutable evidence of her death; this narrative strategy invites us to see the tale as something more than a historical account. After they leave Lahardane, Captain and Mrs. Gault spend the next thirty years preoccupied by avoidance and denial: they avoid true grief and consolation, just as they avoid contact with their Irish home and friends, contact which would have made them aware of the truth about Lucy's survival. The Gaults bury their lives in denial as surely as the servant in Jesus' parable buries the talent he has been entrusted with. Ironically, their flight from Lahardane mirrors Lucy's act of running away from home; in her case, however, this childish act of avoidance and irresponsibility is more understandable than in theirs.

Always a master of prose style, Trevor enhances these avoidances with a series of ambiguous statements in a narrative voice that uses conditional verbs and passive voice syntax. So much, the narrator insists, *could have been* or *might have been*. Repeatedly, these structures reveal the Gaults' failure in a crisis to face and discuss the full truth among themselves. In fact, Lucy is compelled to run away in part by the half-truths and innuendos she picks up by eavesdropping. To emphasise the point, Trevor arranges for the news of Lucy's disappearance to coincide with Captain Gault's speculations about his lack of openness. As the search for Lucy begins, his doubts surface:

> Had he been right not to reveal to Heloise, or to his child, the finality he had begun to sense in this departure? Should he have gone back to that family in Enniseala to plead a little longer? Should he have offered more than he had, whatever was felt might settle the misdemeanour he had committed, accepting that the outrage of that night was his and not the trespassers who had come? … He might have said to himself on this last night that he had too carelessly betrayed the past and then betrayed, with easy comforting, a daughter and a wife. … Yet when he searched his feelings there was nothing there to guide him, only confusion and contradiction. (Trevor, 2003, p. 27)

The emptiness and confusion recorded here indicate that Captain Gault's good intentions are subjugated by his self-doubts. By the same token the intentions of the bad servant in Christ's parable are never questioned; no matter what his reasons might be, his failure to act indicts him. Both the servant of the parable and Everard Gault lack confidence in the future and that lack of confidence breeds paralysis.

Tragically, when Lucy's disappearance leads everyone to assume she has met an early death, Captain Gault realizes to some degree his errors, though he does not change his behaviour. 'We told her lies,' he confesses to Heloise (Trevor, 2003, p. 31). She responds by saying, 'We could not explain more,' though the narrator compromises this statement by adding, 'but her guilt did not lessen: to their child she had not explained enough' (Trevor, 2003, p. 34). In this portion of the novel—the beginning of the second chapter—the narrator's irony and judgment are most pervasive. At this point, when there is still sufficient time to act decisively, Lucy is given up for dead because questions are not asked. Once again, the narrator's syntax indicts the Captain and his wife: 'As if somehow it had acquired a potency of its own in feeding on circumstances and events, the falsity that beguiled the Captain and his wife and their servants, was neither questioned nor denied' (Trevor, 2003, p. 32). Like the servant of the Parable of the Talents, the Gaults might wish to blame conditions beyond their control, but Trevor's language pointedly reminds readers that these characters are self-beguiled. Indeed, most of what the Captain and Heloise say at this crucial point seems to contradict reality.

In choosing to flee their estate, Heloise and Everard Gault repeat a familiar pattern of Anglo-Irish behaviour. Throughout Ireland's troubled colonial past many of its economic and social problems were either caused or exacerbated by the poor management of estates by Anglo-Irish landlords. A common problem was the absentee landlord, who left the Irish estate either to live the high life in England or sometimes to avoid potential civil rebellion from the peasants. Absentee landlords drained Irish estates and the Irish economy of resources that were spent profligately in England. Maria Edgeworth's 1812 novel *The Absentee* is one of many literary appeals to these landlords to remain faithful to their estates. The call echoes that of the parable, which urges faithfulness, steadfastness, and a willingness to invest in the future, despite the dangers of the present.

Inherent in Christ's parable of the talents is the belief that investing in the future is the proper cure for waste and the only way to assure survival. As Mary-Hoyt Fitzgerald said several years before the publication of *Lucy Gault*, Trevor's Protestants face the threat of decline through sexual incapacity and childlessness (1995, p. 41). Not only do the Gaults lose their one child, but their later attempts in exile to give birth end in miscarriage, a judgment, it seems, of their abandonment of Lucy. Nor does this pattern of waste end with the parents. Driven by guilt and remorse for her misdeed, Lucy refuses to marry Ralph and lives out her life in isolation. Trevor reinforces this theme by filling his novel with images of waste and ruin, from the ruined graveyard of the monks which Ralph visits with his wife (Trevor, 2003, pp. 162-4) to the ruined grounds of Lahardane and finally the declining condition of the nearby town, Enniseala. The sins of one generation breed unhappiness and waste even in later generations. Though Ralph is an outsider to the Gault family tragedy, his life is also affected by it, and he feels the frustration of waste that results from their unresolved problems.

Trevor's rhetoric of waste and lost opportunity is especially poignant in the scenes preceding Captain Gault's death. While readers might expect his almost incidental return to Lahardane to foreground a happy ending, it is at best a bittersweet homecoming, which causes the Captain to see the full account of his failure. Initially,

Lucy refuses to speak to the father who abandoned her. His return only serves to make her realize the waste in having lived a life dedicated to receiving the forgiveness of her parents. She thinks, 'What terrible folly had possessed her? All these years to have so stubbornly waited for no more than an old man's scattered words?' (Trevor, 2003, p. 170). Having failed to take the appropriate action when he should have, Captain Gault lives out his days in the vain hope that Ralph or his replacement will magically appear to restore Lucy with life-giving love. Lucy, however, 'was aware that her father hoped for what would never be: that out of a racecourse crowd or a theatre audience a man would step, as so long ago Ralph had stepped out of nowhere' (Trevor, 2003, p. 194). As the analogy makes clear, given Lucy's extreme isolation, Ralph's original visit was miraculous enough, as though to suggest that miracles are of little avail when people fail to seize the opportunity they offer.

Trevor's narrator almost mocks the Captain's futile efforts to conjure up a second suitor. Trevor uses the passive voice to show that Lucy's reunion with her father, remarkable as it is, makes her future no less bleak:

> Their companionship—on Lucy's side edgy with resentment, on her father's anxiously seeking too much—settled for what there was… Circumstances had shaped an emptiness in her existence; and love's ungainly passion belonged, with so much else, to the undemanding past. (Trevor, 2003, p 194)

Things happen to the Gaults because they fail to take decisive steps to secure their future. The narrator's final judgment of Captain Gault, a military man and a minor hero of World War I, is couched in conditional verbs and the devastating metaphor of retreat:

> Simple man that he was, he might have gone that afternoon to find the rifle that had been fired from an upstairs window and with a soldier's instinct might have threatened its use again. Instead, he had withdrawn from an occasion that was beyond him; and he had done so since. (Trevor, 2003, p. 195)

In so many ways it is fitting that the Captain goes to sleep for the final time without a word passing between him and the daughter to whom he has been reunited: 'There had never been the convention of wishing one another good-night in this house and there was not now' (Trevor, 2003, p. 197). The Captain's return really does not change much, as silence continues to dominate the house. This kind of authorial comment makes us realise how flawed the home life of the Gaults has always been. While the opening chapter casts the primary burden of fear on Heloise, Trevor does not allow her husband to escape blame for his failures to act. After his wife's death, he manages to do little to effect real healing in his relationship with Lucy. In some ways he is more severely punished than his wife, being left to see the utter isolation to which their fears have banished Lucy.

Andrew Parkin (2001), who has argued that Trevor's work often contains a 'malign vision' of life, nonetheless believes that the later work does offer some emphasis on hope and the mysterious power of good (pp. 94-5). And indeed, *The Story of Lucy Gault* does offer some redemptive vision. Consistent with the Christian framework of the novel, the source of hope is the transformation of Horahan, the instigator of the Gaults' fear. Like the return of Captain Gault, Horahan's return to Enniseala and Lahardane bears resemblances to another parable, that of the Prodigal Son. The Prodigal, himself a symbol of waste, demonstrates that action can be taken to correct the errors of the past before it is too late. In stark contrast to Captain and Mrs Gault, Horahan takes some responsibility for his past and finally takes some steps toward atonement. Horahan's insanity and his years spent in institutions are signs of the real guilt he feels, as are the dreams which torment him for years. But his guilt leads him to take some steps forward towards reconciliation. In some respects, he ironically becomes the man Captain Gault searched for in theatre crowds and at racecourses, the man who would bring some resolution and meaning back into Lucy's life. In a story filled with incomplete and unfinished things, the completed embroidery becomes a life-giving symbol of the reconciliation achieved between Lucy and Horahan. Her frequent visits to the asylum become the stuff of legend, an inspiration to all who hear about them.

Earlier, I mentioned that Trevor's use of the novel as historical fiction suggests a desire to comment on Ireland's present as well as its past. The novel does turn towards the present, and the future, in its final pages. Here the parabolic function of Trevor's novel could easily escape us if we did not have well-tuned ears to hear. As old age approaches for Lucy, who is left with no heir for Lahardane, Trevor's narrator raises questions about the future of the estate. In these final pages the novel presents numerous images of the new world which are transforming Ireland; these images include the Internet, cell phones, and global tourism. As she considers the future of the house which has been the site of so much disappointment and heartache, Lucy speculates that it will become a hotel:

> She lay sleepless and the transformation lingered: a cocktail bar, a noisy dining room, numbers on the bedroom door. She doesn't mind. It doesn't matter. People coming from all over, travellers like never before: that is the way in Ireland now. (Trevor, 2003, p. 225)

It is clear that Trevor is not content merely to judge the actions of the Gaults and leave us with their results. In turning toward the future, Trevor increases the parabolic impact of his novel, pointing the way for Ireland not to repeat old mistakes. Contemporary Ireland, a leader in the European Union, has demonstrated some uneasiness with the changes that the world brings to its doorstep in the form of tourism and, especially, growth through immigration. Lucy's acceptance of this future in her vision of Lahardane as a hotel is a positive gesture towards Ireland's future. Commenting on Trevor's parabolic imagination, Hoyt-Fitzgerald contends that 'the moral of his parables is that those who lock their identity in a vanishing past are doomed to exclusion from Ireland's future' (1995,p. 45). Too many characters in this novel have lived in the past; Lucy demonstrates here a willingness to face the future and change.

There is some kinship between parable and allegory, and we might conclude by reflecting on the allegorical nuances of Trevor's novel. Lucy Gault is a name worth considering. Lucy, of course, means light-bearer, an ironic image for people like her parents, who gave their child this hopeful name but then chose to condemn her to their own darkness. Once again, the thoughts of the good servant Henry affords us an alternative perspective. When Ralph is courting Lucy, Henry concludes that 'it was not bad that the Captain's child should be taken from this place, separated at last from the dark that clung to it' (Trevor, 2003, p. 115). But Lucy is too paralysed by guilt to accept Ralph's proposal, and so her light is extinguished in the darkness of Lahardane.

Christ's parable of the Talents makes it clear that the punishment one deserves for failing to invest in the future is to be cast into the outer darkness. Gault bears a certain similarity to Gael, and this invites us to consider the possibility that the Story of Lucy Gault—the story of the War for Independence, of failed responsibilities, and of failed relations within families and between Catholics and Protestants in Ireland—has been given to us as an apt story of Ireland. Like the country she represents, Lucy bears the weight of a tragic history. She is, in this sense, a new version of the familiar figure, Mother Ireland. In the context of a new world of global opportunity, Trevor suggests that Ireland needs to pay careful attention to the lessons of its past, but not to bury itself in those failures and pains. Trevor's novel suggests that the reconciliation effected between Horahan and Lucy needs to become an emblem of the new Ireland. That kind of positive action is the proper corrective to a bitter history of things left unsaid and undone.

References

Barclay, W. (1970), *The Parables of Jesus,* Westminster John Knox, Louisville, KY.

Doloff, S. (1977), 'The Prudent Samaritan: Melville's "Bartleby, the Scrivener", as Parody of Christ's Parable to the Lawyer', *Studies in Short Fiction,* 34, pp. 357-61.

Hoyt-Fitzgerald, M. (1995), 'William Trevor's Protestant Parables', *Colby Quarterly,* 31, pp. 40-45.

MacNeice, L. (1965), *Varieties of Parable,* Cambridge University Press, Cambridge.

Miller. J. H. (1991), *Tropes, Parables, Performatives: Essays on Twentieth-Century Literature*, Duke University Press, Durham, NC.

Naveh, G. S. (2000), *Biblical Parables and Their Modern Re-Creations: From 'Apples Of Gold in Silver Settings' to 'Imperial Messages'*, State University of New York Press, Albany, NY.

Parkin, A. (2001), 'The Malign Vision in William Trevor's Fiction', *Journal of the Short Story in English,* 37, pp. 81-96.

Trevor, W. (2003), *The Story of Lucy Gault,* Penguin, London.

Westbrook, D. (1997), 'Wordsworth's Prodigal Son: "Michael" as Parable and as Metaparable', *The Wordsworth Circle,* 28, pp. 109-19.

'Gallous Stories and Dirtier Deeds': Brian Friel's *The Gentle Island*

Alison O'Malley-Younger
University of Sunderland

> What shall become of the ancient race,
> The noble, Celtic, island race?
> Like cloud on cloud oe'r the azure sky,
> When winter storms are loud and high,
> The dark ships shadow the ocean's face –
> What shall become of the Celtic race?
> (Michael Tormey in Leersen, 1996, p. 166)

'Nationalism', according to Ernest Gellner, 'usually conquers in the name of a putative folk culture. Its symbolism is drawn from the pristine vigorous life of the peasant' (Gellner, 1983, p. 57). Within the rhetoric of Irish cultural nationalism the peasantry has incarnated an imagined golden age of Gaelic unity and moral certainty, while the invocation of the rural ideal encompassed ideas of nation, Catholicism and Gaelic romanticism. Poems such as Michael Tormey's 'The Ancient Race', published first in *The Nation*, are indicative of this train of romantic cultural nationalist thought which believed that the loss of the indigenous language, and threatened Anglicisation represented a real and imminent threat to a distinctive 'Irish' way of life. In an attempt to halt what they perceived as cultural deracination and construct a coherent, palpable sense of 'Irish' uniqueness, romantic cultural nationalists located the essence of Irishness in what Joep Leersen describes as 'a people, distant in place, distant in time and distant in ontology' (Leersen, 1996, p. 160), evolving the otherworldly, communally living time-warped peasantry of the west, incarnated in the figure of the *duine uasal* or noble peasant.

With the coming of the Irish Literary Renaissance the *duine uasal* became somewhat of a leitmotif in Irish drama, resulting, in no small part from the endeavours of the Irish Literary Theatre to establish the quintessence of 'Irishness' in the pre-Teutonic, pre-lapsarian peasantry of the West. Thirty years after Matthew Arnold discussed 'the fairy dew of that natural magic that is Celtic' (cited in O'Connor, 1998, p. 137), racially typifying the Celts as sentimental, spiritual, charming and beautiful, members of the 'Irish' intelligentsia including William Butler Yeats, Lady Augusta Gregory, Edward Martyn, John Millington Synge and George Moore were making a Mecca of the Aran Islands, and issuing a *cri de coeur* on behalf of an essentially Celtic peasantry as inheritors and custodians of a culture thousands of years old, avatars of timeless, heroic 'Irishness', versed in folklore, telluric tradition, myth and legend, the archetypal unconscious of Ireland. The pastoral vision of noble peasantry and the myth of the noble peasant which emerged from this period established the terms of an argument that has affected much Irish literature since. From James Joyce to Myles na gCopaleen, from Kavanagh's *The Great Hunger* to Seamus Heaney, Irish writers have felt a compulsion to explode 'the revivalist myth of the saintly western peasantry' (Kiberd, 1995, p. 482) as 'ahistorical and unaffected by social change' (ibid). These versions of Antipastoral attempted to clear what Declan Kiberd describes as the 'sentimental haze of sentiment and nostalgia' (ibid, p. 481) surrounding the imagined peasantry with more realistic depictions of the changing, often harsh and brutal realities of rural life. Brian Friel's 1971 play, *The Gentle Island* is one such work, 'a bitterly ironical working of [certain] romantic fictions of the past' (Andrews, 1995, p. 125) in which Friel, according to Seamus Deane, 'turned on all the illusions of pastoralism, ancestral feeling and local piety that had been implicit in his dramatization of the world of Ballybeg' (Deane, in McGrath, 1999, p. 77) and in which he 'unmasks the myth of Gaelic innocence with anger and bitterness [...]' in an (uncharacteristically) 'almost vengeful spirit' (ibid).

In this discussion of *The Gentle Island* I argue that Friel challenges the myth of the noble peasant by foregrounding the futility of the xenophobic and violent attitudes expressed by the main protagonist in the play, Manus Sweeney. I address the notions of violence and scapegoating in the play and suggest that Friel draws an oblique parallel with varieties of romantic nationalism to explore the dynamics of a culture shaped by persistent and pervasive violence. Central to the play is an implicit critique of nationalistic discourses that display a myopic fidelity to the past; those that according to Eugene O'Brien believe in an 'optative future sanctioned by a monological reading of history' (O'Brien, 1996, p. 19) and which are driven by 'ideas of mother ground, four green fields, blood sacrifice, the necessity for violence and the necessity for a purging of those who are not part of the national community' (ibid). These are *leitmotifs* which resonate throughout a play which is unremittingly iconoclastic, a presentation of the noble peasant which is, as F. C. McGrath suggests 'nothing less than a savage attack on that myth' (McGrath, 1999, p. 76).

The play begins in the kitchen of Manus Sweeney's cottage and the area around his home. In these first lines we have a challenge to the nationalist notion of the 'ideal Irish home' described by Mary Butler in the *United Irishman* of January 1903 as 'the nursery of patriots; the source and centre of national life, the origin of national well-being and the inspiration of national greatness' wherein 'there is no shoddy, no make believe, no pretence or imitation', and where everything including the language, the furniture, the books and the songs sung are of native origin, 'Irish hands and heads have fashioned them and they are suited, in consequence to be used and enjoyed by Irish people' (Butler, 1903, p. 6). In contradistinction, Manus' Irish home is filled with the detritus of warfare and the relics of death scavenged from the shores of Inishkeen, the 'gentle island' of the title. We find Manus 'sitting in an airplane seat' and we are informed later that:

> That clock came off a Dutch freighter that broke up on the Stags; and that table came off a submarine; and those lamps came off a British tanker; and these binoculars came off a French minesweeper. My father used to sit all night waiting for the wreckage. All the men did. And they got bales of rubber and butter and tins of cigarettes and timber and whiskey and whatnot. (Friel, 1973, p. 31)

It is no small irony that Manus, who constantly attempts to turn the island into an impenetrable fortress of Irishness has constructed his homestead from items culled from a wider context. Moreover, he himself is equally 'inauthentic', a performed stereotype who, below the surface is a liar, a violent, xenophobic, racist homophobe who is prepared to maim and kill when his fictitious pastoral idyll is threatened by those he perceives as outsiders. His belief in the sanctity of origin combined with his sentimental regard for an heroic past, aligns him to volkish notions of an all Irish Ireland hermetically sealed from the encroachments of modernity and Anglicisation. For Manus, nothing is more important than the primordial bonds of kin, a shared history and the mystical blood-ties of the Volk, hence his suggestion that the departing Islanders: 'Belong here, and they'll never belong anywhere else! Never!' (p. 10).

It becomes quickly apparent, however, that there is a deep ontological sickness on the gentle island. There is no evidence that anyone other than Manus Sweeney sees being, or essence rooted in the soil of Iniskeen. In the early scenes we see a haemorrhage of islanders abandoning their roots out of necessity, to escape the privations and isolation associated with life on their home ground. By allowing the drunken Con to ask 'Do you think was the Flight of the Earls anything like this?' (p. 14). Friel draws our attention to two things: the incipient myth-making of the islanders, and the undignified nature of this particular diaspora. What is also made clear in these early lines is the level of violence, both manifest and threatened that has become the norm to the 'gentle islanders'. Norah Dan is being dragged into a boat, 'biting and spitting and butting and flinging' (p. 12), Aul' Barney is shaking his clenched fists; Joe is suggesting that the inebriated Con, 'wants his bloody head kicked in' (p. 14) and Mary, the matriarch is suggesting in her 'brisk' and 'efficient' manner the best way to dispose of the dog they are leaving behind:

> I'm at that fool of a father of yours for the past month to throw the dog in the tide but he has to leave it to the last minute. And then what happens? The rope breaks and the dog bites his hand and he falls into the water

himself and destroys his Sunday shoes. (To Joe) He's bound to come about looking for food. Put a shot in him will you? (p. 15)

Mary, unlike Manus, is a pragmatist rather than an idealist. She is leaving due to material pressures for a 'better life' in Manchester with the promise and expectation that she will return when her daughter Sarah becomes pregnant. Within a romantic, cultural nationalist paradigm, the act of her leaving hearth and homestead constitutes an act of betrayal. She is abdicating from what Susan Cannon Harris describes as 'her sacrificial duty, which is not only to bear and rear children but also to preserve the peasant cottage in which they grow up as a repository of all that is Irish' (Cannon Harris, 2002, p. 77). However, she passes down from mother to daughter an inheritance of maternity as the primary cultural function of women. This is a function that Sarah has not yet achieved and, as the play progresses it seems unlikely that she will achieve due to the fact that her marriage is sterile and her husband is impervious to her needs and desires. Desperate to leave and yet desirous to fulfil her role as mother Sarah becomes increasingly frustrated until she offers herself to Shane in the vain hope of producing the much-wanted child which will ensure the continuation of the island race:

> SARAH   I want to lie with you engineer.
> SHANE   I snore in my sleep. And my elbows are like daggers.
> SARAH   Will you lie with me?
> SHANE   Philly.
> SARAH   He's no good to me.
> SHANE   He's your husband.
> SARAH   Will you lie with me?
> SHANE   No, Sarah. (p. 39)

What is evident in Sarah's words is that she desires Shane, not as a lover but as a surrogate to her husband who is 'no good' to her. Her desire is therefore fastened upon a substitute; the resultant frustration, according to Rene Girard, can result in violence:

> Like violence, sexual desire tends to fasten upon surrogate objects if the object to which it was originally attracted remains inaccessible; it willingly accepts substitutes. And again like violence repressed sexual desire accumulates energy and sooner or later bursts forth, causing tremendous havoc. (Girard, 1977, p. 13)

It is clear that the object to which Sarah's desire was originally attached, Philly, has remained inaccessible to her. The tension between them is palpable from the start of the play when Sarah informs him that she wants to leave the island with her family suggesting that if she is forced to stay: 'I'll go out of my head with loneliness, I know I will' (Friel, p. 24). When Philly's half-heartedly responds that they should 'stick it out' until the end of summer she obliquely points out that all is not well in their marriage:

SARAH	Maybe if you spent less time on it [fishing] we might be better off.
PHILLY	Farming? Here?
SARAH	You and me.
	(Pause)
PHILLY	I'm tired.
SARAH	You're always tired when you're at home.
PHILLY	I was up all night, woman. When you and the rest of them were away drinking and dancing I was working.
SARAH	So you were. (p. 25)

Philly's indifference to Sarah is evident in these lines. He works or he is too tired to spend time with his wife. The reasons for this become apparent later in the play when she alleges that she has caught him engaging in some kind of homosexual act with Shane:

> SARAH (to Shane) I seen you – in the boathouse – you and Philly stripped – I seen you – I watched it all – with my own eyes – you and him, you dirty bastard – I seen it all – you dirty dancing bastard. (p. 67)

Her words are a sinister echo of an earlier scene in which Shane attempts to dance first with Philly and then with Sarah. It is notable that both Philly and Sarah react violently to Shane's invitations to dance. Sarah 'slaps his face viciously' (p. 45) while Philly 'shoves him roughly' (p. 45) then 'punches him again and again' (p. 45) shouting 'Dance, you bastard! Dance! Dance!' (p. 45). The sexual tension in this scene is palpable. Philly's aggression towards Shane could (and very possibly does) suggest his repressed homosexual leanings and aversion toward his own arousal to homosexual stimuli. If this is the case it is an early instance of Shane being scapegoated – made symbolically responsible for Philly's repressed desires. This motivates in Philly a hyper-masculine and hyper-aggressive reaction in which he can enact in the guise of the outraged husband, thereby fulfilling the role demanded by a culture which demands aggressive displays of machismo. Philly's aggression could therefore be seen as a savage breaking point within such a prohibitive culture of compulsory heterosexuality in which homosexuality is seen as both taboo and aberrant and, as Manus suggests, after the shooting of Shane, a curse:

> (Shouts) It's them – them queers! I should have killed the two of them when I had them! What we had wasn't much but what there was decent and wholesome! And they blighted us! They cankered us! They blackened the bud that was beginning to grow again! My curse on them! My curse of hell on the two of them! *Agus marbhfaisc orthu* – an early shroud on them. (p. 72)

This is an act of retrospective wish – fulfilment which substitutes the problems of his disintegrating society onto the outsiders; those he labels as semiotically and sexually 'queer'. Only a ritual of *pharmakos* or scapegoating (the murder of 'them queers') can purify the blight and remedy the canker for which Manus blames them. The expulsion and destruction of Peter and Shane represents to Manus a means of purification and remedy to the calamities which have befallen the gentle island. In his conception they are a contaminant that should have been eliminated in the same way that the 'niggerman' was eliminated for allegedly stealing five golden sovereigns when Manus was a boy. Yet Manus cannot do it. Although he views Shane's 'crime' of stealing his son as far worse than the niggerman's, he hesitates to shoot and it is Sarah fuelled by the urge to mate and a desire for revenge who fires the gun.

In his presentation of the women in the play Friel infuses an element of subversion into retrograde romantic national stereotypes that conflate the nation with the female body. Sarah is neither virgin nor mother. She cannot regenerate the nation or ensure the integrity and continuation of the race. As Susan Cannon Harris observes, the duty of Irish women within a romantic nationalist paradigm was: 'to function as guardians of the untainted essence of Irish identity … by maintaining their own sexual purity, by conceiving and bearing Irish children within the confines of the ideal Irish family, and by preserving the domestic interior as an inviolable shrine to national identity' (Cannon Harris, p. 68). When she is thwarted in her desire to be a material mother, Sarah adopts the role of Mother Ireland, issuing a call to arms and vengeance to her male protector (Manus) to regenerate her by the shedding of blood. She does this by drawing his attention to the alleged tryst between Philly and Shane in the boathouse, an act which threatens the pure continuity of his line and compromises his dynastic fantasies. Forced to acknowledge that his son is 'doing for that tramp what he couldn't do for me' (Friel, p. 61), Manus Sweeney is taunted by Sarah to shoot Shane in order to protect and preserve his imagined, primitive, peasant culture. However, Manus cannot fulfil his role. Despite the verbal bravado he has displayed hitherto he cannot either defend Sarah or avenge what he sees as the wrong done to him. In the closing scenes of the play Sarah is seen to possess something which Manus lacks – the ability to act. In a reversal of the traditional role assigned to women Sarah takes control while Manus becomes the passive recipient of female intervention. In this instance the female of the species is clearly more deadly than the male as Sarah shoots and paralyses Shane, a defenceless surrogate for the husband she feels has failed her. In doing this, according to Jose Lanters, she is able to 'symbolically cast out Philly's impotence and the violent tensions evoked by it' (Lanters, 1996, p. 165). Yet as the play makes clear any abeyance in conflict is temporary. Philly never learns of Shane's fate and Sarah has accepted hers as indicated in her final words, 'we'll get used to it' (Friel, p. 77).

Shane is not the only scapegoat in the play, but his otherness and difference renders him the obvious choice to be a sacrificial substitute to eliminate the ills of society and restore a sense of community. He is the serpent in the Manus Sweeney's fictive, Irish Eden; an outsider or other, a man without origins who breaks the rules and transgresses the taboos of the Island community. A mimic, a mocker and a desecrator of authority, Shane enacts his world with an *ad hoc* combination of what is at hand; the epitome of paradox he is the breacher of norms, the violator of taboos, a vicarious conduit for expression of otherwise forbidden desires and prohibited behaviours, and the destroyer of myths. His behaviour, according to Elmer Andrews, is 'an affront to ancient piety' which activates 'deep springs of violence' (in Peacock, 1993, p. 32). Significantly, it is Shane who penetrates the façade of rural primitivism which Manus adopts, and Shane who mocks and mimics this mask in Act 1:

> Be Jaysus, Shane boy, you're a quare comedian. You should be on the stage. Like me. Look at the act I have – the simple, upright, hardworking island peasant holding on manfully to the real values in life, sustained by a thousand-year-old culture, preserving for my people a really worthwhile inheritance. (Friel, p. 40)

The language Friel employs here allows Manus to be placed on an imaginative stage on which he attempts to re-enact, restage, rememorize and reinterpret his renditions of the past as he sees it. In order to do this he has to adopt a role, that of the ambiguously aristocratic peasant descendant of a pristine and prehistorical culture. Shane is 'quare' on a number of counts. Though he uses it here to mean 'exceptional' or 'good', the pun on his homosexuality is evident. Moreover, 'translated' from Dublin slang, it comes to define Shane as exactly what he is, a 'stranger' on Inishkeen. It is due in part to this strangeness or otherness that he becomes scapegoated, to preserve the purity of the Gentle Island.

There are clear parallels between Friel's subversive pastoral and Synge's *Playboy of the Western World*. In both plays a stranger enters an enclosed rural community and becomes celebrated for their eloquence. Both of these strangers, Christy and Shane, become the object of the female protagonist's affections, both plays challenge the 'cult of the hero' in their portrayals of the male protagonists; both have central characters who create romantic fictions of themselves and both have violence and poetry cheek by jowl. However, Friel presents a much grimmer vision of rural life than we see in Synge's dark comedy. While Pegeen Mike is attracted to Christy as a prospective marriage partner in favour of the feckless Shawn Keogh, the married Sarah Sweeney in Friel's play is attracted to Shane out of frustration at her loveless, childless marriage and out of desperation to conceive. As the play makes apparent, Shane is more of a 'gay boy' of the Eastern coast than a playboy of the Western world so Sarah's hopes of a procreative union with him cannot come to fruition. Again, while Christy in Synge's play is celebrated for a self-proclaimed act of parricide, Shane's metaphorical surrogate father, and probable lover, Peter is psychologically and emotionally smothering the younger man. The overriding image of the play is of futility, fruitlessness and stasis as exemplified in the tale of the petrified monks, cursed to remain forever for falling in love with an old monk's niece.

Elmer Andrews and Michael Parker observe that the play is about narratives, versions and storytelling. This notion of narration is equally true of scapegoating theory wherein 'sacred' violence is mythicised and narrativised to sustain the camaraderie and social cohesion generated by the original violence. These stories and myths attempt to turn *chronos* (profane time) into *chairos*; (sacred time) to recreate, renew and sustain the world before its fall into profane, quotidian experience. They seek to take the teller, and the listener back to a pre-lapsarian sacred time; the source, or point of origin wherein ontological plenitude or 'being' lies. The same can be said of the myth-making tendency in nationalistic discourse wherein versions of events are manipulated to define and valorise a nation as a distinct entity. In a society of 'fixed forms and binarisms' such as Northern Ireland each side will posit a history, which is teleological and aspires to narrative closure. Causality and origin can be cited as indices of racial discreteness or exceptionality in a homogenising drive which excludes those without the requisite cultural credentials such as lineage or religious affiliation. History becomes a univocal commentary voicing the indisputable truth. For Friel there are no irrefutable facts or historical absolutes. History is narrativised, a collection of stories recounted by a collection of storytellers. The tale is changed in the interpretation. There is no objective standard of 'truth'. There is no consensus, no communal and shared sense of memory, no essence, no source, and no point of origin. This is evident in the competing narratives that occur in *The Gentle Island*, none of which agree or cohere. The romantic/heroic narrative which Manus constructs around his past is refuted and de-romanticised by Sarah as a 'gallous story' based on 'dirty deeds'. The loss of his arm was not, she asserts, due to a mining accident in 'Butte, Montana', but an act of revenge undertaken by the barbaric uncles of 'Rosie Dubh' the gentle girl he impregnated and abandoned:

> And he got Rosie Dubh pregnant … and as soon as she told him, off he skited to England … And after twelve months he came home – God knows why – maybe he was running away from some English girl. And the night he arrived down at the harbour there, the two uncles were waiting for him with the knives they use for gutting herring. And that's how the arm was lost – in that fight. (p. 57)

His retort, that 'There's ways and ways of telling every story. Every story has seven faces' (p. 57) acquiesces to Fintan O'Toole's contention that 'Ireland is not one story any more … What we have instead are fragments, isolated pieces of a whole story that no-one knows (in Boss, 1998, p116). Arguably this is the central theme of *The Gentle Island*; a play which Friel described as 'a metaphor for Ireland' in which 'we see most facets of Irish life, love, hate, loneliness …' (cited in Madden, 2000, p. 110). In the rhetoric of Romantic nationalism, Ireland is presented as a single, authentic and unfinished story of heroic resistance and eventual liberty from colonial 'enslavement', when the island will be, in the words of the Young Irelander Thomas Davis's famous nineteenth-century song, 'a nation once again'. In *The Gentle Island* Friel highlights the dangers implicit in such a myopic fidelity to a discourse that relies on notions of essence and othering for its existence, to the point that it must annihilate the other in order to preserve the race within consolidated and demarcated borders. He points out that such a discourse, based on an authentic spirit of nation is entirely fictitious and rooted in a mythic past that never was; it celebrates stasis, eschews renewal and guarantees, not continuance but the extinction of the peoples it attempts to protect. In *The Gentle Island,* Manus Sweeney represents these beliefs, whose folly is the folly of nationalist purists in the North of Ireland who, according to Dermot Bolger, 'are so bizarrely entangled with history that we must go back three centuries to explain any fight outside a chip shop'. (Bolger, 1996, p. 62). Manus's abjection and descent into madness at the end of the play highlight the disabling nature of this ideology. In insisting on his authenticity he becomes a static object, much like the petrified 'Monks' off the coast of Inishkeen. Furthermore, he fulfils the colonial stereotype of the colonised Irish as savage and primitive, thus requiring civilisation. Inishkeen is a microcosm for Ireland. Manus has been constructed by the imagined discourse of Irishness; thus he is unable to comprehend Ireland as a living and changing culture, but as a dead and static image rooted in the past.

The play ends with images of utter futility and stasis. Manus Sweeney is huddled over a dead fire mumbling inarticulately to himself. Joe, the younger of his two sons has left for London leaving only Manus, Philly and Sarah on the island. As Jose Lanters points out: 'Whatever the Sweeneys believe their treatment of Shane has accomplished, in actuality their situation has deteriorated: the cow is giving less milk, the salmon are increasingly elusive and Joe is gone' (Lanters, p. 169). What is left is a culture in its death throes. The scapegoat has been expelled from their midst but there is no society left to be united by this expulsion. Violence has accomplished nothing. It is pointless for Manus to invoke ancient wrongs such as the story of the petrified monks; nor can he legitimate his position by invoking narratives of violence, blame, retribution and recrimination. There is no-one left to blame and there is no-one other than Sarah and Philly left to listen. Sarah is a broken woman, Philly will clearly never leave; none of the remaining islanders will ever change.

It can be argued that *The Gentle Island* is a tragic statement of the mental and sexual frustrations of rural island life. The play focuses on issues of identity and belonging centred on the myth of an essentialised rural nation as a site of indigenous culture and authenticity. It is also perhaps Friel's most sustained challenge to Romantic Nationalist discourse in its repudiation of the myth of the *duine uasal*. Friel excoriates this myth of the noble peasant by painting a stark, harsh picture of isolation and poverty, the hopelessness, ignorance and desperation of the rural poor. More than this, the play undermines the notion that violence can be good, redemptive, acceptable even attractive. Violence in the play is never heroic but nauseating and indiscriminate: a dog is paralysed, a 'niggerman' is paralysed, a donkey is tortured to the point of madness and death, and a young man is shot and dumped on the mainland. All of this is undertaken to defend an 'authentic' insular island culture from outsiders. Violence has become part of a mythic narrative which allows the past to justify the present.

Yet, as Manus says, 'Every story has seven faces' (Friel p. 56). There is no irrefutable truth, nothing is incontrovertible. We do not know whether the central conflict of the play, the alleged liaison between Philly and Shane occurred at all. As Ulf Dantanus points out, 'a jury would have great difficulty in disentangling the facts' (Dantanus,

1988, p. 125). Friel shares his circumspection. In *The Gentle Island* there are no external verities, only differing versions; each narrative operates as a retaliatory mechanism in which the protagonists justify their actions against a perceived wrongdoing which they believe has been inflicted upon them. Each teller determines the point at which the narration begins and ends, and which details are included and omitted. All the characters exist in a perpetual state of self-deception and stasis, slowly calcifying like the monks, unable to escape, trapped by their obsessive fixation on a past that may or may not have been. As the play suggests, the point of origin - and consequently a sense of resolution or closure - is never reached: history becomes a palimpsest of half-truths in which the fiction of truth is the most apocryphal discourse of all.

References

Andrews, E. (1993), 'The Fifth Province', in *The Achievement of Brian Friel*, ed. A. J. Peacock, Colin Smythe, Gerrards Cross, Bucks.

Bolger, D. (1996), 'Shift your Shadow or I'll Burst You', *Sunday Independent*, 16 August 1992, cited in *Dancing to History's Tune: History, Myth and Politics in Ireland*, ed. B. Walker, Belfast Institute of Irish Studies, Belfast.

Boss, M. (ed.) (1998), *Ireland: Towards New Identities*, Dolphin, Aarhus, Denmark.

Cannon Harris, S. (2002), *Gender and Modern Irish Drama*, Indiana University Press, Indiana.

Dantanus, U. (1988), *Brian Friel: A Study*, Faber & Faber, London.

Friel, B. (2000), in 'Brian Friel's Other Island', an interview with A. Madden, 1971 in *Brian Friel in Conversation*, University of Michigan Press, Michigan.

Friel, B. (1993), *The Gentle Island*, Gallery, London.

Gellner, E. (1991), *Nations and Nationalism*, Blackwell, Oxford.

Kiberd, D. (1995), *Inventing Ireland*, Cambridge, Mass., Harvard University Press.

Girard, R. (1977), *Violence and The Sacred*, trans. P. Gregory, John Hopkins University Press, Baltimore and London.

Lanters, J. (1996), *Violence and Sacrifice in Brian Friel's The Gentle Island and Wonderful Tennessee, Irish University Review*, 26 (1), pp. 163–176.

O'Connor, U. (1984), *Celtic Dawn: A Portrait of the Irish Literary Renaissance*, Black Swan, London.

O'Toole, F. (1998), *Irish Theatre The State of The Art*, in *Ireland: Towards New Identities*, ed. M. Boss, Aarhus University Press, Aarhus, Denmark.

Tormey, M. (1996), 'The Ancient Race', in *Remembrance and Imagination: Patterns in the Literary Representation of Ireland in the Nineteenth Century*, in J. Leersen, Field Day Monographs, Cork University Press, Cork.

Brian Friel's Love Scenes

Paddy Lyons
University of Glasgow

Early twentieth-century modernism launched a new kind of love scene, and it soon became a convention of the art of the century, one that lives on in many areas of culture such as film and popular song. This scene is one of total surrender, of swooning, melting, and even abject abandonment to a moment felt as endless and as surpassing time. Here is an early example:

> He took her into the dark gardens and … he kissed her. He kissed her passionately, violently, with a sudden explosion of the passion that had been bridled all his life … and he passed the night in her bed.
>
> When the palpitating creature was at last asleep in his arms [Edward] discovered that he was madly, was passionately, was overwhelmingly in love with her. It was a passion that had arisen like fire in dry corn. He could think of nothing else; he could live for nothing else. (Ford, 2004, p. 227)

This scene of love, from Ford Madox Ford's *The Good Soldier* (1915), presents love as fusion, a fusion of sexuality with sentiment, which becomes an all-absorbing yieldingness and invites identification. Ford's narrator is as much in thrall to Edward's passion as Edward is to his new beloved, La Dolciquita, the mistress of the Grand Duke. A further characteristic of the convention is that it can accommodate – and indeed thrives on – contradiction, as in this very dazzling version from W. B. Yeats:

> Slim adolescence that a nymph has stripped,
> Peleus on Thetis stares.
> Her limbs are delicate as an eyelid,
> Love has blinded him with tears;
> But Thetis' belly listens.
> Down the mountain walls
> From where Pan's cavern is

> Intolerable music falls.
> Foul goat-head, brutal arm appear,
> Belly, shoulder, bum,
> Flash fishlike; nymphs and satyrs
> Copulate in the foam.
> ('News for the Delphic Oracle'; Yeats, 1990, p. 386)

Here sensitivity and coarseness are set up as contraries that nonetheless blend together, held in suspension; everything is in the present tense; and opposed urges take over simultaneously. As in the scene from Ford, high rhetorical skills also are in play – and again they're veiled, thanks to the rhythmic insistence that makes all other devices subordinate – mere means to an end - sweeping the reader into vicarious identifications. This can take possession of and hold as if spellbound even the most unexpected and unlikely souls, even such a one as Beckett's Krapp, whose cheerful devotion to eating bananas and recording his ramblings completely deserts him once he becomes mesmerised by a high modernist love scene found on an old tape; Krapp is soon in its grip, and he plays and replays it, over and over again:

> TAPE: ... I asked her to look at me and after a few moments - [*Pause.*] - after a few moments she did, but the eyes just slits, because of the glare. I bent over her to get them in the shadow and they opened. [*Pause. Low.*] Let me in. [*Pause.*] We drifted in among the flags and stuck. The way they went down, sighing, before the stern! [*Pause.*] I lay across her with my face in her breasts and my hand on her. We lay there without moving. But under us all moved, and moved us, gently, up and down, and from side to side. (Beckett, 1986, p. 221)

Until he happens upon this scene, Krapp can occupy himself contentedly thanks to his command of words, relishing the sounds words make, and marvelling over their dictionary meanings; but as he listens he falls silent, and is at the mercy of the words he hears. Between the stripped-back minimalism of Krapp's life-style and the lushness of the recorded love-scene there's a stark misfit, and this split, this cleft, in turn suggests where the appeal of the high-modernist love scene lies: it provides a fullness where otherwise boredom and emptiness might enter and reign. That is to say, this genre of love scene exemplifies quite exactly Jean-François Lyotard's comment that 'modernity takes place in the withdrawal of the real and ... the emphasis can be placed on ... the nostalgia for plenitude felt by the human subject ...' (Lyotard, 1984, p. 79). In short, it's so all-embracing it leaves no blanks.

My contention in this essay is that Brian Friel's love scenes amount to a radical departure from the practice of early modernism. This is so, I will argue, because Friel persistently delights in putting his theatrical devices on open display, unlike the high modernists, whose love-scenes achieved their special effects by masking or occluding the rhetorical and linguistic devices on which they relied. In other words, Friel breaks with the theatre of identification, and develops a dramaturgy comprehensible in relation to those late twentieth-century thinkers who queried more broadly identification and its mechanisms – Althusser, Lacan and Badiou. Whereas the early modernist love-scene tended to be solemn, and awe-stricken, a last gasp of the romantic movement, Friel introduces an understanding of the difference between solemnity and seriousness, interested in how love can encompass intelligence and amusement and thereby be seriously tender.

Friel's love-scenes – and they are many, and often very radiant — are never less than tender, and instead of dissolving into the modernist prolonged moment, Friel's dramaturgy of devices on display makes space for a wider sense of how people can inhabit time feelingfully. Here is an instance, from his 1994 play *Molly Sweeney* - the speaker is Mr Rice, the eye-surgeon who attempts to restore Molly's sight, and Mr Rice is telling what passed between himself and his ex-wife Maria at the funeral of the man for whom she'd left him:

> ... she took my hand and kissed it and held it briefly against her cheek. It was a loving gesture. But for all its tenderness, because of all its tenderness, I knew she was saying a final goodbye to me. (Friel, 1999, p. 505)

A loving gesture is presented and described with care, then the gesture is reread – but in reverse. This in miniature is a tendency prevalent in Friel's dramaturgy, where any quick or easy response is soon turned inside out, thoughtfully and interrogatively. To an expression of feeling Mr Rice brings an understanding of feeling – '*because* of all its tenderness, I knew she was saying a final goodbye'. Unlike Ford's Edward, for whom unleashed passion was overwhelming, unlike Yeats' lovers, for whom passion was blinding and consuming, and unlike Beckett's Krapp, held in fascination by the magic moment when the boat 'drifted in among the flags, and stuck', Friel's Mr Rice is at once lucid and responsive: rather than insulating or closing off his awareness, feeling informs his intelligence. Not lost in enrapturement within a single moment, he can at once inhabit that moment, and also - in noticing how *briefly* his hand is held against Maria's cheek – he has access to a more extensive time-span: he can measure the brevity that allowed her gesture to become legible. For the audience, too, perception is dispersed across several non-intersecting time-zones: on stage nothing is seen to be enacted, everything is narrated. This dramaturgy stages a gap between seeing and understanding and it does so primarily to place the spectator in a position not unlike that of Molly herself, the blind woman whose recovered vision never comes fully into correspondence with her grasp on the world. The audience watches Molly, and her husband Frank, and the surgeon Mr Rice, as one after the other they narrate the events that led up to and followed after Molly's operation; the audience is invited to construct and attempt to understand those events, while never seeing the events directly, and seeing only the participants who tell them over afterwards, as events that are already past. As so often with Friel, a distance is established for the spectators, and the means whereby that distance is established are palpable, up front, and visibly on show. It is - very exactly - a dramaturgy that rests on 'forms of temporality that do not achieve any mutual integration', and which brings to life a 'dissociated structure'; those are terms Louis Althusser devised to describe what struck him as the bedrock of progressive non-identificatory theatre (Althusser, 1975, p. 142; p. 147).

For his first extensive venture into the love scene, in *Winners* (1967), Friel adopted a framing device which fractures any unitary perception of time, and stages temporal dissociation very boldly. Centre stage are two teenagers, Mag and Joe, for whom school is over and exams still to come. Mag is pregnant, and their lives are before them. They've made their way to a hillside overlooking a lake, supposedly to study, but mostly they mimic and caricature their schoolteachers and other local worthies, and fantasise how their own lives will turn out. In other words, instead of surrendering to the moment that they inhabit, they make time their own by imagining themselves elsewhere, in space and in time, skittishly, and quite defiantly:

> MAG: If we put a lace curtain across the kitchen window, we wouldn't actually *see* down into the slaughterhouse yard.
> JOE: And if we wore earplugs all the time we wouldn't actually *hear* the mooing and the shooting.
> MAG: (*Softly to herself.*) And even if a curtain did make the room darker, it'll still be lovely …
> JOE: There's a bullock that looks like the president of Saint Kevin's. Bang! Bang!
> MAG: A sheep the image of Sister Paul! Bang! Bang!
> JOE: Drag 'em away!
> MAG: Slice 'em open!
> JOE: Joan O'Hara's white poodle. Tweeny.
> MAG: Bang! And Philip Moran's mother.
> JOE: Bang! Bang! Doctor Watson.
> MAG: A friend. Pass, friend, pass. (Friel, 1969, pp 17-19)

They banter, quarrel, make up, and in the end, to 'begin the future now' they set off running, intending to steal a boat and sail away, recklessly, to invent paradise right where they are:

> MAG: The lake! We'll dance on every island! We'll stay out all night and sing and shout at the moon!
> JOE *does a wolfhowl up at the sky.*
> Come on, Joe! While the sun's hot.
> JOE: O mad hot sun, thou breath of summer's being.
> MAG: Away to the farthest island.
> JOE: We've no boat.
> MAG: We'll take a boat. (Friel, 1969, pp. 85-6)

But sitting on either side of the stage throughout, and speaking intermittently through lulls in the love-talk, are two commentators, an unnamed man and woman. They introduce a second perspective, a broader time-frame, and another narrative, one which disrupts focus on the lovers. These commentators read out from books that tell how this day in the life of the young couple is to be the day of their death by drowning. They speak impersonally and without emotion; an opening stage direction insists: 'At no time must they reveal an attitude to their material' (Friel, 1969, p. 5).

Their attention is as much on people who will live afterwards, and on how the lovers' deaths will impact on them: parents, teachers, and the local community. That the lovers' death is impending is flashed forward, proleptically, from early on, thus inserting the audience into two time perspectives at once: one wherein the lovers advance in their courtship, and one wherein these lovers engaged in love-play are already to be imagined as dead and buried, and present only through the distancing perspective of a postmortem. Until the final moments, when the lovers dash off to look for a boat, both couples remain on stage, though separate and apart; neither pair looks at the other pair, a constant visual reminder to the theatre audience that this is indeed theatre.

At the close of *Winners,* the young couple dash off uttering wordless cries, variations on Joe's wolfhowl:

> MAG: We're away!
> JOE: Easy – easy –
> MAG: Wheeeeeeee –
> JOE: Aaaaaaaaah –
> *They run down the hill, hand in hand.* (Friel, 1969, pp. 87-8)

This motif will reappear, again and again: Friel habitually links the initial moment of love to liveliness of movement combined with sound that is conspicuously empty, sometimes taking the form of expressive noises, sometimes words fallen into meaninglessness and nonsense. Frank's recollection of how he fell for Molly Sweeny while they were dancing is exemplary: 'she didn't have to say a word – she just glowed' (Friel, 1999, p. 479). Molly remembers in more detail – 'we were doing an old-time waltz' - and recalls how Frank touched her feelings, first by paying her a compliment and then by launching endearingly into what were to her entirely fatuous speculations, asking if because of her blindness 'you question not only the idea of appearance but probably the existence of external reality itself' (Friel 1999, p. 479). Moved by the meaninglessness of his chatter Molly concludes: 'And I knew too, after that night in the Hikers' Club, that if he did ask me to marry him, for no very good reason at all I would probably say yes' (Friel, 1999, p. 480). With this mix of babble and wolfhowling Friel makes prominent in the love-scene what the early modernist version masked or elided – the dimension of the new and the strange that resists ready-made words and phrases, that area which Lacan designates 'the real' because it's not yet tamed and contained in the web of familiar words. Friel dramatises love as beginning as Badiou would describe it – in 'pure encounter … not preceded by anything … practically without measure' (Badiou, 2003, pp. 27-8); and love's start-off is, as Lacan described such encounters, 'apprehended in its experience of rupture, between perception and consciousness, in that non-temporal locus' (Lacan, 1998, p. 56). So it is for Hannah and Andy, the middle-aged couple who feature in *Losers,* Friel's companion-piece to *Winners.* Their courting is kick-started through experience not yet sifted into sense by language. If they lapse into silence Hannah and Andy are at constant risk of interruption from Hannah's demanding invalid mother, and to be free to thrash around on the parlour sofa, they are obliged to punctuate their intimacies with bawling out shopping-lists and shouting random stanzas from Gray's 'Elegy Written in a Country Churchyard'. The lists and the stanzas become farcical nonsense, meaningless sounds that, ironically, have the effect of intensifying rather than dampening their lust.

The charm and appeal of love that begins in non-sense, outside meaningfulness, is notably evident in the love-scene recalled by the traveling players Crystal and Fox, as they sit despondent after their son Gabriel has been arrested for manslaughter, and their vaudeville world is undergoing collapse:

> FOX: ... you got a mad notion of going for a swim at dawn. And this morning, just about this time, you woke me up, and we slipped out and raced across the wet fields in our bare feet. And when we got to the sea, we had to wade across this stream to get to the beach.
> CRYSTAL: [*suddenly remembering.*] The channel!
> FOX: D'you remember? And you hoisted up your skirt and you took my hand and we stepped into the –
> CRYSTAL: Fish! Flat fish!
> FOX: Hundreds of them! Every step you took! D'you remember?
> CRYSTAL: Oh my God!
> FOX: Every time you put a foot down!
> CRYSTAL: The wriggling of them! Under your bare feet!
> FOX: And you couldn't go forward! And you couldn't go back!
> CRYSTAL: And you split your sides laughing!
> FOX: Trying to keep hopping so that you wouldn't touch bottom!
> CRYSTAL: Squirming and wriggling!
> FOX: And then you lost your balance – and down you went!
> CRYSTAL: And pulled you down, too.
> FOX: And then you started to laugh!
> CRYSTAL: It was the sight of you spluttering!
> FOX: The water was freezing!
> CRYSTAL: We were soaked to the skin!
> FOX: And we staggered over to the beach.
> CRYSTAL: And you, you eejit, you began to leap about like a monkey!
> FOX: The seagulls – remember? – they sat on the rocks, staring at us.
> CRYSTAL: And you tied a plait of seaweed to my hair.
> FOX: And we danced on the sand. (Friel, 1970, pp. 60-1)

What was once wordless hilarity has been put into words – to be sure, words of great lyrical delight – but that is also to say it has now been mapped, encodified, and moved from the Lacanian real into everyday reality. The gorgeousness of these shared memories is in vivid contrast with the situation of Crystal and Fox, and is not a cue for fusion. Though Fox takes heart enough to feel he can go forward – '… we'll laugh again at silly things and I'll plait seaweed into your hair again' (Friel, 1970, p. 63) – Crystal falls sombre. Henceforth this remarkable and twisting play hurls onwards to its dark and final turns, the scene of early love that is recollected but not staged soon giving way to Friel's bleakest on-stage anti-love scene.

In Friel's plays, direct statements of love are frequently prone to reversal and doubt, and Crystal is to make such a statement with a sudden tipsy declaration of her love for Fox – 'I'd marry you a hundred times again … Every day. Every hour … My sweet Fox … This is all I want' (Friel, 1970, p. 70). Her declaration unleashes in Fox his very worst destructive impulses: he claims it was he who informed on their son Gabriel to the police, and that he did so for money. Crystal abandons him, in horror and dismay:

> CRYSTAL: What … are … you? [*He puts out a hand to touch her. She recoils. She screams.*] Don't – don't – don't touch me! [*She backs away from him.*] … I don't know who you are. [*She runs off.* FOX *takes a few steps after her.*]
>
> FOX: Crystal! Crystal! [*Quietly, tensely.*] It's a lie, Crystal, all a lie, my love, I made it all up, never entered my head until a few minutes ago and then I tried to stop myself but I couldn't, it was poor Papa that told the police and he didn't know what he was saying, I don't know why I said it, I said it just to – to – to [*Roars.*] Crystal! [*Again quiet, rapid.*] Lies, lies, yes I wanted rid of the Fritters and Billy Hercules, yes I wanted rid of Cid and Tanya, and I wanted rid of the whole show, even good Pedro, because that's what I saw, that's the glimpse I got for the moment the fog lifted, that's what I remember, that's what I think I remember, just you and me, as we were, but we were young then, and even though our clothes were wet and even though the sun was only rising, there were hopes – there were warm hopes; and love alone isn't enough now, my Crystal, it's not, my love, not enough at all, not nearly enough. (Friel, 1970, pp. 72-4)

No matter which part of what Fox says here is taken for truth, Fox is fearsome because his darkness is so fluent and so lucid. Lacan once remarked of the protagonists of tragedy that 'The only thing one can be guilty of is giving ground relative to one's desire … the voice of the [tragic] hero trembles at nothing' (Lacan, 1992, p. 319; p. 323). Fox's desire, set out in the hilarity among the flat fish, began in and belonged to a wordless nonsensical moment, unmapped and uncharted, promising a space for hope and for risk. The comfort of words, meaningful words, is contrary to that desire.

The radical contrast between the remembered off stage scene which opened onto possible futures and the relatively limited comfort of what's present on stage – familiar words – propels him to destroy all he has now. Fox's tragedy is that he has, like the play itself, discovered in love those 'forms of temporality that do not achieve any mutual integration' which Althusser saw as underlying the theatre of non-identification (Althusser, 1975 p. 142). The play ends on desolation, Fox performing his showman's patter with his wheel of fortune, a game of risk and chance, Fox not giving ground relative to his desire for what's become absent from love, though he thereby loses Crystal ('my Crystal … my love') and is left to occupy only bare, blank space.

Absence and off-stage scenes continued to interest Friel. 'The play should not have its centre in itself but outside …' remarked Althusser, applauding 'Brecht's stroke of genius … in not showing the great scene of the trial in his play *Galileo*' (Althusser, 2003, pp. 143-4). Through the 1970s Friel was to experiment with love encounters which are not exhibited on-stage, and are powerful in their effects because taboo. In *The Gentle Island* (1971) it's never conclusively established whether or not, in an off-stage boathouse, the fisherman Philly and Shane, the tourist from Dublin, have indeed shared same-sex love, love that in 1971 was not supposed to speak its name in the Irish Republic because that could and did give rise to grave criminal charges. However, Philly's wife Sarah rushes on stage and is quite adamant to her father-in-law Manus as to exactly what she's witnessed:

> That he's down there in the boathouse at the far slip, your Philly, my husband. That he's down there with that Dublin tramp, Shane. That they're stripped naked. That he's doing for the tramp what he couldn't do for me. (Friel, 1993, p. 61)

In consequence, Manus assents to Sarah maiming Shane, with shocking and would-be murderous brutality, even though Manus will later envisage an alternative boathouse scenario that introduces an undertow of sanctioned bestiality and takes doubt further:

> One night when I went into it there was a sail hanging from the roof and as sure as God I thought it was a sheep making for me. I could have sworn it was a sheep making for me … it's that dark in yon place you could imagine anything. (Friel, 1993, p. 74)

Uncertainty is maintained to the bitter end, and enables the chilling anti-love-scene that concludes this play. As Philly sits impassively in a chair and Sarah kneels beside him unlacing his boots, Sarah and Philly make low-key small talk, about the salmon catch, and about how the island will be quiet without Philly's younger brother Joe, who has emigrated to Glasgow; the audience is meantime held in wonder at the potential for violence and cruelty that the couple's steadfastly humdrum conversation appears to be leaving unspoken. In *Living Quarters* (1977) there is no doubt an illicit love affair did occur between Ben and Anna, the son and the second wife of Commandant Frank Butler – and that their affair is the cause of the Commandant's suicide – but again the love encounter which crosses a taboo line is not shown on stage, and only becomes apparent in refractions and in its tangled aftermath. Instead, what's unremittingly present to the audience is the repressiveness of everyday chatter, which consigns to absence whatever it is unable to come to terms with. At the end of the decade, with *Translations* (1980), Friel's preoccupations with transgressive love, and with the functioning of language and nonsense, were to coalesce again on-stage, largely thanks to a new and highly ingenious device to distance the audience.

It's imagination that distances the audience at *Translations*. Although throughout this piece the actors on stage speak almost all their lines in the language system prevailing among the audience, the audience is invited to imagine that on stage two language systems are in play, that while the two soldiers from England who are mapping the district of Ballybeg are speaking English, the native inhabitants are in the main speaking Irish – although in fact no Irish is used on stage other than for place-names. How much importance Friel attached to sustaining this device became evident when a translation of *Translations* into Irish was mooted. Friel insisted that if the play was to be performed in Irish, for an predominantly Irish-speaking audience, then everything the two English soldiers say must also be spoken in Irish. In other words, although the performance is given in the single predominant language of the audience, the audience is to imagine on stage two languages strange to each other and mutually incomprehensible without translation. This convention is established gradually, and its first effect is to give rise to casual comedy, as for example over the verbal confusion imagined when Irish-speaking Maire brings news there's to be a dance, and the English soldier Yolland can only understand through the mediation of the translator, Owen.

MAIRE:	(*To* OWEN) Did you tell him?
YOLLAND:	(*To* MAIRE) Sorry-sorry?
OWEN:	(*To* MAIRE) He says may he come?
MAIRE:	(*To* YOLLAND) That's up to you.
YOLLAND:	(*To* OWEN) What does she say?
OWEN:	(*To* YOLLAND) She says –
YOLLAND:	(*To* MAIRE) What-what?
MAIRE:	(*To* OWEN) Well?
YOLLAND:	(*To* OWEN) Sorry-sorry?
OWEN:	(*To* YOLLAND) Will you go?
YOLLAND:	(*To* MAIRE) Yes, yes, if I may.
MAIRE:	(*To* OWEN) What does he say?
YOLLAND:	(*To* OWEN) What does she say?
OWEN:	Oh for God's sake! (Friel, 1984, p. 425)

What's amusing here is that the mutual incomprehension is completely fictional. Neither Maire nor Yolland can – or so we imagine, though it's contrary to all we actually hear – follow what each other means, what is signified. Later, after the dance, in the love-encounter between Maire and Yolland which will occupy the last scene of the play's second act, this distance that spectators necessarily take up to imagine incomprehension will be mirrored in shifts of emotional distance between the would-be lovers. Regarding distance between a play and its spectators, Althusser observed: 'it is essential that in some way this distance should be produced within the play itself' (Althusser, 1975, p. 146). That is exactly how distance is orchestrated in this justly celebrated scene.

This love-scene moves through three main sequences. It begins in mutual embarrassment, with increasingly frustrated efforts to cross the communication barrier. Maire and Yolland have run in together from the dance, holding hands, but they're taken aback as they become aware of their sudden intimacy, and they draw apart and attempt polite conversation. Yolland tries speaking loudly, with equal emphasis on every syllable:

> YOLLAND: Every-morning-I-see-you-feeding-brown-hens-and-giving-meal-to-black-calf- *(The futility of it.)* O my God…
> (Friel, 1984, p. 427)

Maire tries speaking the one English phrase she knows, to the confusion of them both:

> MAIRE: George, 'In Norfolk we besport ourselves around the maypoll'.
> YOLLAND: Good God, do you? That's where my mother comes from – Norfolk. Norwich actually. Not exactly Norwich town but a small village called Little Walsingham close beside it. But in our own village of Winfarthing we have a maypole too and every year on the first of May – (*He stops abruptly, only now realising. He stares at her. She in turn misunderstands his excitement.*)
> MAIRE: (*To herself.*) Mother of God, my Aunt Mary wouldn't have taught me something dirty, would she?
> (Friel, 1984, p. 428)

In these exchanges what each is imagined as conveying to the other is arrant nonsense joined to an urge to make contact through what words signify. A second sequence takes over as they cease these efforts at signification and instead employ signifiers without any regard to meaning, enjoying the blissful nonsense of pure sound. They utter the Gaelic names for neighbourhood places – place-names familiar to Yolland as a would-be cartographer, and familiar to Maire as a local – but in joyous indifference to all actual reference other than the come-hither this speaking nonsense enables. Lifted off the map, signifiers taking precedence over the signified, place-names become the raw materials for a love-song, a free-form duet. Then in the final sequence of the scene, the couple return to speaking their feelings, but now with no concern for whether or not the words convey any sense to each other:

(*She holds out her hands to* YOLLAND. *He takes them. Each now speaks almost to himself/herself.*)

YOLLAND: I wish to God you could understand me.
MAIRE: Soft hands; a gentleman's hands.
YOLLAND: Because if you could understand me I could tell you how I spend my days either thinking of you or gazing up at your house in the hope that you'll appear even for a second.
MAIRE: Every evening you walk by yourself along the Trá Bhán and every morning you wash yourself in front of your tent.
YOLLAND: I would tell you how beautiful you are, curly-headed Maire. I would so like to tell you how beautiful you are.
MAIRE: Your arms are long and thin and the skin on your shoulders is very white.
YOLLAND: I would tell you …
MAIRE: Don't stop, I know what you're saying.
YOLLAND: I would tell you how I want to be here, to live here – always – with you – always, always.
MAIRE: 'Always'? What is that word 'always'? …
YOLLAND: I'm not going to leave here.
MAIRE: Shhh – listen to me. I want you too, soldier.
(Friel, 1984, p. 429-30)

Interestingly, these lovers are not lost in rapture. If each is past worrying over the significance of their own words, each is also listening as well as speaking, and listening with enough distance to halt, and to reflect questioningly, in puzzlement over whatever may seem strange. 'What is that word "always"?' As well as these internal distances, between them there is, too, further distance perceptible to the audience: Yolland wants to stay in Ireland, whereas Maire wants to leave Ireland and to live with him 'anywhere – anywhere at all' (Friel, 1984, p. 430). In short, corresponding to the imaginative distance established between the play and the spectators are internal psychic distances and discords that at once divide the lovers and fuel their drive to reach across each to the other. The scene ends on disruption. As the lovers kiss, there's no pause for the audience to melt into their bliss. On dashes Sarah, the girl with the speech impediment, and as she catches sight of them she howls for Manus, her teacher and Maire's intended. Darkness follows, and the play turns abruptly into a new direction, the centre of gravity shifting as the effects of this scene ripple through the community.

Yolland has disappeared, and Manus leaves town. Has Manus beaten out Yolland's brains with a stone and disposed of the body in a limn-kiln? The possibility is raised. Or has Yolland been kidnapped by the roving Donnelly twins, proto-guerrillas and the most likely culprits for any and every skullduggery, all the more so since they never appear on stage? This possibility too is floated, and the matter is not settled by the time the play ends, leaving what Friel elsewhere extols as 'the necessary uncertainty'. But while there's uncertainty, the community faces punishment, and the list of place-names which gave Yolland and Maire the elements for their love duet is recited again, but this time with the sounds tied firmly to the places they signify, which are to be targets for sacking and destruction by the army. The translator, Owen, Manus's brother, learns the discomfort of attempting to straddle both sides of a fence. And while the younger men go to hide the cattle from the wrath of the army, the old school-master, Hugh, the father of Manus and Owen, sits with an elderly pupil to reminisce over their lost youth and the fate of empires. According to Seamus Deane, the play is tragic. Its theme has been 'the death of the Irish language', and it concludes on 'final incoherence' because 'The crisis [*Translations*] is concerned with is experienced directly by people who are trapped ... the failure of the lovers to find the opportunity to express their feeling ....' (Deane, 1984, pp. 21-2). Declan Kiberd concurs with Deane's drift, and cites Edward Said to embed the love scene in a reading of the play which indicts imperialism for how it warps culture:

> No Orientalist text, Said adds, was complete without a ritual infatuation ... with some mysterious woman of the native tribe, much along the lines of Yolland's assignation with Maire Chatach, an infatuation often experienced by the wayward son who is sent to an outpost because he can find no suitable job or partner at home. The woman, like the colony, is a mystery to be penetrated ... (Kiberd,1995, p. 620)

The larger trouble with such readings – still prevalent in commentaries on this play - is that to absorb the fate of the lovers into an anti-colonial outlook they fudge the geometry and invoke simplistic identification: distance between the audience and the world of the play is collapsed as the imaginative dimension is supplanted by 'crisis ... experienced directly by people who are trapped'. Politically, this is to deplore past injuries while leaving the post-colonial present unaddressed. Artistically, this is to presume that a love-scene should display the plenitude of early modernism, and close off all that is contradictory and beyond signification, all that is reached towards under Lacan's concept of 'the real'. Gender trouble is evident too, with Maire dragooned into allegory, as that venerable anti-colonial image of Ireland as a needy and abandoned woman otherwise known as Dark Rosaleen.

In a poem by Seamus Heaney, it is likely that Maire's fate would indeed have been just so wretched, and even tragic. Heaney's poem 'Punishment' appeared in 1975, five years before *Translations,* and is explicit about the stigmatisation a Northern Irish Catholic girl could meet with at home if she went walking out with a British soldier in the 1970s; 'betraying sisters', he records, were tarred and feathered and publicly shamed - 'cauled in tar' to weep 'by the railings'; this cruel punishment replaying a tribal past, continuing brutality over which Heaney presents himself as understanding everything while standing 'dumb' (Heaney, 1985, p. 119). However, Friel's dramaturgy offers no such transparent window onto an unchanging world, and truly is a *post*-colonial text, its distances allowing Maire's immediate audience an opportunity to imagine its own communal past quite differently, to imagine a young woman *not* as ostracised but as accepted back without hostility into her community after a brief fling with a soldier-boy from the other side of the lines. When Maire reappears in the last act, she is indeed concerned because Yolland is missing, but she's not an abandoned or a tragic figure, and is already rewriting their love scene – cheerfully, and minus intensity:

> He left me home, Owen. And the last thing he said to me – he tried to speak in Irish – he said – 'I'll see you yesterday' – he meant to say 'I'll see you tomorrow.' … And off he went, laughing, laughing, Owen. Do you think he's all right? (Friel, 1984, p. 437)

She expands and recounts not so much what the audience has seen but a version that sounds as if she has been studying to make sense retrospectively from what to her at the time was sheer nonsense. She drops to her hands and knees and traces a map on the ground:

> Look. There's Winfarthing. And there's two other wee villages beside it; one of them's called Barton Bendish – it's there; and the other's called Saxingham Nethergate – it's about there. And there's Little Walsingham –that's his mother's townland … He drew a map for me on the wet strand and wrote the names on it. I have it all in my head now. (Friel, 1984, p. 437)

Her highly detailed cartography seems to have come from a geography book, very likely the same geography book Maire disingenuously claims she didn't have time to study the previous night. Then, as if Sarah hadn't arrived to interrupt the start of a kiss with her screaming, Maire compliments Sarah on the colour of her dance-frock. She even persuades old Hugh to start teaching her English, and begins by asking him, 'Master, what does the English word "always" mean?' (Friel, 1984, p. 446). Clearly it's Maire who's out to penetrate the mysteries of English and she's hardly a victim, or a Dark Rosaleen, but someone recovering command of her life on her own terms. Unlike the gloomier critics among his contemporaries, Friel imagines a girl well capable of bouncing back with no lasting damage after the thrills of a one-night stand – and, unlike the poet Heaney, Friel puts before his immediate audience a history where their community is seen to conduct itself with rather more tolerance than now.

The Yalta Game (2001) can be read as itself both extending and theorising Friel's concept of the love scene. It is based on and displays another ingenious device to distance the audience. The published text of *The Yalta Game* distinguishes between speech that is addressed directly to the audience (printed in a roman typeface) and speech between the on-stage characters, which appears not to recognise there is a theatre audience (printed in bold). The stage directions are printed in italics. In the script as on the stage, Friel's devices are on display. And in these switches between explicit acknowledgement of the theatre audience and seeming indifference to the theatre audience, Friel establishes with the theatre audience a game of identification and dis-identification, recognition and non-recognition, a game of presence and absence which will also play out through the love relation between Anna and Gurov, the two protagonists of *The Yalta Game*. Their names, and the outline of the course their love takes, are borrowed from Chekhov, from his famous short story usually translated into English as 'The Lady with the Lapdog', but the Chekhov story is only a starting-point, to which Friel has added the idea of a game between Anna and Gurov, a game repeated as the interface with the theatre audience shifts, and shifts about again. Again Althusser is pertinent, for remarking:

> If [the spectator] is kept at a distance from the play by the play itself, it is not to spare him or to set him up as a Judge – on the contrary, it is to take him and enlist him in this apparent distance, in this 'estrangement' – so as to make him into the distance itself, the distance which is simply an active and living critique. (Althusser, 1975, p. 148)

The Yalta Game has its protagonists at once falling in love and themselves actively engaging on a close analysis of love, a living critique.

To begin with, Gurov chats to the audience about the passing scene at Yalta, and this is a game – the only person on stage is Gurov. He breaks off abruptly to address a waiter, though what he addresses is in actuality a blank space – the waiter's role is not performed by an actor. Anna enters, and they talk among themselves about her dog, which also does not appear on stage to the audience. And so they play what they will call the Yalta Game, devising stories for each other about people who may or may not be present to them, shuttling between presence and absence, just as they both shuttle between talking out to the audience and behaving as if they were alone together. Here, for example, it's Anna taking the initiative:

> *She takes his arm and leans into him and speaks very softly, almost conspiratorially.*
> ANNA: Look at the pair across the street. Don't stare! See them?
> GUROV: I see them. And that's my role.
> ANNA: Where is his left hand?
> GUROV: What?
> ANNA: His left hand - where is it? - can you see it?
> GUROV: I see a man in a grey -
> ANNA: But no left hand visible. And why not?
> GUROV: I see a staid couple enjoying a brisk -
> ANNA: The beast! Oh my God! In broad daylight!
> GUROV: What are you talking - ?
> ANNA: She's trying to walk normally, but how can she? God!
> GUROV: Are you telling me he's - ?
> *She whispers quickly into* GUROV's *ear - then explodes with laughter. He laughs too, and stares at her in pretended shock and amazement.*
> **Well, aren't you a naughty child!**

ANNA:	*I swear!*
GUROV:	*Very naughty.*
ANNA:	*But I'm right, amn't I?*
GUROV:	*Absolutely!* (Friel, 2002, pp, 18-19)

These games constitute a form of verbal nonsense, exercises in mutual entertainment played with signifiers that have tenuous connection to their apparent referents: presence and absence intertwined as impropriety is ascribed to a hand that can't be seen.

Gurov and Anna enjoy a holiday romance, they name the (invisible) dog 'Yalta', they suffer uncertainty as to whether or not to lock up the dog while they spend a night together in a hotel room, and – the holiday over – Anna returns to her husband Nicolai. Because the romance was based in a game where presence and absence, the actual and imaginary could change places, Gurov confides to the audience he's uncertain in what sense their affair was 'real':

GUROV:	Did it happen at all? I began to think - truthfully! - I began to wonder had I made it all up! Maybe it was not more actual than the fictional lives I invested the people in the square with. (Friel, 2002, p. 23)

Anna in turn confides to the audience how the very impalpability of their love gave it an uncanny – and highly sensual – afterlife, as she was tending to her husband's illness:

ANNA:	Nikolai was a month in hospital. … It was a bleak time. The snow had come early It was almost an hour's walk to the hospital every day. And I was anxious about Nikolai … He had become so dependent on me, as if we had switched roles. He usually cried when visiting time was over. Dmitry was with me all the time. But his presence had different manifestations and different levels of intensity Sometimes I wouldn't see him for days; only the echo of his voice; and I'd strain to hear was he calling me … And sometimes he'd come up behind me stealthily and enfold me in his arms and whisper into the back of my neck, just below the hairline. And when he did that, I was flooded with such a great happiness that I would have collapsed if he had let me go. It was a strange kind of living; knowing with an aching clarity that I would never see him again - ever; and at the same time being with him always, always, happily always in that ethereal presence. There were times when I thought I mightn't be right in the head. (Friel, 2002, pp. 24-5).

Gurov is driven to seek Anna out, and as they meet again, he speaks to Anna and then to the audience, murmuring reassurance and devotion to her, meanwhile to the audience voicing doubt:

> ANNA: Our lives are in ruins, Dmitry.
> GUROV: Why are you so upset today?
> ANNA: We hide from everyone. We lie all the time. We live like fugitives.
> GUROV: You are such a beautiful fugitive.
> ANNA: And we're never going to escape. How can we? Neither of us is ever going to be free. And I love you so much, so much. No, I don't just love you - I worship you. Oh, Dmitry, my darling, you will love me always, won't you?
> GUROV: She believed she did worship me. She believed she would always worship me. And for the first time in my life I had come close to worshipping somebody too. But how could I tell her that this would come to an end one day? Indeed it would. But if I had told her, she wouldn't have believed me. (Friel, 2002, p. 31)

But in a final twist, as Gurov gives verbal reassurance that there is substance to this love of theirs, – and then himself craves reassurance – Anna is so lucid as in putting uncertainties to the audience that it seems all her love-talk has been a shield with which to protect Gurov:

> *They stand back-to-back, facing in opposite directions, holding hands.*
> ANNA: You will love me always, Dmitry?
> GUROV: Yes.
> ANNA: And I will love you always.
> GUROV: I know that.
> ANNA: We are so lucky. Do you appreciate how lucky we are? How many people do you know have had such happiness as we have had? We have been such a ... blessed couple, haven't we?
> GUROV: Yes.
> ANNA: I do believe that. Blessed.
> GUROV: Yes.
> ANNA: At moments like that - and we had so many, so many of them - at moments like that I was convinced we would find a solution to our predicament. No, not a solution - why not a divine intervention? Yes, a miraculous solution would be offered to us. And that release would make our happiness so complete and so opulent and ... forever. But I knew that until that miracle happened, we would have to stumble on together for a very long time; because the

	end was coming even though it was still a long way off. But the drawing to a close had already begun and we were now embarked on the most complicated and most frightening and the most painful time of all.
GUROV:	**Kiss me, Anna. Please.** *They kiss.* *Bring up the exuberant military music in the background.* (Friel, 2002, pp. 31-2)

The disruptive brass band fractures attention on their kiss, just as did the entry of Sarah when Maire and Yolland were kissing. The play ends on this formal flourish, and not on the end of their story. Anna and Gurov remain projected into dissociated timespans, at once looking towards endless fulfilment and opulent happiness, while also, and quite knowingly, facing a slower journey into rawness, exposure, hurt, and finality.

It's as if Maire and Yolland have found a common tongue, but therefore find themselves needing to establish other and inner distances, employing the audience to hold themselves away from fusion, from melting in each other's arms – while exactly this tension is propelling them to wish for just that. It's also Friel's demonstration how by restoring both the nonsense and the lucidity excluded from the early modernist love scene, and by playing openly on absences and on dis-identifications, the love scene can become not a site of abandonment but a creative and to some extent a hopeful space.

References

Althusser, L. (1977), *For Marx,* trans. B. Brewster, New Left Books, London and New York.

Althusser, L. (2003), 'On Brecht and Marx', trans. M. Statkiewicz, in Warren Montag, *Louis Althusser,* Palgrave Macmillan, London and New York, pp. 136-49.

Badiou, A. (2003), *On Beckett,* trans. N. Power and A. Toscano, Clinamen, Manchester.

Deane, S. (1984), 'Introduction', in Friel, 1984, pp. 11-22.

Ford, F. M. (2004), *The Good Soldier,* Green Integer, Kobenhaven and Los Angeles.

Friel, B. (1970), *Crystal and Fox,* Faber & Faber, London.

Friel, B. (1993), *The Gentle Island,* Gallery Press, Loughcrew, County Meath.

Friel, B. (1969), *Lovers: Two Plays,* Faber & Faber, London.

Friel, B. (1984), *Selected Plays,* Faber & Faber, London.

Friel, B. (1999), *Plays 2,* Faber & Faber, London.

Friel, B. (2002), *Three Plays After,* Gallery Press, Loughcrew, County Meath.

Heaney, S. (1980), *Selected Poems, 1965-75,* Faber & Faber, London.

Kiberd, D. (1995), *Inventing Ireland,* Jonathan Cape, London.

Lacan, J. (1992), *The Ethics of Psychoanalysis,* trans. D. Porter, Norton, London and New York.

Lacan, J. (1998), *The Four Fundamental Concepts of Psychoanalysis,* trans. A. Sheridan, Vintage, London.

Lyotard, J-F. (1984), *The Postmodern Condition,* trans. G. Bennington, Manchester University Press, Manchester.

Yeats, W. B. (1992), *The Poems,* ed. Daniel Albright, Everyman's Library, London.

Revolution and Revelation: Brian Friel and the Postcolonial Subject

Ulf Dantanus

Gothenburg Programme at the University of Sussex

During the last 25 years or so, the announcement of a new conference or publication in Irish Studies might well have been greeted with the phrase 'Postcolonialism, I presume'. In the recent *Cambridge Companion to Brian Friel*, in an article entitled 'Brian Friel as postcolonial playwright,' Csilla Bertha can quite confidently and probably correctly state that 'by now the postcolonial approach has gained dominance in Irish Studies' (Bertha, 2006, p. 155). In a call for papers for a special issue on Ireland in the new online periodical *Postcolonial Text*, the extraordinary growth of Irish Studies was causally linked with the rise of postcolonial theory: 'Indeed it is arguable whether Irish Studies as an international academic and critical discipline would be the force that it undeniably has become without the impetus of Ireland's inflection of postcolonial studies' (Mendis, 2006, n. p.). The rise and rise of Irish Studies thus owes its success to postcolonial theory. This is a potentially unhealthy relationship in that it may encourage a form of sycophantic dependence associated with the bandwagon syndrome.

The connotations of the lexeme 'dominance' are ominous. The ascendancy of one form of critical discourse at the expense of others may threaten to restrict and constrain by the very force of its extraordinary ubiquity. It involves much more than just an 'approach' or an 'inflection' in Irish studies. In the empire of academic criticism its 'force' has at times threatened to overrun and even oppress other approaches or methods by its paradigmatic tendency and application. Mining this rich seam and extracting its resources for domestic use pays dividends for the individual academic. Conversely, failure to buy into the theory may imply ignorance of the state of play both in the generic and in the specific case. Its ascent to the zenith of the Irish academy has displayed some of the conventional characteristics of the rise of a fashionable trend. It is often salutary in this context to keep in mind Liam Kennedy's condemnation of the post-colonial fad in criticism: 'Like jackdaws to shiny objects, literary and cultural critics seem to be drawn to labels and packaging' (Kennedy, 2000, p. 668).

Many of these negative concerns have been voiced before and form part of the 'contentious' role of postcolonial theory in Irish Studies (Howe, 2003, n. p.). The fact that its very legitimacy has been questioned and that it has been, and still is, 'the cause of vigorous debate' (Richards, 2004, p. 607) suggests that the case of Ireland may be more complex than mainstream global postcolonialism, or, at least, different. If Homi Bhabha's oft-quoted dictum that 'the construction of the colonial subject in discourse, and the exercise of colonial power through discourse demands an articulation of forms of difference' means anything at all (Bhabha, 1986, p. 150), it must allow for distinctive and specific differences within the 'difference' that is 'the colonial discourse'.

I have set out my stall in order to locate this essay in the chiasma between postcolonial studies and Brian Friel's work. It is not a call for a return to critical orthodoxy by ignoring or erasing the considerable contribution of postcolonial theory to the expansion and theorisation of Irish Studies (as if that were possible today), but it asks some critical questions about the way the theory has been deployed in the specific case of Friel Studies. The broad history of the engagement between postcolonial theory and Irish Studies is too well-known to be replayed here (see, for instance, Graham, 2001, Hooper and Graham 2002, Richards 2004), but since the zest and zing of that debate is an intrinsic part of any treatment of Irish postcoloniality, it may be necessary to wade into it from time to time to set the scene for my own specific discussion. Three general points will be assayed: (1) that postcolonial discourse may have marginalised literature in the academy by putting the abstract idea of theory before the 'scrupulous meanness' of the literary word, (2) that the roneo effect of duplicating concepts and conditions globally may confuse and dilute the original impact of the theory and (3) that its blanket coverage may encourage an undiscriminating and indulgent use of the term in works and contexts where it does not genuinely belong. It is in particular in the last case that I wish to refer to Friel Studies.

In its omnipresent popularity, 'the postcolonial' has sometimes been administered as a critical placebo to treat any cultural and literary condition. The original impact of its novel, provocative and eye-opening power has been weakened by its bland, global sameness. During the period of its dominion, I have on numerous occasions been struck by the many instances where the little village in Sweden where I grew up has come to exhibit many of the typical characteristics of a postcolonial society. There can be no doubt that the original thrust of postcolonial theory provided a new and welcome shot in the arm for literary and cultural criticism in the English-speaking world. That is not at issue here. Nor can there be much doubt that its most immediate and urgent application came through an engagement with African, Asian and Caribbean literatures, where the racial, non-European element and an obvious, direct and confrontational dialectic between colonizer and colonized provided an easy and unmistakable point of entry. When the theory is transposed to other historical and contemporary contexts the success of its application is more variable.

The notorious unwillingness of the very earliest postcolonial prospectuses to engage with Irish literature got relations between the postcolonial and Irish Studies off to a shaky start. *The Empire Writes Back* (Ashcroft, Griffiths and Tiffin, 1989) includes Ireland only as a momentary afterthought, and *The Post-Colonial Studies Reader* (Ashcroft, Griffiths and Tiffin, 1995) anthologizes an abbreviated article by David Cairns and Shaun Richards from their book *Writing Ireland: Colonialism, Nationalism and Culture*, 'What ish My Nation,' which does not deal with Ireland at all. Some quarters of Irish Studies do not seem to have recovered from this early snub of the 'no Irish need apply' variety. The sense of hurt exclusion from the mainstream has grated on many critics and is a recurring and ongoing theme in Irish postcolonial discourse. Shaun Richards, who has monitored the appearance and development of the term and the theory in relation to Friel, complains that '[i]n the wider field of literary and cultural criticism, however, Ireland is often marginalised or excluded from the mainstream of postcolonial criticism' (Richards, 2004, p. 607). Around the same time Dawn Duncan was trying to 'enjoin the broader postcolonial community to accept Irish writers into their consciousness as full members of the debate' (Duncan, 2004, p. 4), as if there is a perceived need for and value in a theoretical superstructure of global application. In the foreword to Duncan's *Postcolonial Theory in Irish Drama from 1800-2000*, Michael Kenneally commends her work for its efforts to 'establish a critical relevance beyond the specific and transitory,' thereby seemingly conjoining specificity with transitoriness, and regarding them as outmoded, ephemeral and irrelevant in relation to Duncan's 'post-colonial analysis' (Duncan 2004, p. xiii). The conclusion we are supposed to draw is that postcolonial theory somehow confers unspecified longevity and universality on a particular kind of critical analysis. This questioning and downgrading of other critical approaches and theories is an unattractive by-product of the work of some missionary postcolonialists, and may emanate from the dominant position of the theory in Irish Studies. It is often achieved by attributing a lack of sophistication to and levelling a charge of critical idiocy against competing discourses. Joe Cleary may be accused of displaying this attitude towards 'modernization discourses,' where, he claims, 'the past is consistently understood as calcified "tradition" that simply impedes progress' (Cleary, 2002, p. 103). 'Modernization discourses,' can, of course, be as complex and refined as the best postcolonial theory. In the specific case of Brian Friel, for instance, a close reading (still a very useful model of literary analysis) of the short stories (and perhaps even more so his *Irish Press* journalism in the early 1960s) shows the disturbing (not to say traumatic) effects of the modernisation process on the individual. Typically, these effects often appear under the guise of light, ironic comedy, a well-known psychological evasion technique. Furthermore, Friel's *Translations*, the focus (as we shall see) of much Irish postcolonial discourse, also fits nicely into a European or global modernisation discourse where Ireland has more affinities with Sweden than with Nigeria or India. Glenn Hooper, too, ironically devalues critics opposed to the postcolonial models by suggesting that some of them believe that 'Irish literary studies – whether these models are applicable or not – should simply be divorced from political readings that only distract from the "true", sometimes simply the aesthetic, intentions of their authors' (Hooper, 2002, p. 4). There can be few genuine academic critics worth their salt who at the beginning of the twenty-first century harbour such illusions of a prelapsarian, theory-free reading of Ireland.

The crucial battles in this debate have often been fought somewhere between the global and the specific, or to express it in a more nuanced manner; it has been a question of perspective, balance and focus. How postcolonial is Ireland and how Irish is postcolonialism? These are important questions that can be seen to define the relationship between postcolonialism and Irish Studies and suggest a balance between global theorem and Irish specificity. When Duncan quotes a statement by Declan Kiberd that 'Ireland is, for me, a supreme postcolonial instance' in support of her argument for the postcolonial community to include Ireland (Duncan, 2002, p. 323), Kiberd's syntax and word order actually suggest the opposite. They clearly show which critical world order he favours: the focus and emphasis should be on Ireland as a specific example of the postcolonial experience. It should not be taken to mean that a globalised postcolonial theoretical model should be imposed as a critical paradigm and somehow include Ireland at the expense of Irish specificity. Indeed, Kiberd's *Inventing Ireland* is a study which, in spite of its 'sins of omissions' (O'Toole, 1996, p. 15) and its clear nationalist bent (or perhaps because of it), clearly keeps its global postcoloniality subordinate to its Irish literary specificity. Although Kiberd does establish some general and important parallels between Ireland and other parts of the British Empire (India, basically) his postcolonialism is light years away from its globalised version, and he seems careful to temper the 'striking analogies' in 'the wider world' with specific 'differences' in the Irish case (Kiberd, 1995, p. 251). In his review O'Toole complains about Kiberd's 'colonial' approach to Irish literature and goes on to argue that 'Irish writers have long since left the Anglo-Irish paradigm behind them, preferring to place themselves in a wider context and to look more unflinchingly on the realities of their own society rather than in the evasions of colonial theory' (O'Toole, 1996, p. 15). Here 'colonial theory' seems to equate 'the Anglo-Irish paradigm' and 'a wider context' is the same as 'the realities of their own society'. The point is well made, and what may, in relation to global postcolonialism, at first look like contradiction and confusion makes perfect sense. O'Toole sees colonialism/postcolonialism as specifically Anglo-Irish, and he seems to suggest that Irish writers cannot be bothered any more (although Friel's *The Home Place* in 2005 would in itself be enough to refute that argument). But what is clear from the references by Richards, Duncan, Kiberd and O'Toole is that the words 'wider' and 'broader' have different meanings in relation to Irish postcolonialism. Is the 'wider' Irish context Ireland itself (ignoring 'the Anglo-Irish paradigm'), the history of Anglo-Irish conflict or globalised postcolonialism? Richards and Duncan seem to favour a top-down model where postcolonialism includes Ireland, whereas Kiberd and O'Toole, in their different ways, emphasise or at least include postcolonialism in Ireland. It is difficult to understand why so much energy has been expended on arguing about whether Ireland should be part of the globalised postcolonial paradigm or not. This is, in itself, clearly a critical 'cul de sac' which encourages only circularity and reversion. Postcolonialism may be on offer as a wholesale prototype, but the retail or smorgasbord model of postcolonial theory will allow a critic to test for Irish specificity inside its alleged universality.

Richards, Duncan, Kiberd and O'Toole (and many others) keep returning to *Translations* as a key text of Irish postcolonialism. For that reason it may (or may not) be relevant and interesting to begin by examining the author's own interpretation of that play. In *Inventing Ireland*, Kiberd attributes to Friel an awareness that *Translations* is 'a postcolonial text to precisely the extent that its powerful diagnosis of a traumatized Irish consciousness nonetheless adds to the glories of the English language' (Kiberd, 1995, p. 624). Here Kiberd's postcolonialism is strikingly and specifically Anglo-Irish. Is this how Friel sees his play? In the wake of the success of the original Field Day production, he gave an interview where he elaborated on some of the important issues raised in the play. When asked if he felt that 'the play has a relevance to places like Belgium and Quebec, where there is a problem of two cultures,' he replied: 'Yes, I think so. Those are places where I would love to go with this play. I am sure there are areas of Russia, perhaps Estonia or southern Russia, where their languages have faded, as has Irish' (Agnew, 1980, p. 59). Although Friel here sees parallels with cultural and linguistic conditions elsewhere in the international world, he does not at this stage seem ready to situate his play in the general postcolonial theorem of Africa, Asia or the Caribbean. In fact, in a reference to Hugh's well-known line 'Confusion is not an ignoble condition' (Friel 1980, p. 67), Friel stresses the play's geographical specificity: 'Other countries perhaps have access to more certainties than we have at the moment. I was thinking specifically about Ireland' (Agnew, 1980, p. 61). For this confusion to have genuine meaning in *Translations* it needs to be specifically Irish. On another occasion two years later he was openly dismissive about interpretations that make claims of global relevance for the play: 'You know, when you get notices especially from outside the island, saying "if you want to know what happened in Cuba, if you want to know what happened in Chile, if you want to know what happened in Vietnam, read *Translations*," that's nonsense. And I just can't accept that sort of pious rubbish' (O'Toole, 1982, p. 21). This is how Friel saw his own play in 1980-82. Perhaps it also explains why 'early' postcolonialists placed Ireland outside their pale. It offers too much Irish specificity to be included in the generalised (basically African, Asian, Caribbean) postcolonial discourse.

Over the course of the 1980s the emergence of postcolonial theory moved the goalposts for criticism of Friel's play. Joe Cleary sees the first production of *Translations* as 'the formative moment' of postcolonial studies 'within the Irish academy' (Cleary, 2002, p. 101). But this theoretical after-construction took root very gradually. It was a few years before the Field Day context was expanded into the colonial paradigm, and it is possible that it was the production of Athol Fugard's *Boesman and Lena* in 1983 that first suggested, certainly outside the academy, clearer parallels between Irish literature and the postcolonial. According to Stephen Rea, the choice of Fugard's play seemed in some quarters to provoke a 'do you think you are as oppressed as the blacks?' kind of response (Gray, 1985, p. 5). The 1988 series of Field Day pamphlets on *Nationalism, Colonialism and Literature* established the critical discourse of Irish postcolonialism in an international context and might be more usefully seen as the birth of Irish postcolonial studies. There is a striking internationalisation and postcolonialisation of the solidly Irish/Northern Irish context in the earlier pamphlets.

In the same year the theme of the IASAIL conference in Coleraine was 'The Internationalism of Irish Literature and Drama' (proceedings published in 1995) and although the majority of contributions were on Irish themes there were also a few papers on African and other postcolonial contexts. By then, certainly, the postcolonial was beginning to establish itself in the Irish academy. But it was the appearance of international superstars like Terry Eagleton, Frederic Jameson and Edward Said in Irish postcolonialism that represented a major new development.

The effect of the trend of emerging postcolonialism on Friel Studies was dramatic. When Richard Pine published a revised version of *Brian Friel and Ireland's Drama*, originally from 1990, as *The Diviner: The Art of Brian Friel* in 1999, it had become compulsory for him to deal with Homi Bhabha, hybridity and the postcolonial condition. Some slightly earlier studies of Friel, however, just missed the cut, and probably escaped the postcolonial edict, which now seems to necessitate a reference to Bhabha et al., by a couple of years. *The Achievement of Brian Friel* in 1993, edited by Alan Peacock, uses largely conventional literary-critical terms and methods and mentions neither the postcolonial nor Bhabha, whereas Elmer Andrews's *The Art of Brian Friel*, published in 1995, although it includes discussions about 'displacement, exile and [in quoting Frank O'Connor] submerged population groups,' mentions Edward Said only as the author of the Field Day pamphlet. Tony Corbett's *Brian Friel: Decoding the Language of the Tribe* from 2002, on the other hand, satisfies the requirement by supplying, in a reference to *Translations,* Bhabha's rather generalistic quote about 'difference' cited above (Corbett, 2002, p. 19). The use of Bhabha here introduces the question as to whether the rather general and simplistic concept of 'difference' can do justice to artistic expressions of the complex and often traumatic real-life experience of modern Ireland and of the work of somebody who, like Friel, lived and worked in Derry, Northern Ireland, between 1939 and 1967. The wholesale subscription in many quarters of Irish Studies to the kind of cranked-up levels of abstraction that came as a by-product of postcolonial theory may be trying to make Ireland a *bona fide* member of the postcolonial club at the expense of localised historical, cultural and literary specificity. It has, in fact, introduced a large element of selective arbitrariness in the application of the term. In discussing Yolland's worries about the hermetic nature of the language of the tribe, Corbett rather curiously refers to Yolland's '*almost* post-colonial awareness of himself as an outsider' (Corbett, 2002, p. 27, my italics). This looks very much like a case of the term for the term's sake, when the fashionable use of a word or theory is 'required' by the popularity of a particular discourse. This vague and indulgent delivery of the term risks turning critics into imperfect speakers of postcoloniality.

The only book-length, purportedly postcolonial approach to Friel's work so far is F. C. McGrath's 1999 study *Brian Friel's (Post)Colonial Drama: Language, Illusion, and Politics*. Here McGrath deploys many of the well-known forces of postcolonial theory (Said, Bhabha, Spivak) but nevertheless labours when trying to find the postcolonial ghost in Friel. Even in his dealings with *Translations*, where postcolonial theory, especially in relation to language, can illuminate and expand the Anglo-Irish context (as Friel was obviously aware), McGrath's references to Bhabha are far outnumbered by his reliance on George Steiner's *After Babel* as a discursive medium and critical tool. McGrath's book illustrates one of the major weaknesses of postcolonial theory as a critical panacea for all Irish literature or all Friel's work. To argue in the case of *The Loves of Cass McGuire*, for instance, that '[t]he device of direct address to the audience, like the other devices in the play, also highlights the nature and structure of illusion and its (post)colonial function' does not usefully extend our understanding of that play (McGrath, 1999, p. 94). In fact, it actually obscures it. Friel's use of these distancing effects in the play cannot be postcolonial (with or without the parentheses) because they are also available and applicable elsewhere, from the Greek chorus to the Brechtian use of the 'Verfremdungseffekt'. And the direct address to the audience, for instance, here and generally in Friel's work, and specifically in *Faith Healer*, can also be locally and specifically related to the tradition of the storytelling Irish 'seanachie,' a distinctly pre-colonial practice.

If everything is postcolonial, nothing is. For the critical term 'postcolonial' to have genuine meaning it has to be activated in the specific orbit of a postcolonial experience. This, I believe, is more or less what Shaun Richards means when in a more recent article called 'Irish Studies and the Adequacy of Theory: The Case of Brian Friel,' he criticises McGrath's postcolonial bent: 'If there is no cultural political dimension to postcolonial theory then its function as a mode of analysis has to be seriously questioned' (Richards, 2005, p. 270). Where I disagree with Richards, for whom it seems to be enough for this 'dimension' to be generally and globally 'cultural political' for the analysis to be relevant in the case of Ireland, is in my insistence on the primary specificity of the Irish situation. In progressive postcolonial theory critical space must always be found for the geographies of specific postcolonialisms and their social and political characteristics. In a survey of the historical and contemporary geographies of Irish place names (a theme of particular relevance in relation to Friel and *Translations*), Catherine Nash argues the need for 'locating post-colonial theories, dismantling their globalizing implications by attending to the specificities of different post-colonial contexts' (Nash, 1999, p. 475). Her primary focus in 'locating' theory is the whole island of Ireland and in particular contemporary projects to reinstate Gaelic place names both in the North and in the South. A similar critical distinction needs to be made in the specific context of Friel's plays and, rather than coerce all or most of them into the postcolonial paradigm, the theory should be applied more discriminately and with greater precision in plays and contexts that are Irish-postcolonial rather than postcolonial-general.

In Friel Studies two contradictory processes seem to be at play in relation to postcolonial theory. In many critics who go a-Frieling today, as exemplified in McGrath's study, there is at times a tendency to use the term and the theory indiscriminately and indulgently. Even a perspicacious and nuanced critic like Richard Pine seems to have been seduced by postcolonial hyperbole into seeing traces of it in unexpected places. Pine's basic handling of *Wonderful Tennessee* is consistently centred on the ideas of 'The Imagined Place' (which was Friel's working title for the play), the mysterious, the pagan and the sacred, but on one occasion he is tempted into placing Bhabha on Ballybeg Pier and to refer to the three married couples waiting there in terms of postcolonial theory: 'In post-colonial terms, they are "missing persons" whose identity is migrant and whose being is transitive' (Pine, 1999, p. 284). Again, as in the case of McGrath and Friel's distancing effects, since a number of different historical and contemporary conditions other than the postcolonial can produce 'migrant identities' and 'transitive beings' (modernisation and secularisation processes, for instance) there seems to be nothing distinctively 'postcolonial' about their situation, unless Beckett's Vladimir and Estragon, who are also waiting for their Godot, are in some way postcolonial. When global postcolonial terms are superimposed on Irish specificity in a way that dilutes and confuses both, their valency must be questioned.

In her survey of Friel as postcolonial playwright in the recent *Cambridge Companion to Brian Friel,* Csilla Bertha mentions no fewer than thirteen of his plays, therefore, I assume, claiming for them some kind of postcolonial significance. Interestingly, and revealingly, in view of McGrath's advocacy of its postcolonial credentials, one of the plays Bertha does not deal with is *The Loves of Cass McGuire*. On the other hand, she makes seven references to *Wonderful Tennessee*. On closer analysis, however, her citations of this play seem to have more in common with the conflict between tradition and modernity, a mode of critical thinking derided by Cleary. Bertha's remarks about *Wonderful Tennessee* deal with urbanisation, 'metaphysical exile,' vestiges of primitive and pagan practices, storytelling, the competing claims of the sacred and the secular and with reviving a lost cultural memory, all of them, of course, recognisably Irish subjects and themes, but none of them describing a specifically colonial or post-colonial experience. When, in her conclusion, Bertha has to provide some proof positive of Friel's testament as a postcolonial playwright, however, she is forced to fall back on Edward Said's championing of *Translations* in the afterword to Carroll and King's *Ireland and Postcolonial Theory*. But, as Stephen Regan has shown, it may be a little risky to rely on Said's reading of Irish affairs. In an article on 'W. B. Yeats, Irish Nationalism and Post-Colonial Theory,' Regan finds that Said sometimes misreads Yeats's relationship with the land. It is, he argues, 'more complex and ambiguous than Said's anti-colonial label suggests' (Regan, 2006, p. 92). The specific and localised context of the Irish experience of colonialism, including the anti- or post- variants, seems to defeat Said's great reputation for handling generalised, abstract theory. The same concerns about Said's relevance in the Irish context have been voiced elsewhere: his 'scattered, mostly brief writings on Ireland often lacked the subtlety of perception so evident in much of his other work' (Howe, 2003). The willingness to enlist the support of the big, global guns in your own local battles carries the risks inherent in a lack of specificity. 'Parochialism,' as Patrick Kavanagh knew, 'is universal; it deals with the fundamentals' (Kavanagh, cited in Heaney, p. 139). It is very doubtful whether, in postcolonial theory, the opposite is true.

Bertha's reliance on *Translations* for her clinching argument is paralleled by Richards in his article 'Throwing Theory at Ireland'. This seems to be the second current trend in Friel Studies concerning the postcolonial subject. The first, the seemingly arbitrary appropriation of all or nearly all of Friel's plays for the purposes of postcolonial debate is implicitly felt to be ineffective and *Translations* has to be brought in to shore up the general argument. Richards chronicles the constant revision of the term and concept of postcolonial theory in Irish Studies in general and in Friel Studies in particular, and develops an idea that he picked up from Cleary, which claims contemporary global capitalism for the jurisdiction of postcolonial theory. In one sense, this may look like an Irish Studies version of old wine in new bottles, but it is also a significant renovation of the theory and leads Richards to a new way of reading *Translations*:

> That the play captures the fraught movement into an imminent capitalism is clear, but while its dramatic location is the 1830s, its thematic preoccupation is equally with Ireland's twentieth-century engagement with modernity in the aftermath of T. K. Whitaker's 1958 *Report on Economic Development* and its injunction that 'it would be well to shut the door on the past and to move forward'. (Richards, 2004, p. 620)

This is a valuable point and reminds us that Friel's history plays tend to be set at the cusp of great change, at a moment in the past when Irish history congeals into a fateful pattern with clear implications for the future. But it simply will not do to argue the case for Friel as a postcolonial playwright generally and then bank on *Translations* always to balance the argument. That this is a play that, as a result of its complex and radical in-betweenness and ambiguity on a number of issues (empire, nationality, culture, language) provides a perfect battleground for debates about Irish (or any kind of) colonialism, anti-colonialism or postcolonialism is beyond any doubt.

Richards's dependence on *Translations* is particularly obvious in an earlier article from 1997 ('Placed Identities for Placeless Times: Brian Friel and Post-Colonial Criticism'), where, out of thirteen and a half pages, he spends (approximately) 6.5 on *Translations*, 3 on *Dancing at Lughnasa* (interspersed with references to *Translations*), 1.75 on *Wonderful Tennessee* and less that 2 pages on *Molly Sweeney* (with interspersed references to *Translations* and *Faith Healer*). Richards then uses a much later article (from 2005) to extend his argument by drawing examples from three of Friel's plays. With neat chronological progression he moves from the 1830s (with the onset of global capitalism in *Translations*) through the mid twentieth century (*Dancing at Lughnasa* with 'the eradication of the cottage economy of the sisters' and 'the post-Whitaker discontents of Michael') to the 1980s (with 'the depthless discontents of the couples in *Wonderful Tennessee*'), but the argument is still heavily dependent on echoes of *Translations* (Richards, 2005, p. 277). Although Richards prefers to ignore the fact that the discontents of the couples in *Wonderful Tennessee* seem to have spiritual rather than economic causes, his advocacy of a new direction in Irish Studies and in Friel's plays adjusts postcolonialism's focus and introduces a new, significant and specific target:

> Friel's work is certainly concerned with the cultural realm and issues of representation and identity, but the plays are grounded in an appreciation

of the economic structures and their discontents within which those identities are formed and located. This is the essence of Friel's postcolonialism and of productive readings of his plays and, by extension, of parallel readings into the expanding canon of 'postcolonial' Irish literature. (Richards, 2005, p. 278)

Again, we are asked, for the sake of fitting Friel into this new strand of postcolonialism, to subordinate his Irish specificity to general and global theory. To boil down mindsetting influences like the overall history of Anglo-Irish conflict, the clash between Irish and English and between tradition and modernity, the experiences of a young boy and grown man commuting between the city of (London)Derry in British Northern Ireland and the village of Glenties in the Irish Free State and Republic (across a border he has deliberately tried to erase from his writing), a nationalist father politically active in a gerrymandered polity, himself marching for Civil Rights on Bloody Sunday, for instance, to a question of 'economic structures and their discontents' seems an extremely reductive and simplistic exercise. To make that question 'the essence of Friel's postcolonialism' and to coerce a complex and rich variety into a Marxist straitjacket risks seriously unbalancing the relationship between Friel's work and the world. If Richards had turned his attention to *The Freedom of the City*, he would have seen how Friel's own claim that the play started as 'a study of poverty' (Boland, 1973, p. 18) was very soon overtaken by the Irish specificity of Derry on 30 January 1972. In that play, Dr Dodds and his academic theories about 'the culture of poverty' are separately superimposed onto the reality of the daily lives of Michael, Lily and Skinner and cannot be said to explicate the complex and specific causes and effects of the situation (Friel, 1973, p. 51). Friel clearly sympathises with the three Irish victims in the Guildhall, and Dr Dodds' sporadic, abstract and general theory seems to offer a pretty ineffectual not to say ironic contrast.

On a lighter note, to allow 'economic structures' to dominate to such an extent the reading of Friel's work may convert the famous note in Bill Clinton's 1992 presidential campaign about the decisive factor in politics, 'It's the economy, stupid,' into Irish Studies discourse. More seriously, this artificially resuscitated version of Marxism and its rather single-minded focus on the economics of literary content at the expense of the aesthetic, the spiritual, and the political seems to promote a new book-keeping approach to literary theory. The theory as described by Richards may be sweepingly universal and global, but it is not specific to colonial or postcolonial societies, unless, of course, you count capitalism as the coloniser and (basically) the whole world as the colonised. Arguing that 'economic structures and their discontents' are 'the essence of Friel's postcolonialism' also weakens the impact of *Translations*, which, for all the various speculative theories that have been expended on it, can never lose its relevance as a pre-colonial, colonial, anti-colonial and post-colonial text. Friel's treatment of the historical relationship between England and Ireland allows the true complexity and radical ambiguity of the postcolonial to be heard in a specific postcolonial context. Of all the lively arguments that that play has generated, for or against, none has dealt with its capitalist economics.

In administering postcolonial theory to Friel, it is not so much a question, as Richards will have it, of 'the case of Brian Friel' as the case of which of his plays. What an analysis of his plays demands is a sharper tool, a set of performance indicators that will, like a litmus paper, allow in a more precise and specific manner a distinction to be made between two fundamentally different kinds of plays like *Translations* and *Wonderful Tennessee*. To unconditionally make these two plays fit the postcolonial paradigm seems to diminish both the theory and the specifically Irish qualities of each play. They need instead to be tested for their Irish specificity of content in a way that allows at its most basic a separation to be made between plays dominated by the visible world we know, and plays dominated by the hidden world we cannot deny, or between revolution and revelation. The postcolonial tends to move mainly in the orbit of the former and to largely ignore the latter. The concepts that I shall include within the sphere of 'revelation,' like religion, interiority, spirituality, providence, eternity, for instance, are not included in mainstream postcolonial theory as promoted by Ashcroft, Griffiths and Tiffin's *Post-Colonial Studies: The Key Concepts*.

In some external and very obvious respects, the two plays are very different in their relations with the world at large. Briefly, at first, we have in *Translations* a play that has been (1) famously described in *The Times* as 'a national classic', (2) seen by some as Irish nationalist criticism of British colonialism, (3) welcomed into the British Royal National Theatre, (4) near the centre of revisionist debate in Ireland since its first performance, (5) enjoying worldwide popular success and (6) acknowledged as a near-perfect text for postcolonial treatment. Then there is *Wonderful Tennessee*, one of Friel's problem plays, which has caused confusion and incomprehension in the critics and neglect in the play-going public, notoriously closing after nine performances on Broadway. Internally, in an analysis of the texts and textures of the two plays their differences persist in shapes that mirror the contrast between revolution and revelation. Although today our first understanding of the lexem 'revolution' is of a visible event of often violent upheaval or change, some of its earliest meanings derive from the movement of celestial objects. These orbits were observed and the time they took measured in the same way that history is studied, interpretations made, and conclusions drawn. The word revolution was formed from 're-volve,' the original Latin meaning to 'roll' or to 'turn back' or 'anew,' again implying the study and interpretation (and re-interpretation) of openly visible and measurable events shared and experienced in the external world in recognisable, physical places and spaces. These activities imply active and deliberate thought and calculation, using spoken and written language in a rational attempt to understand and describe the link between cause and effect in a scientific world. It is controlled by the idea that existence, and, in terms of the study of history, particularly the past, can be known and interpreted. The historical progression of colonialism from geographical exploration, the excavation of raw materials, the establishment of trade, the opening of markets for industrial products, through to western dominance in the form of political and cultural imperialism, followed by the withdrawal of the colonizer and a form of (often partial) political freedom, division and civil war, followed by 'Civil Peace,' to quote the ironic title of a story by Chinua Achebe, and, in many cases, neo-colonial chaos and confusion. Key concepts in this revolution are the measurement of time, development and change, history and the reading of the past, rational thought and external action, national and international relations.

Key concepts in 'revelation,' all excluded (I repeat) from *Post-Colonial Studies: The Key Concepts*, are timeless eternity, an unknown future, emotional intuition, the fear of internal vacuum and waiting, God, providence, the thought patterns of religion and paganism. Such categories are always conditional, and, by no means, perfect or absolute classifications, but by using them as themed indicators it is clearly possible to place *Translations* and *Wonderful Tennessee* in different groups. The Irish characters on the island of Ireland in *Translations* experience their home place as real and historical. This is the primary field of postcolonial studies. The Irish characters in *Wonderful Tennessee* see the 'Island of Otherness' as a mysterious and symbolical quest. This does not seem to be the primary jurisdiction of postcolonial studies.

In the study of history dates are important, but dates in these two plays offer different kinds of histories. Two decisive dates in *Translations* carry enormous significance: 1789, the year of the French Revolution (a completed orbit and a successful revolution) and 1798, the doomed Irish revolution against the English. In *Wonderful Tennessee*, the year 1294, in Berna's story about the flying house, is associated with fairytales (Trish introduces it with: 'Once upon a time . . .), and is appreciated by her because it is 'an offence to reason' (Friel, 1993, p. 46). Another important date mentioned in the play, 26 June 1932, describes an event where a young boy was 'sacrificed' in a religious or pagan ritual in a reason-defying atmosphere of uncontrollable fervour and ferment. It happened in the aftermath of the Eucharistic Congress in Dublin, an event that 'symbolically celebrated' the nation's Catholic ethos (Foster, 1988, p. 537). From the assumed killing for political reasons of Yolland in *Translations*, and its historical extension up to the latest victim of the British security forces in Northern Ireland, these deaths have political, colonial or postcolonial causes. The flying house and the pagan ritual in *Wonderful Tennessee* are beyond time and outside reason. The concept of measured time is so tangible and real in *Translations* that Hugh dismisses Maire's question about a translation of the immortality and eternity implied in 'always': 'It's not a word I'd start with. It's a silly word, girl' (Friel, 1980, p. 67). An alternative title to *Wonderful Tennessee*, in deference to Beckett's place and timeless settings and characters, is, of course, 'Waiting for Carlin,' a reference to the allegedly real and at the same time symbolic ferryman on the boundary between the real world and Hamlet's 'undiscover'd country from whose bourn / No traveller returns' (III.1.85-6). Terry's remark about Carlin that '[t]ime has no meaning for a man like that' seems to double up both as an Irish contrast between the primeval and rural west as opposed to modern and urban Dublin (Charlie, the minibus driver, who ferries them back from their failed encounter with eternity, 'is always on bloody time') and, which is more relevant to this discussion, and as a symbol of the timelessness of death and eternity (Friel, 1993, p. 29 and p. 71). Carlin and the characters in the play, who depend on him, are thus placed in chronological abeyance. Frank's 'clock book,' *The Measurement of Time and its Effect on European Civilization*, although it may just be, in his own words, '[a]nother apparition' (it may never realise) clearly shows how the measurement of scientific time has upset natural routines of life. The intimations of timelessness and eternity exist in stark contrast to the historical and chronological specificity of *Translations*.

Revolution looks back in time in a rational and interpretative mode. Revelation looks forward beyond time in a spiritual and apocalyptic mode. In 'The Second Coming' Yeats's sense of an impending event of cataclysmic proportions, '[s]urely some revelation is at hand' (Yeats, 1961, p. 211) was caused by the increasing political violence in his contemporary world (Ireland and Europe), but it remained a mysterious and timeless apprehension on the level of the individual's human experience of a shared religious context (Bethlehem). It remains hidden behind the veil.

As Friel's title makes clear, language and communication between languages (or the failure of), speaking and writing to people in the known world and in the historical context of the 1830s, play a major part in *Translations*. The experiences in *Wonderful Tennessee*, on the other hand, are about '[w]hatever we desire but can't express. What is beyond language. The inexpressible. The ineffable' (Friel, 1993, p. 41). This is a human and immemorial form of spiritual communication with the unknown. The play obviously deals with the spiritual climate of thought and feeling in Ireland in the early 1990s, but reading or describing *Wonderful Tennessee* in terms of the postcolonial seems to do violence to the very soul of that play and at the same time to diminish or confuse the real spirit of postcolonial discourse.

References

Agnew, P. (1980), 'Talking to Ourselves', *Magill* 4, (3), pp. 59-61.

Andrews, E. (1995), *The Art of Brian Friel*, Macmillan Press Ltd, Basingstoke.

Ashcroft, B., Griffiths, G. and Tiffin, H. (eds.) (1989), *The Empire Strikes Back: Theory and Practice in Post-Colonial Literatures*, Routledge, London.

Ashcroft, B., Griffiths, G. and Tiffin, H. (eds.) (1995), *The Post-Colonial Studies Reader,* Routledge, London.

Ashcroft, B., Griffiths, G. and Tiffin, H. (eds) (2000), *Post-Colonial Studies: The Key Concepts*, Routledge, London.

Bertha, C. (2006), 'Brian Friel as Postcolonial Playwright', in *The Cambridge Companion to Brian Friel*, ed. A. Roche, Cambridge University Press, Cambridge, pp. 154-165.

Bhabha, H. (1986), 'The Other Question: Difference, Discrimination and the Discourse of Colonialism', in *Literature, Politics and Theory: Papers from the Essex Conference 1976-84*, eds. F. P. Barker, P. Hulme, M. Iversen, and D. Loxley, Methuen, London, pp. 148-172.

Boland, E. (1973), *Hibernia*, 16 February, p. 18.

Carroll, C. and King, P. (2003), *Ireland and Postcolonial Theory*, Cork University Press, Cork.

Cleary, J. (2002), '"Misplaced ideas?" Locating and dislocating Ireland in Colonial and Postcolonial Studies', in *Marxism, Modernity and Postcolonial Studies*, ed. C. Bartolovich and N. Lazarus, Cambridge University Press, Cambridge, pp. 101-124.

Corbett, T. (2002), *Brian Friel: Decoding the Language of the Tribe*, The Liffey Press, Dublin.

Duncan, D. (2002), 'A Flexible Foundation: Constructing a Postcolonial Dialogue', in *Relocating Postcolonialism*, ed. D. T. Goldberg and A. Quayson, Blackwell, Oxford.

Duncan, D. (2004), *Postcolonial Theory in Irish Drama from 1800-2000*, The Edwin Mellen Press, Lampeter.

Foster, R. F. (1988), *Modern Ireland 1600-1972*, Allen Lane, London.

Friel, B. (1973), *The Freedom of the City*, Faber & Faber, London.

Friel, B. (1980), *Translations*, Faber & Faber, London.

Friel, B. (1993), *Wonderful Tennessee*, Faber & Faber, London.

Friel, B. (2005), *The Home Place*, Gallery Press, Loughcrew.

Graham, C. (2001), *Deconstructing Ireland: Identity, Theory, Culture*, Edinburgh University Press, Edinburgh.

Gray, J. (1985), 'Field Day Five Years On', *Linenhall Review*, 2 (2), pp. 4-10.

Heaney, S. (1980), *Preoccupations: Selected Prose 1968-1978*, Faber & Faber, London.

Hooper, G. and Graham, C. eds. (2002), *Irish and Postcolonial Writing: History, Theory, Practice*, Palgrave, Basingstoke.

Howe, S. (2003), review of C. Carroll and P. King, eds., *Ireland and Postcolonial Theory* (2003), University of Notre Dame Press, Notre Dame, H-Albion, H-Net Reviews, December 2003.

<http://www.h-net.msu.edu/reviews/showrev.cgi?path=205071078751422>.

Kennedy, L. (2000), 'Modern Ireland: Post-Colonial Society or Post-Colonial Pretensions?', in *Postcolonialism: Critical Concepts in Literary and Cultural Studies*, ed. D. Brydon, Routledge, London, pp. 658-671.

Kiberd, D. (1995), *Inventing Ireland*, Jonathan Cape, London.

McGrath, F. C. (1999), *Brian Friel's (Post)Colonial Drama: Language, Illusion, and Politics*, Syracuse University Press, Syracuse, New York.

McMinn, J. (1995), ed. *The Internationalism of Irish Literature and Drama*, Colin Smythe, Gerrards Cross, Bucks.

Mendis, R. (2006), CFP *Postcolonial Text*, viewed 15 October 2006, the Literary Calls for Papers Mailing List CFP at <http://cfp.english.upenn.edu>.

Nash, C. (1999), 'Irish Placenames: Post-colonial Locations', *Transactions of the Institute of British Geographers*, 24 (4), pp. 457-480.

Peacock, A. (ed.) (1993), *The Achievement of Brian Friel*, Colin Smythe, Gerrards Cross, Bucks.

O'Toole, F. (1982), 'The Man from God Knows Where', *In Dublin*, 28 October 1982, pp. 20-23.

O'Toole, F. (1996), review of Declan Kiberd, *Inventing Ireland*, *Observer*, 7 January, 'Review' section p. 15.

Pine, R. (1990), *Brian Friel and Ireland's Drama*, Routledge, London.

Pine, R. (1999), *The Diviner; The Art of Brian Friel*, University College Dublin Press, Dublin.

Regan, S. (2006), 'W. B. Yeats: Irish Nationalism and Post-Colonial Theory', *Nordic Irish Studies*, 5 (1), pp. 87-99.

Richards, S. (1997), 'Placed Identities for Placeless Times: Brian Friel and Post-Colonial Criticism', *Irish University Review*, 27 (1), pp. 55-68.

Richards, S. (2004), 'Throwing Theory at Ireland? The Field Day Theatre Company and Postcolonial Theatre Criticism', *Modern Drama*, 47 (4), pp. 607-623.

Richards, S. (2005), 'Irish Studies and the Adequacy of Theory: The Case of Brian Friel', *Yearbook of English Studies*, 35, pp. 264-278.

Yeats, W. B. (1961), *Collected Poems*, Macmillan, London.

'Fearful equivocal words': Virgil, Dante, and the Hells of Heaney

Gareth Reeves
University of Durham

Much has been written about Heaney and Dante, less about Heaney and Virgil. While this essay attempts to make some amends, it is difficult, if not impossible, to separate out these two poetic presences in Heaney's work, because the Italian made the Latin poet his guide through the *Divina Commedia*. Of course this is the situation for any poet inspired by Dante, but, I want to argue, it is crucially so for Heaney, since the convergence of Virgil and Dante takes on symbolic significance in the development of his poetics.

When, in Canto VIII of his Dantean pilgrimage, 'Station Island' (1984), Seamus Heaney makes his murdered second cousin Colum McCartney question the poet's earlier poetic practice, specifically that of the elegy 'The Strand at Lough Beg' (*Field Work*, 1979), he implicitly raises issues of poetic language in relation to politics. McCartney is made to say that the elegy 'confused evasion and artistic tact', and, in particular, that the poet 'whitewashed ugliness and drew / the lovely blinds of the *Purgatorio* / and saccharined my death with morning dew' (Heaney, 1984, p. 83). But, as several critics have pointed out, this is hardly fair to Heaney's earlier poetic self. When the 'blinds of the *Purgatorio*' are drawn at the end of 'The Strand at Lough Beg', the effect, if 'lovely', is not 'saccharine'; on the contrary, much of its linguistic effort is spent resisting the sickly-sweet. As the epigraph from the *Purgatorio* indicates, the poem recalls Dante's guide Virgil ritually cleansing the infernal filth from the Italian's face before their ascent of Purgatory. The poem's mixed diction sounds symptomatic of the attempt to hold the saccharine at bay. For instance, towards the close of the poem, the aureate phrase 'the sweeping of your feet' gives way before the quotidian horror of McCartney's death: 'to find you on your knees / With blood and roadside muck in your hair and eyes' (Heaney, 1979, p. 18). As Stephen Regan points out, in his account of the poem as 'both summoning and resisting traditional elegiac conventions', here 'an imaginative reunion with McCartney is brutally displaced by the actuality of his death', and 'the submissive and compliant suggestions of a victim on his knees are countered by the more priestly and prayerful suggestions of that same physical attitude'. In terms of the present argument, this doubleness produces a linguistic mingling of the aureate and the quotidian, ritual and reality. A similar to and fro, between bringing the facts home and keeping them at a distance, is audible in the disjunction between the lachrymose 'brimming grass' and the 'drizzle out of a low cloud' (as Regan writes, Heaney has the cloud 'come down to earth rather than risk the suggestions of an ascension into heaven'), or the disjunction between the flat phrase 'and lay you flat', and the latinately ceremonial 'scapulars' of the final line. 'The Strand at Lough Beg' sounds as if it wants to ward off the impulse to anaesthetize the murder (Regan, 2006, pp. 29-30).

This mixture of the aureate and the earthy is a poetic premonition of the tug between two versions of Dante – T. S. Eliot's universalist poet of Western Christendom and Osip Mandelstam's poet of the local and vernacular – which Heaney was to articulate in prose six years later, in 1985, in his essay 'Envies and Identifications: Dante and the Modern Poet'. Here Heaney distances himself from Eliot's influential view of Dante. First and foremost the issue involves how you hear Dante's language: 'Eliot was recreating Dante in his own image', the Dante of a 'confident and classically ratified language'. Heaney continues, 'To listen to Eliot, one would almost be led to forget that Dante's great literary contribution was to write in the vernacular and thereby to give the usual language its head'. By contrast Mandelstam, in his essay 'Conversation about Dante', brings out what Heaney calls 'the swarming, mobbish element in the Italian'. Heaney's rallying-cry, that Mandelstam's Dante is 'a woodcutter singing at his work in the dark wood of the larynx', internalises Dante's '*selva oscura*' as the poetic voice, but it also strongly intimates that Mandelstam's single-minded dedication to his art represents an abandonment of self to something greater, to the language. As ever with Heaney, politics shadows the language issue: total dedication to poetry was the only possible form of protest for the Russian poet when he turned to Dante as personal fortification in his political exile (Heaney, 1985, pp. 12, 18).

It is no coincidence that this tug between two ideas of Dante first made itself felt in Heaney's work, in 'The Strand at Lough Beg', with an allusion to a Virgilian juncture in the *Divina Commedia*, for the issue of Dante's relationship with Virgil is crucial to the case Heaney makes in 'Envies and Identifications'. Heaney implicitly turns Eliot's version of Virgil on its head. Eliot based his argument on the time-honoured view of Virgil as 'the pagan precursor of the Christian dispensation' who anticipates the Dante whose Italian is 'the product of universal Latin'. But this Virgil who looks to a future by the same token comes out of a past, and so, 'as the great poet of the Latin language', Virgil can be seen to 'walk naturally out of the roots of [Dante's] Tuscan speech' (1985, pp. 11, 8, 11). Heaney's desire to remove what he calls the 'latinate-classical-canonical' (1985, p. 13) label from Dante is evident from another poem in *Field Work*, 'An Afterwards' (1979, p. 44), a secularized ('afterwards' for 'afterlife') domestic version of the bottommost pit of Dante's Hell, and a poem which again refers to Virgil. The poem parades the vernacular and demotic. For instance the phrase 'as some maker gaffs me in the neck' mocks the envies and identifications, the internecine ructions, of the poetic community (the medieval word for poet, 'maker', giving the poetic 'backbiting' an ancient lineage). The poet's wife being 'aided and abetted by Virgil's wife' mockingly turns the poet into a latter-day Dante with Virgil as guide. As R. J. C. Watt writes, 'To put oneself ... into the Ninth Circle is to be in the most famous of disgraceful company, a case of modest immodesty indeed' (Watt, 1994, p. 232). The mockery and self-mockery are savage, the irruption into the poem of the horrific Ugolino episode from the Ninth Circle of the *Inferno* reminding us that the poetic stakes are high:

> Unyielding, spurred, ambitious, unblunted
> Lockjawed, mantrapped, each a fastened badger
> Jockeying for position, hasped and mounted
> Like Ugolino on Archbishop Roger.
> (Heaney, 1979, p. 44)

Heaney has himself translated the Ugolino episode (*Inferno*, 32 and 33). His version concludes the *Field Work* collection, and it is even more distant from the 'latinate-classical-canonical' than is 'An Afterwards'. The version is striking for the boldness with which it makes the *Commedia* a sounding-board for riven Ulster. In Neil Corcoran's words, 'the picture of enemies eternally locked in a literal enactment of "devouring hatred" has, of course, its relevance to Northern Ireland, just as dying of hunger has its reverberations in Irish history and politics' (Corcoran, 1986, p. 132) – the last point reinforced by Heaney's rendering of '*e come il pan per fame si manduca*' as 'Like a famine victim [gnawing] at a loaf of bread' (Heaney, 1979, p. 61). Literally the Italian means, simply, 'and as bread is chewed for hunger' (Temple Classics, *Inferno* 32, l. 127). In 'Envies and Identifications' Heaney writes: 'What I first loved in the *Commedia* was the local intensity, the vehemence and fondness attaching to individual shades, the way personalities and values were emotionally soldered together, the strong strain of what has been called personal realism in the celebration of bonds of friendship and bonds of enmity' (Heaney, 1985, p. 18). At the start of his version of the Ugolino episode Heaney renders the symbiotic relationship between Ugolino and the Archbishop with the words 'soldered in a frozen hole' (The Italian literally means 'frozen together in one hole'; Temple Classics, *Inferno* 32, l. 125). Heaney's phrase, echoing as it does the sentence from 'Envies and Identifications', demonstrates his preoccupation with 'bonds of enmity' – if any such demonstration were needed. Corcoran also remarks on how two of Heaney's additions to the original, the comparison of the Archbishop's brain (which Ugolino is gnawing) to 'sweet fruit', and of his head to 'spattered carnal melon', 'point up the comparison between this hideous act and the eating of a meal' (Corcoran, 1986, p. 132). There are more additions, one of which has Virgil asking Ugolino, 'What keeps you so monstrously at rut?', and Ugolino is made to say 'I act the jockey to his mount' (Heaney, 1979, p. 61). These and other additions signify very forcibly how Heaney hears the episode, and the reason for translating it the way he does, conspicuously shunning the 'latinate-classical-canonical'. The language is highly physical – sensual, sexual, physiological – more so even than that of the original. It is the language of 'intimate revenge', to quote the concluding words of 'Punishment' (Heaney, 1975, p. 38): it is that sort of language, but with a savage twist.

The Ugolino episode contains a significantly Virgilian moment. Ugolino begins his narrative '*Tu vuoi ch'io rinnovelli / disperato dolor che il cor mi preme*' ('Thou willest that I renew desperate grief, which wrings my heart', Temple Classics, *Inferno* 33, ll. 4-5). These words echo the start of Aeneas's narration to Dido and her Carthaginian court of his heartrending experiences and the fall of Troy: '*Infandum, regina, iubes renovare dolorem*' (*Aeneid* 2, l. 3). Heaney translates the Italian thus: 'The thought of having to relive all that / Desperate time makes my heart sick'. In the context of Heaney's version 'relive that time' is better than the more literal 'renew', both because it is nearer the colloquial, and also because it emphasizes the sense that the teller is not merely remembering or recalling a bitter experience, but is living it again, perpetually renewing it in all its agony, for it has become a living part of his psyche, breaking his heart again and again. That is essential to the infernal state in the *Commedia*: tormentedly to relive past enmities keeps the grief and the punishment – and the enmities – alive; which is the point Ugolino goes on to make:

> Yet while I weep to say them, I would sow
> My words like curses – that they might increase
> And multiply upon this head I gnaw.
> (Heaney, 1979, p. 61)

To 'sow / My words like curses' is the atavistic danger which, in the context of Ireland's 'house divided against itself', Heaney's poetry courts, fears, and would forestall. Seamus Deane, making a similar observation about Heaney's Ugolino translation, goes on to comment: 'The thought of having to repeat the tale of the atrocity makes Ugolino's heart sick. But it is precisely that repetition which measures the scale of the atrocity for us, showing how the unspeakable can be spoken' (Deane, 1985, p. 115). Speaking the unspeakable (*infandum*) is a central Heaneyish preoccupation.

In the *Station Island* collection (1984) this importunity of political consciousness coincides at significant moments with Dantean allusion, in both 'Sandstone Keepsake' and 'The Loaning', in the former poem warded off, in the latter given full voice. In 'The Loaning' again the Dantean allusion comes loaded with Virgilian freight. The allusion is deliberately self-conscious, for this is a poem about poetic inspiration, 'in the limbo of lost words' – an inspiration that, so the poem's first part hints, knows violence, 'the spit blood of a last few haws and rose-hips'. The hint is picked up in the third part, in the poem's final lines:

> When you are tired or terrified
> your voice slips back into its old first place
> and makes the sound your shades make there...
> When Dante snapped a twig in the bleeding wood

a voice sighed out of blood that bubbled up
like sap at the end of green sticks on a fire.

At the click of a cell lock somewhere now
the interrogator steels his *introibo*,
the light motes blaze, a blood-red cigarette
startles the shades, screeching and beseeching.
(Heaney, 1984, p. 52)

The involuntary regression enacted here, the 'voice slip[ping] back into its old first place', implicitly denies that the poet's 'state of image and allusion' can be 'free', in the words of 'Sandstone Keepsake' ('my free state of image and allusion', Heaney, 1984, p. 20). It is as if the allusion to Dante forces itself upon the poet. As Alan Robinson writes: 'Heaney reminds us in his allusion to *Inferno* XIII that the "dark wood of the larynx" is also the "bleeding wood" of the suicide Piero delle Vigne, the statesman accused of treason against Frederick II and blinded and imprisoned'. Robinson continues, 'Just as Mandelstam could find an experimental modernity in Dante's linguistic bravura, so his own persecution under Stalin enforced the contemporaneity of Dante's political interests' (Robinson, 1988, p. 148). But the poem arrests because such conclusions are not rationally arrived at. The poetry enacts the terrifyingly destabilizing sense of the poet losing his bearings and then relocating himself 'somewhere' he had not anticipated – in that cell.

There is something culpably blood-curdling about this poetic witness to torture, about this speaking the unspeakable, about the note of 'screeching and beseeching' on which the poem ends. But such has invariably been the burden of Heaney's poetry: he may be 'a feeder off battlefields', in the words of 'The First Flight' (Heaney, 1984, p. 102), but the poetry shows that it knows this. The snapping twig in 'The Loaning' signals the poet's apprehension of involvement, of oracular possession, that the state of image and allusion is out of his control. 'Freedom' has turned into its opposite, into possession, into being taken over, importuned. Moreover, it is significant that in *Inferno* 13 Dante has Virgil unambiguously inform the poet that by snapping the twig he, Dante, renews the pain of the shade who has entered the tree, thus making the poet an accessory in the shade's torture. Once again Heaney has encountered a strikingly Virgilian episode in the *Commedia*. When Dante stands terrified at the words and blood that issue from the broken splint, Virgil is made to say to the pained shade: 'If he [i.e. Dante] ... could have believed before, what he has seen only in my verse, he would not have stretched forth his hand against thee; but the incredibility of the thing made me prompt him to do what grieves myself' (Temple Classics, *Inferno* 13, ll. 46-51). Virgil takes on himself some of the guilt and blame for renewing the shade's pain, and, as his words here reveal, Dante borrowed the famous episode of the bleeding wood from the *Aeneid* – as did Ariosto, Tasso and Spenser after him. Thus Heaney has placed himself in a long line of poets to have used the episode as an image for the pain which the poet guiltily renews; and the very act of alluding to this Dantean incident, resonant with the poetic involvement of Virgil and so many others, is emblematic of how poetry reaches back beyond the individual practitioner, the 'voice slip[ping] back into its old first place', 'mak[ing] the sound' that the shades of other poets make in 'the limbo of lost words'; of how, on the other hand – and this is the defence that lies buried in such poetic confessions by Heaney – it gives voice and bears witness to the importunate blood.

To recapitulate: 'giv[ing] the usual language its head' is associated for Heaney with that un-Eliotic version of the Dante-Virgil relationship, a version which stresses the past in which Dante was rooted more than the future to which he aspired: the local ('Tuscan') and vernacular more than the universal and imperial. At the end of his 'Station Island' pilgrimage, the poet may want to follow the Daedal example that lies behind the advice he makes James Joyce's shade give him, to fly by the nets of linguistic and religious nationalism (Heaney, 1984, p. 93); but Heaney's dealings with Dante involve descent as will as flight, a descent that on occasion takes on a distinctly Virgilian resonance: Virgil cleansing the infernal filth from Dante's face, or Dante's Virgilian 'bleeding wood' which renews the torture of an infernal shade. Aeneas must descend to the underworld in order to continue his journey, and one can sense a similar imperative in the progression of Heaney's poetry. But in the later poetry the convergence of Virgil and Dante becomes intriguingly involved, Virgil's example ensuring the Dantean Daedal flight does not soar out of visionary sight, and Dante's example ensuring the Virgilian descent returns to daylight.

The *Seeing Things* collection (1991) registers loud and clear the Virgilian aspect to Heaney's reading of Dante. The opening poem, a translation of Aeneas's visit to the Cumaean Sibyl in *Aeneid* 6 before his descent to Avernus, gives specific gravity to the closing poem, a translation of the passage in *Inferno* 3 describing the outset of Dante's descent into Hell, about Charon ferrying the dead souls across Acheron. According to John D. Sinclair, this Canto has been called 'the most Virgilian in the whole poem' (Sinclair, 1961, p. 56). The title Heaney has given his translation of the Dante, 'The Crossing', strongly intimates one of the preoccupations of the *Seeing Things* collection. The third section, called 'Crossings', of the 'Squarings' sequence of poems, finishes with a poem (no. *xxxvi*) that begins after a street march, 'In darkness. With all the streetlamps off', proceeds via what it calls 'one of [Dante's] head-clearing similes' and the 'unpredictable, attractive light' of 'policemen's torches', and ends with the protagonists feeling like Dantesque-Virgilian 'herded shades who … cross' with a sense of relief to the safety of their car, which is compared in the last line to 'Charon's boat under the faring poets' (Heaney, 1991, p. 94). The crossings in the *Seeing Things* collection are between different states of being and consciousness, not so much into darkness as out of darkness into light, a visionary crossing, the quotidian crossing over into the imaginary, memories out of the past crossing into realms beyond time. 'Yet', as Elmer Andrews writes, 'installed at the heart of Heaney's visionary seeing (and encoded in the double meaning of his title, *Seeing Things*) is the continual awareness that vision may be delusional' (Andrews, 1998, p. 155) – which is an apt description of the ambiguous feelings elicited by 'Crossings *xxxvi*'. It is significant that the passage Heaney has translated from *Inferno* 3 contains a (possibly delusional) alternative way to cross: Charon says to Dante, a living soul who should not therefore cross with the dead, 'By another way, by other harbours / You shall reach a different shore and pass over. / A lighter boat must be your carrier' (Heaney, 1991, p. 11). Much of the poetry in the *Seeing Things* collection takes a 'lighter', in both senses of the word, way for the poet's visionary crossings. For instance in the title poem, for the crossing to what turns out to be a visionary moment on the Isle of Inishbofin in preparation for an extraordinary conjuration of the father's 'immanent' 'ghosthood', the boat is piloted by a 'ferryman' over

> The deep, still, seeable-down-into water,
> It was as if I looked from another boat
> Sailing through air, far up, and could see
> How riskily we fared into the morning,
> And loved in vain our bare, bowed, numbered heads.
> (Heaney, 1991, p. 16)

– a possibly delusional crossing (since the passengers' heads are 'numbered'), but certainly a 'lighter boat', which takes off 'free into space', in the words of the Dantean encounter with Joyce at the end of the 'Station Island' pilgrimage (Heaney, 1984, p. 93).

The immediate appeal to Heaney of the episode from *Aeneid* 6 is clear: the title of his translation, 'The Golden Bough', recalls Sir James Frazer's researches into autochthonous mythology, the journey back into cultural memory which is the ground-base of the *Aeneid* – as it is of Heaney's poetry. The Sibyl's words about plucking the golden bough before entering Avernus bring with them imagery of dark woods, in the midst of which lies the key (the bough) that will unlock the underworld to release its secrets. The famous passage beginning '*facilis descensus Averno*' conjures up the Heaneyish preoccupation with disinterring the past so that it may speak to and for the present:

> [T]he way down to Avernus is easy.
> Day and night black Pluto's door stands open.
> But to retrace your steps and get back to upper air,
> This is the real task and the real undertaking.
> A few have been able to do it, …
> (Heaney, 1991, p. 2)

As these lines indicate, Heaney's translation may at times sound rough and ready, but this is undoubtedly the effect of shunning the 'latinate-classical-canonical'. Often in this translation the diction that sounds most distant from what is commonly understood as 'latinate' is uncommonly effective. The unremarkable opening phrase, 'So from the back of her shrine', prepares for the way 'the usual language [is given] its head' later, in such locutions as 'The *murk* of Tartarus' and 'Hidden in the *thick* of a tree' (emphases added). This Virgilian 'dark wood' inspires Heaney's 'larynx' to sing with a particularly 'mobbish' vernacular. Sibylline frenzy is called up not in the sort of sonorities many were brought up to think of as 'latinate', but in more rugged sounds: 'As soon as her fit passed away and the mad mouthings stopped', for instance. To put it another way, Heaney's idea of 'latinate' is a long way from '*classical*-latinate'. This style, this voice, is one of 'fearful equivocal words'. Like Heaney, the Cumaean Sibyl is obliged to speak out, and it is well known how in her usual vein she both does and does not, how she speaks in riddles, allowing the sibylline leaves to be blown higgledy-piggledy about her cave:

> So from the back of her shrine the Sibyl of Cumae
> Chanted fearful equivocal words and made the cave echo
> With sayings where clear truths and mysteries
> Were inextricably twined. Apollo turned and twisted
> His spurs at her breast, gave her her head, then reined in her spasms.
> (Heaney, 1991, p. 1)

The phrase 'gave her her head' is decidedly rough-and-ready and un-classical-latinate. In giving the Sibyl 'her head' Heaney boldly gives the language of his translation its head, with the word 'spasms' reading innuendo into the original where there is none; for in the Latin the governing metaphor is of the Sibyl being ridden as a horse by Apollo, no sexual subtext present.

This translated passage from *Aeneid* 6 looks back to certain motifs in Heaney's earlier poetry and forward to much of what follows in the *Seeing Things* collection. In *Field Work* there was the Sibyl of the second poem of the 'Triptych' sequence, whose words are decidedly 'fearful', but not so 'equivocal' perhaps ('My people think money / And talk weather. Oil-rigs lull their future / On single acquisitive stems'), and who invokes that 'bleeding wood' to reverse its fateful signs:

> 'Unless forgiveness finds its nerve and voice,
> Unless the helmeted and bleeding tree
> Can green and open buds like infants' fists …'
> (Heaney, 1979, p. 13)

– although these lines are indeed somewhat equivocal: 'green' as a (possibly) transitive verb does not sound very 'forgiving' in conjunction with nascent, possibly pugilistic, 'fists'. (In 'Easter 1916' Yeats may have changed 'motley' near the start of the poem to 'green' at the end – 'Wherever green is worn' – but he did not try to turn 'green' into a transitive verb (Yeats, 1961, p. 202)). In the passage from *Aeneid* 6, Aeneas refers to the story of Orpheus descending to the underworld to 'call back the shade of a wife' (Heaney, 1991, p. 2), a story that conjures up the 'looking back' motif, the impulse to descend into the past to recover and renew it, and that lies buried in the richly layered poem 'The Underground' which opened the *Station Island* collection. (It is a rich mythic layering: Pan and Syrinx, Hansel and Gretel, Orpheus and Eurydice…). The poem ends with a resonant equivocation: 'all attention / For your step following and damned if I look back' (Heaney, 1984, p. 13). This is equivocal in various ways: linguistic, in that the colloquial 'damned' takes on a hellish underground air; autobiographical, because 'looking back' is exactly what the poem has been doing;

and more generally equivocal in the context of the trajectory of Heaney's poetry, behind which so often lurk the exhilaration and danger of 'mak[ing] germinate' the past, in the words of 'The Tollund Man' (Heaney, 1972, p. 48). It is remarkable how Heaney uses these motifs to illuminate both private and public (historical, political) spheres, thus showing that the one invariably involves the other.

Encountering the dead father, another motif in the passage from *Aeneid* 6, wonderfully shadows the *Seeing Things* collection:

> I pray for one look, one face-to-face meeting with my dear father.
> Teach me the way and open the holy doors wide.
> I carried him on these shoulders through flames
> And thousands of enemy spears.
> (Heaney, 1991, p. 1)

There is a loud Virgilian resonance to the father-son image in 'Man and Boy' (a poem which characteristically reviews and re-envisions Heaney's early poem 'Follower'; for 'Man and Boy' is itself an instance of how the father, in the concluding words of 'Follower', 'keeps stumbling / Behind [the poet], and will not go away'). The Virgilian resonance to the father-son image in 'Man and Boy' was emphasized by the poem's original publication, in *Poetry Review,* alongside the *Aeneid* 6 translation. The end of the poem conjures up the poet's father as a young boy at the moment of learning of the death of *his* father (that is, of the poet's grandfather), in a beautifully managed recession into memory and beyond, into the imagined and imaginary:

> My father is a barefoot boy with news,
> Running at eye-level with weeds and stooks
> On the afternoon of his own father's death.
>
> The open, black half of the half-door waits.
> I feel much heat and hurry in the air.
> I feel his legs and quick heels far away
>
> And strange as my own – when he will piggyback me
> At a great height, light-headed and thin-boned,
> Like a witless elder rescued from the fire.
> (Heaney, 1991, p. 15)

Virgil's 'holy doors' into the underworld blend here with a rural 'half-door'. Later in Heaney's translation they become 'black Pluto's door', but in 'Man and Boy' the dark aspect of what turns into the buried life of the poet's psychological underworld is alleviated by a breathtakingly simple line of visual and audible echoes: 'The open, black half of the half-door'. That 'black half' wondrously and wonderingly opens up, not 'into the dark' as in the younger Heaney's 'All I know is a door into the dark' (Heaney, 1969, p. 19), but into a 'light-headed', lighter, insubstantial and a temporal realm, not an underworld, nor an afterworld, but an *other*world. The episode, as re-created and imagined by the poet from his father's words, slips from an historical present ('My father is a barefoot boy') into a more actual and felt present ('I feel much heat') into a memorial present ('I feel…far away') and then into an historical future ('when he will piggyback me'), to alight in an atemporal realm reconciling dark and light, the imagined and the actual, the near ('eye-level') and the distant ('far away'), the present and the absent. In the process poet and father uncannily coalesce and change places. Into this realm enters the Virgilian motif of the son (Aeneas) who carries the father (Anchises) on his shoulders away from a flaming Troy. In 'Man and Boy' it is the father who is remembered and imagined as carrying the son, so that their Virgilian roles are reversed and the son turns into the 'witless elder' who is rescued. That is to say, in manhood the fact of (lovingly) recalling the father is in itself an act of psychological renewal: to recall has the potential to redeem and be redeemed – just as the word 'witless' has been redeemed by its context, by its collocation with 'light-headed'. The whole poem, like many in *Seeing Things*, enacts the mental state of being suspended out of time. This is a 'light-headed' if 'dangerous' 'step[ping] free into space', in the words of the encounter with the Joycean shade in 'Station Island' (Heaney, 1984, p. 93). Passage through the door of memory can mean rescue ('rescued from the fire') and redemption, as opposed to damnation ('damned if I look back'). Here Virgil is made party, as it were, to Heaney's effort, in his own words, 'to make space in my reckoning and imagining for the marvellous as well as for the murderous' (Heaney, 1998, p. 458).

'[T]o retrace your steps and get back to upper air', in those words of Heaney's *Aeneid* 6 translation; 'Man and Boy' enacts a retracing of memory's steps into the past to bring the poet back to a renewed and redeemed present, or at any rate a renewable and redeemable present. Thus Virgil can be made to signify, not only the dark downward aspect of recession, but also its lighter-headed opposite, the return 'back to upper air'. A similar dynamic is at work in another poem in the *Seeing Things* collection, 'A Retrospect', which stratifies and layers personal memories, blending them with political and historical allegory to create a kind of 'republic of conscience' out of contemporary Ireland, in so doing covertly and overtly appropriating the *Aeneid*. Part I is a timeless pre-diluvial pastoral – although only *just* 'pre-', for 'The whole country [is] apparently afloat', 'As if we moved in the first stealth of flood'. The second part begins by re-figuring this visionary memory in preparation for crossing over into a landscape of Virgilian echoes, in the process transforming part I's first person into the third person. Part II begins:

> Another trip they seemed to keep repeating
> Was up to Glenshane Pass – his 'Trail of Tears',
> As he'd say every time, and point out streams
> He first saw on the road to boarding school.
> And then he'd quote Sir John Davies' dispatch
> About his progress through there from Dungannon
> With Chichester in 1608:
> 'The wild inhabitants wondered as much

To see the King's deputy, as Virgil's ghosts
Wondered to see Aeneas alive in Hell.'

They liked the feel of the valley out behind,
As if a ladder leaned against the world
And they were climbing it but might fall back
Into the total air and emptiness
They carried on their shoulders.
(Heaney, 1991, pp. 42-3)

Playfully echoing 'vale of tears', 'Trail of Tears' seems to conjure up Virgil's *'sunt lacrimae rerum'* (*Aeneid* 1, l. 462). This Virgilian echo is likely in view of the piece of Virgiliana a few lines later, lifted from a dispatch written by the poet John Davies in his capacity as attorney-general for Ireland. The dispatch's nightmare-vision of Ireland as a Virgilian netherworld, historically in thrall to England, is then somewhat mitigated by lines that again come to rest on the Virgilian motif (with a bit of biblical Jacob's dream thrown in) of the shouldered burden – or in this instance non-burden. The visionary headiness of 'total air and emptiness' balances the riskiness, against the need, of 'step[ping] free into space' and 'upper air', the effort to 'climb' against the danger of 'falling back'. This is one of those equivocal, suspended moments of assured tentativeness familiar in later Heaney: assured in its visionary sensing, its seeing and 'feeling' ('the feel of the valley'), tentative in its manner of expression – 'as if' ('As if a ladder…') alerting us to the fact that this is, in Heaney's words, a 'radiant' moment 'swim[ming] up into memory … com[ing] back in the light of a more distanced and more informed consciousness' (Heaney, 2001b, p. 9). Here we are made to savour the visionary moment before the poet reveals, or possibly discovers with his 'more informed consciousness', its purport, which is to evoke the emotionally precarious position of lovers, who, as we learn later in the poem, are now 'Young marrieds, used … to the licit within doors' as opposed to the illicit outdoors, the sexy pastorals of old. The young marrieds have 'the fasted eyes / Of wild inhabitants', which, with arresting explicitness, recalls those starving Irish of John Davies' dispatch. As Virgilian ghosts of their former selves the young marrieds, in a sort of anti-Thelma-and-Louise moment towards the end of the poem, parked their car 'A bit down from the summit', envisioned a life that was and was not for them ('gazed beyond themselves'), and then drove back 'with all their usual old / High-pitched strain and gradual declension' – this, the conclusion of the poem, articulating a linguistic decline from the un-latinate sounding phrase 'high-pitched strain' to the (classically?) latinate 'gradual declension'. This last point may be fanciful, but decidedly unfanciful is the wider historical context in which the young marrieds find themselves, for the landscape overlooked by their parked car comprises 'baronies and cantreds', that is pre-Norman Invasion Ireland ('cantreds') and post-Invasion Ireland ('baronies'). (A barony is thought by historians to be a Norman division, into which the cantreds were grouped.) Superior to ('they saw down through', that is, they looked down and they saw through) such historical-territorial divisions, their predicament, as lovers and spouses, for better or for worse, outlasts, 'gazes beyond', such mere spatial-temporal confinements: 'The scene stood open', open to any eventualities which the future may hold. And the poem's Virgilian backdrop ('the valley out behind') reinforces the sense that this 'retrospect' goes beyond the grave and beyond time (Heaney, 1991, pp. 43-4).

Another equivocal and suspended moment is poem *xlii* of the 'Squarings' sequence. Yet again the poem calls on Virgil, and reads like a commentary on 'A Retrospect'. It composes a characteristically Heaneyish ambiguous frieze of the quotidian-sublime, and with a knowing restraint almost crosses over into Virgil's Elysian Fields: 'fields of the *nearly* blessed' (emphasis added). With its reticently loaded diction, its ambiguities and double-speak, its 'territorial' 'apparitions' which are 'active still', the poem invites even as it wards off the pressures of Irish history: it is unsure, like its denizens, 'how far / The country of the shades has been pushed back', how far this is a picture of life or of afterlife, of the living or of the dead, unsure whether or not it has crossed over (Heaney, 1991, p. 102.) But this poem is already moving away from the Virgil of the *Aeneid*, and therefore beyond the territory of this essay, the hells of Heaney, towards the Virgil of the *Eclogues*, the territory Heaney went on to explore in his later collection, *Electric Light* (2001), which contains adaptations of the fourth and ninth *Eclogues*. The fourth, 'Bann Valley Eclogue', has the 'poet' invoke 'my hedge-schoolmaster Virgil', who is made to give instruction, with measured optimism, on the role of the poet in Ireland's nascent peace process. Here Heaney's version of pastoral, with its rural effects at times ostentatiously rough and ready ('Big dog daisies will get fanked up in the spokes'), participates directly in his meditation on contemporary Irish life and the poet's role within it (Heaney, 2001a, pp. 11-12).

References

Andrews, E. (ed.) (1998), *The Poetry of Seamus Heaney*, Icon Critical Guides, Icon Books, Cambridge.

Corcoran, N. (1986), *Seamus Heaney*, Faber & Faber, London.

Dante Alighieri (1900), *The Inferno of Dante Alighieri*, Temple Classics, Dent, London.

Deane, S. (1985), 'The Timorous and the Bold', *Celtic Revivals*, Faber & Faber, London, as excerpted in *The Poetry of Seamus Heaney*, ed. E. Andrews, Icon Critical Guides, Icon Books, Cambridge, pp. 110-16.

Heaney, S. (1969), *Door into the Dark*, Faber & Faber, London.

Heaney, S. (1972), *Wintering Out*, Faber & Faber, London.

Heaney, S. (1975), *North*, Faber & Faber, London.

Heaney, S. (1979), *Field Work*, Faber & Faber, London.

Heaney, S. (1984), *Station Island*, Faber & Faber, London.

Heaney, S. (1985), 'Envies and Identifications: Dante and the Modern Poet', *Irish University Review*, 15, pp. 5-19.

Heaney, S. (1991), *Seeing Things*, Faber & Faber, London.

Heaney, S. (1991), 'Two Poems by Seamus Heaney: "Man and Boy", "The Golden Bough"', *Poetry Review*, 81 (1), 1991, pp. 72-3.

Heaney, S. (1998), 'Crediting Poetry: The Nobel Lecture', *Opened Ground: Poems 1966-1996*, London, Faber & Faber, pp. 445-67.

Heaney, S. (2001a), *Electric Light*, Faber & Faber, London.

Heaney, S. (2001b), 'Lux Perpetua', *Guardian, Saturday Review*, 16 June 2001, p. 9.

Regan, S. (2006), 'Seamus Heaney and the Modern Irish Elegy', *Foundation: The Annual Periodical of the St. Chad's College Foundation*, 3 (1), pp. 19-33.

Robinson, A. (1988), *Instabilities in Contemporary British Poetry*, Macmillan, Basingstoke.

Sinclair, J. D. (trans.) (1961), *The Divine Comedy of Dante Alighieri*, Oxford University Press, New York.

Virgil (1986), *Eclogues, Georgics, Aeneid I-VI*, 2 vols, Loeb Classical Library, Harvard, Cambridge Mass.

Watt, R. J. C. (1994), 'Seamus Heaney: Voices on Helicon', *Essays in Criticism*, 44, (3), pp. 213-34.

Yeats, W. B. (1961), *Collected Poems*, Macmillan, London.

Eavan Boland's Revisionary Stance on Nationalism: A 'Post-nationalist' or a 'Post-colonial' Writer?

Pilar Villar Argáiz
University of Granada

This essay discusses Eavan Boland's complex reconstruction of women's images in art and literature, in particular the nationalist icon of Mother Ireland. Although much has been written on Boland's revision of conventional images of femininity in the Irish national tradition (see, for instance, Fogarty (1994, 1999) and Meaney (1993)), her ambivalent attitude towards nationalism as a viable narrative has not been sufficiently explored. In what follows, I will try to reduce this critical imbalance by focusing on Boland's contradictory desire both to surpass, and yet at the same time epitomise, Irish nationality. The assumption upon which this study is based is that Boland's work can be considered as a postcolonial production. When attempting to pin down the meaning of postcolonial literature, it is almost impossible to avoid very large generalisations and simplifications, given the wide range and variety of such writings. In order to define this sometimes overused term, and in order to incorporate the different cultural productions that are considered postcolonial, I would like to embrace Boehmer's definition of the term. For Boehmer (1995, p. 3), postcolonial literature, 'rather than simply being the writing which "came after" empire, is that which critically scrutinises the colonial relationship … that sets out in one way or another to resist colonialist perspectives'. Taking into account Boehmer's definition of postcolonial literature, Boland's work can indisputably be categorised as such. Her poetry, mostly her mature production, constantly scrutinises Irish women's subjugation in terms of imperialist and nationalist practices. In this sense, Boland creates a text committed to cultural resistance towards their double colonisation as Irish citizens and as women (Fulford (2002, pp. 213-214) and Atfield (1997, p. 168) also read Boland's work as one example of 'postcolonial poetry').

There are two views among postcolonial theorists and critics as regards postcolonial literature. First of all, postcolonial theorists such as Said (1994, p. 261), Bhabha

(1995, p. 185), and Spivak (1993, pp. 219-223) tend to focus on those works characterised by an eminent anti-essentialism, anti-nationalism, and postmodernism. This sort of literature discards cultural identity and perpetuates the Western, postmodernist notion of agency and subjectivity which often involves the splintering of the subject, and the celebration of national and historical rootlessness. One postcolonial writer within this branch of literature is Salman Rushdie, whose *Satanic Verses* is praised by Bhabha (1995, p. 185), Said (1994, p. 261), Spivak (1993, pp. 219-223), and Hall (1990, p. 212) for showing the constructed and provisional nature of identity and succeeding in overcoming binary oppositions (such as coloniser/colonised) by parody, mimicry, borrowings, and the metaphor of migrancy. In Ireland, one illustration of this anti-nationalism and anti-essentialism is found in Samuel Beckett's work, which finds freedom in exile (Arrowsmith, 2000: 64). His work has been praised by critics such as Kiberd (1996, p. 531), who asserts that Beckett is 'the first truly Irish playwright ... free of factitious elements of Irishness'.

Secondly, we come across those postcolonial scholars who focus on those texts which, instead of promoting the fragmentation and the rootlessness of the subject, maintain a sense of cultural identity and attempt to create collective selves. As Boehmer (1995, p. 248) notes, postmodern notions of meaning and identity as fictional and provisional can be of no use for those for whom (as women, indigenous peoples, and marginalised groups) the signifiers of nation, home, self, and history might be compelling issues. Mohanty (1991, p. 36) is one of the critics who defends this type of writing on the grounds that the most subaltern group of all, Third World women, need to 'conceptuali[se] notions of collective selves' in order to be politically effective. This is the way these women engage with feminism, by creating an imagined community of women who suffer as they are suffering. This notion of agency, which moves away from the postmodern one advocated by Said, Bhabha, and Spivak, has a location in history and geography, and 'its consciousness is both singular and plural' (Mohanty, 1991, p. 37). This is beginning to be acknowledged in Ireland. As Arrowsmith (2000, p. 66) has explained, current ethnographic studies are demonstrating how for the Irish, home and abroad, cultural identity continues to be of paramount importance, especially 'in contemporary contexts of globalisation and cultural homogenisation'. It seems that some Irish writers are beginning to search for 'the means to construct actively a stable sense of cultural identity' that counters 'the neutralising effects of emigration, anti-nationalism, and globalisation' (p. 67).

Boland's work can certainly be categorised within the second type of postcolonial literature Mohanty identifies. As we will see, she needs to establish a dialogue with the idea of the nation. Cultural identity is very important for this female poet, and, as a consequence, she tries to construct, through her work, a viable national and historical continuity that might give her a sense of stability. In this sense, Boland attempts to move away from the postmodern uncertainty (anti-essentialism and anti-nationalism) of writers such as Rushdie and Beckett, by asserting the importance of notions such as nationhood. Nevertheless, her stance is more complicated than it looks at first sight. First of all, she finds difficulty in accepting those decorative images raised to emblematic status by nationalism. Boland constantly revises and deconstructs nationalist discursive practices in order to show their simplification and misrepresentation of women. Furthermore, she tries to avoid the creation of an essentialist nationalist discourse, by scrutinising the dogmatic and totalitarian use that this ideology has made of notions such as 'Irishness'.

In this sense, Boland's work can be located within both forms of postcolonial literature mentioned above: her attitude towards nationalism is both modernist and postmodernist, essentialist in one way, but deeply anti-essentialist on the other.[1] Boland's liminal stance on the Irish nationalist ideology can be explained from the perspective of Colin Graham's theories. As I will show, she is in-between that 'post-colonialism' and 'post-nationalism' that Graham (1994, p. 35) identifies among contemporary scholars and writers in Ireland. Boland adopts this 'in-between' ideological position with a subversive project in mind, in order to advocate a more inclusive and fluid national identity that encapsulates different heterogeneous experiences.

In his essay 'Post-Nationalism/Post-Colonialism: Reading Irish Culture', Colin Graham (Graham, 1994, p. 35) identifies two contradictory movements within current Irish cultural manifestations. This scholar establishes a distinction between a 'post-nationalism' and a 'post-colonial criticism' (ibid.). Within the first branch he locates critics such as Richard Kearney and his *Across the Frontiers: Ireland in the 1990s* (1988). Although Kearney advocates a pluralised European identity and a redefinition of cultural identity, [1] Graham (1994, p. 36) argues that he leaves nationalism behind 'with a reluctance and a nostalgia' (p. 36). Post-nationalism, according to Graham, does not reject the nation, but evolves from it. Furthermore, it is unable to understand the ideological constructions and limitations of the nation, and 'hopes instead to be able to preserve and move beyond it simultaneously' (p. 37). On the other hand, 'post-colonialism' is, for Graham, more revolutionary, because it is able to adopt a more suspicious attitude towards the nature of nationalism and the ideological restrictions it implies. He names Fanon's *The Wretched of the Earth* and the *Subaltern Studies* group in India as appropriate models to follow (pp. 36-37). Their theories, according to Graham, have succeeded in building a critique of this ideology. They have understood more than Irish critics such as Kearney that 'the post-colonial nation becomes the 'ideological product' of the colonial regime' (p. 37).

Boland's stance on Irish nationalism certainly coincides with what Graham defines as 'post-colonialism'. [2] First of all, she views nationalism as a powerful restrictive ideology. The fusion of the feminine and the national, a monopoly in Irish poetry, is unacceptable to her, for the reality of womanhood is inevitably simplified, as she asserts in an interview with Rebecca Wilson:

> Irish poets of the nineteenth century, and indeed their heirs in this century, coped with their sense of historical injury by writing of Ireland as an abandoned queen or an old mother. My objections to this are ethical. If you consistently simplify women by making them national icons in poetry

or drama you silence a great deal of the actual women in the past, whose sufferings and complexities are part of that past, who intimately depend on us, as writers, not to simplify them in this present. I am conscious of bringing my own perspective into the debate. (Wilson, 1990, p. 87)

In the national tradition, the heroine Hiberna was utterly passive, and her role was almost always as a mother or a virgin. Boland cannot approve of these passive and simplified images of women: she sees them as a 'corruption' of Irish women's reality in the past (Boland, 1996, p. 135). Nevertheless, the worst of nationalist poetry, Boland seems to imply, is not only that it has misrepresented women, but that, in doing so, it 'has structured the position of the poet in such masculine terms' that it has prevented 'women from constructing themselves as [speaking] subjects' (Meaney, 1993, p. 137). Because of this, Boland (1996, p. 66) realises that she has been granted no power of expression as a female artist: 'I was feeling the sexual opposites within the narrative. The intense passivity of the female; the fact that to the male principle was reserved the right not only of action but of expression as well'. This dichotomy established between (male) subject/ (female) object has encouraged the fusion of the political poem and the private poem in Ireland, making the subject always 'representative' and the feminine object always 'ornamental' (p. 178). In short, for Boland cultural nationalist ideals are exclusive and narrow because, firstly, they conceive of poetry as an exclusively male vocation; and, secondly, because they rely on the conventionally fixed dichotomy between the male bard and the female muse/ emblematic object of the poem.

In this sense, Boland's sharp critique of cultural nationalist images and her understanding of the dynamics that underlie such conventions makes her approach 'post-colonial', as Graham (1994, p. 37) would argue. Nevertheless, her position is more complex than it first seems. Boland resembles Kearney in that her cultural identity is still very important for her. When asked by Wilson (Wilson, 1990, p. 84) if she considers herself as an 'Irish poet', she assuredly answers that she wishes to be categorised as such, and that a 'nation' is a 'potent, important image' for her. As she has later admitted, 'I knew that as a poet I could not easily do without the idea of the nation', because her reality is inevitably 'rooted in one country and one poetic inheritance' (Boland, 1996, p. 128). In fact, nationhood, together with womanhood, is one of the two constituent aspects of Boland's fulfilled identity. In her reliance and dependence on nationhood as a still viable narrative, Boland also shares that 'post-nationalism' which Graham (Graham, 1994, p. 36) identifies in Kearney. Boland's rejection of the exclusive tendencies of cultural nationalism does not involve a rejection of nationhood as such. As Said has argued, 'moving beyond nativism does not mean abandoning nationalism; but it does mean thinking of local identity as not exhaustive, and therefore not being anxious to confine oneself to one's own sphere' (Said, 1994, p.277) . It is precisely this position that Boland adopts in her poetry. Boland reinvents the notion of Ireland as a more inclusive country, one which bears witness to the defeats of Irish history and the sufferings of Irish women. In an interview, Boland makes explicit her approach to Irish national identity:

> I am not a nationalist. It isn't always in linear time that nations flow along and define themselves. They crystallise in different individuals, at different times, in different voices and images. A 'nation' is a potent, important image. It is a concept that a woman writer must discourse with. [...] And I know that as a woman, I couldn't accept the idea of nationhood as it was formulated for me in Irish literature, … I would always choose a past that was real and actual and was composed of private, enduring human dignities … That is what a nation means to me. (Wilson, 1990, p. 84)

Thus Boland rejects the traditional exclusive and narrow nationalist conception for a new national identity which includes, in her own words 'private, enduring human dignities', that is, different voices of individual experiences. Simply by being a woman, Boland destabilises narrow poetic identities, becoming the female author of the poem. On the other hand, by moving her female characters from being the objects to the speaking subjects of the poems and by giving voice to women's experiences, Boland widens the previous exclusive national identity.

In order to gain some insight into the ways in which Boland examines nationalist ideals, and imaginatively reconstructs notions of Ireland and Irish identity, I will focus on two of Boland's most significant poems: 'Mise Eire' (*The Journey*, 1987, pp. 10-11) and 'Mother Ireland' (*The Lost Land*, 1998, p. 39). In these two poems, Boland adopts a clear 'post-nationalist' stance, because she maintains, and not rejects, the conventional relation between gender and nation, showing her interest in dealing with discursive practices that, for better or for worse, have helped to define her Irish experience. Nevertheless, the poet also adopts a 'post-colonial' perspective, in her critique of nationalism as a powerful coloniser for women.

This 'in-between' stance is observed in 'Mise Eire', where Boland reclaims the feminine persona often given to Ireland, in particular the Old Woman of Beare. The title of the poem echoes Patrick Pearse's poem 'I am Ireland', a prototype of the passive, patient, and sorrowful Mother Ireland. In the latter poem, the female speaker appears as a dispossessed mother, who has been betrayed and abandoned by her sons, and who fervently hopes for the arrival of another Cuchulain who will restore her dignity. In this sense, she lacks agency and depends on a male hero to 'save' her from the British oppression. In her version of Pearse's poem, Boland rewrites 'I am Ireland' as 'I am a woman', an assertion reiterated twice in the poem:

> I am the woman-
> a sloven's mix
> of silk at the wrists,
> a sort of dove-strut
> in the precincts of the garrison-
>
> who practices
> the quick frictions,
> the rictus of delight

> and gets cambric for it,
> rice-coloured silks.
>
> I am the woman
> in the gansy-coat
> on board the 'Mary Belle'
> in the huddling cold,
>
> holding her half-dead baby to her
> as the wind shifts East
> and North over the dirty
> water of the wharf. (Boland, 1987, pp. 10-11)

Gaining authority, the new muse Mother in 'Mise Eire' suddenly advocates her right to emerge in less idealised roles. The lexical repetition of 'I am the woman' indicates Mother Ireland's ability to be different kinds of women at the same time. First of all, she becomes a whore, who trades sex and practices 'the rictus of delight', a radical revision of the nationalist icon of virginal Ireland being raped by corrupted England. Rather than beautiful, this prostitute is described as 'sloven', careless in her personal appearance. She is portrayed as walking with pompous bearing in the environs of the garrison, in order to impress the soldiers at the military post. In contrast to the former representation of Mother Ireland, she does not incite rebellion. Her strut is 'dove'-like, indicating that she advocates peace, conciliation, and negotiation, instead of confrontation or armed conflict. Secondly, Mother Ireland has the potential to become an émigré, forced to escape from her country. The fact that the woman who is leaving the homeland is on board a ship called 'Mary Belle' is not accidental. The name of the boat embodies the two main virtues imposed on women by patriarchal tradition: they must be like 'Mary' (virginal, pure, and devoted to others), and they must also be 'Belle' (attractive and beautiful). Boland emphasises the patriarchal Madonna/prostitute dichotomy in order to create a new figure of Mother Ireland which encompasses both images: she is both the whore and the devoted mother. As Fogarty puts it, Boland 'depicts female counter-selves that refuse to function as comforting and affirmative mirror images' (Fogarty, 1999, p. 270). In fact, Boland is here rewriting the conventional image of Mother Ireland in order to suggest a more unpleasant reality: how Irish women have had to survive, either by selling their bodies as prostitutes, or by emigrating to a new country where they could start a new life.

In this sense, Boland suggests that nationhood is not something to be praised by nationalist ballads and songs, but a cruel reality of dispossession and oppression. Her poem moves away from the traditional political idea that a defeated nation must be reborn as a triumphant woman. As Kearney argues, 'the more dispossessed the Irish people became in reality, the more they sought to repossess a sense of identity in the realm of ideality' (Kearney, 1985, p. 76). In the poem under discussion, Boland does not intend to follow the Celtic Revival idealisation of triumphant nationhood. She shows instead a nation which has been defeated by a history of colonisation and by an oppressive nationalism. The 'half-dead baby' of 'Mise Eire' is an emblem for a nation half-destroyed by violence and crimes. However, this baby is only half-dead, implying that there is a slight possibility for renewal, for rejuvenation. Despite the 'scalded memory' of the woman in 'Mise Eire', there is a hope for the creation of 'a new language', a new poetry which will replace the 'old dactyls' and 'songs' (Boland, 1987, pp. 10-11). By telling the story of her nation mainly by means of her sexuality, Boland contends that Irish women poets are really empowered to write a new poetry which transforms the received national culture, and hence, their concept of national identity.

Perhaps the sharpest criticism that this poem has received has been that of Gerardine Meaney (Meaney, 1993, p. 149), who maintains that in a poem like 'Mise Eire', Boland's version of Mother Ireland perpetuates feminine stereotypes. Her reconstruction 'leaves maternity and sexuality separated', as those traditional female roles that Irish nationalism has maintained. In this sense, Meaney accuses Boland of being 'content with Pearse's version' and of not using 'the other possibilities offered by the [Gaelic] tradition', which is not always idealising in its representation of women (that is, the interrelation of fertility and sexuality that the cultural Cailleach Bhéarra tradition offers) (ibid). Boland indeed subverts one 'specific Irish variant' (the nationalist trope) by the 'more general Western myth of femininity': the Madonna/prostitute dichotomy, as we have seen (Meaney, 1993, p. 146). Nevertheless, Meaney ignores the speaker's contention at the end of the poem that her reconstruction of nationalist images is only partial and incomplete. Establishing a tension between her aim at recovery and the female voice of the emigrant mother, Boland describes this woman's language as:

> mingling the immigrant
> guttural with the vowels
> of homesickness who neither
> knows nor cares that
>
> a new language
> is a kind of scar
> and heals after a while
> into a passable imitation
> of what went before. (Boland, 1987, p. 11)

Boland's new language is only a 'passable', but not outstanding, 'imitation' of how women in the past were. The poet avoids writing her subversive speech as another hegemonic and dominant (nationalist) discourse. She tries to elude the creation of another essentialist discourse, in which the poet claims to be speaking on behalf of an oppressed community, to act as an authoritarian and privileged spokesperson. In fact, it is quite typical of Boland to undermine her poetic authority as her poems come to a close. [3] In 'Mise Eire', the speaker recognizes at the end that her language is imperfect, scarred, and that her reconstruction of Mother Ireland can only be malleable and workable as a copy of previous constructs. In this sense, whereas she subverts this nationalist and patriarchal icon, she still acknowledges that her reconstruction is incomplete, and shaped by the 'constructs' upon which women have been defined (interview with Villar Argáiz, 2006, p. 66). Boland's search for cultural identity is not a search for an essence, but rather a way of *'positioning'* herself within the discourses of history and culture, as Hall (1990, p. 230) would define it.

In 'Mother Ireland', Boland makes explicit, once again, her new stance on the age-old equation of woman and nation. This poem is written from the personal perspective of Mother Ireland, who is able to recognise that she has been an object and now is also a subject. Thus, here the first person pronoun singular recurs in the majority of the lines. She is both the speaker and the object of discussion, the creative self and the topic of the poem. By including both, poetic image and poetic speaker in the same framed picture, Boland expands the boundaries of what seems at first a fixed national icon. Significantly enough, Boland deliberately produces deviations in the layout in order to reinforce her subversion of traditional national allegories:

> At first
> > I was land
> > > I lay on my back to be fields
>
> and when I turned
> > on my side
> > > I was hill
>
> under freezing stars. (Boland, 1998, p. 39)

These lines serve to illustrate what can certainly be viewed as the traditional feminisation of the Irish land: the woman in the poem asserts that she was 'land', 'fields', and 'a hill'. The transformation that Mother Ireland experiences in her earthly figure is noteworthy. Whereas 'lands' and 'fields' are territories which can be controlled by human beings (in the sense of being exploited in agricultural terms), a 'hill' stands out as a more uncontrollable place, difficult to plough and therefore to conquer. This change in appearance preludes Mother Ireland's imminent transformation. Maintaining the associative pattern of fertility between land and women, the mythological woman in 'Mother Ireland' is going to resurge with the aid of a seed:

> I did not see.
> > I was seen,
>
> Night and day
> > words fell on me.
> > > Seeds. Raindrops.
>
> Chips of frost.
> > From one of them
> > > I learned my name.
> > > > I rose up. I remembered it.
>
> Now I could tell my story.
> > It was different
>
> from the story told about me. (Boland, 1998, p. 39)

The seeds falling upon Mother Ireland enable her to achieve transformation. They represent the source of the beginning of life, the germ of a new female identity. Learning her own name implies gaining insight into what constitutes her own female identity. Remembering her name, on the other hand, involves re-asserting her own female self. Thus, we are witnessing the female process which all literary women artists, according to Gilbert and Gubar (2000, p. 17), follow: self-definition is achieved when Mother Ireland learns her name, what the 'I' means; self-assertion is attained when she remembers her identity, and positively declares her creative 'I AM'. The act of rising up signifies a reaction against her earlier imposed self, her static and inert status. In her elevation, she awakens and comes to the recognition of her female reality, and more importantly, her female potential:

>   I could see the wound I had left
> in the land by leaving it.
>   I travelled west.
>   Once there
> I looked with so much love
>   at every field
> as it unfolded
>   its rusted wheel and its pram chassis
>   and at the gorse-bright distances
>   I had been
>   that they misunderstood me.
>   *Come back to us*
> they said.
>   *Trust me* I whispered. (Boland, 1998, p. 39)

Mother Ireland's potential for change and confidence in her speech parallels her emigration from Ireland. By removing her position and travelling to other places, Boland implies that cultural identity must not be exclusive (of a particular single place), but plural. Postcolonial theorists such as Bhabha (1995, p. 209) and Said (1994, p. 284) believe that postcolonial agency is achieved by (spiritual and/or physical) emigration. This stance is well summarized by Boyce Davies in her 1994 study on the construction of the female subject through black women's literary and cultural texts. As she has it, black female subjectivity 'asserts agency as its crosses the borders, journeys, migrates, and so re-claims as it re-asserts' (Boyce Davies, 1994, p. 37). In 'Mother Ireland', the speaker only 're-claims' and 're-asserts' herself, as she argues, by 'leaving' Ireland and 'travell[ing] west'. She breaks the traditionally strictly-defined borders imposed by nationalism, in favour of a more open and fluid sense of Irish culture. Emigration involves accepting different settings, different speakers, which are equally suitable for defining (Irish) nationalism. Boland's new concept of nation recognises the need to move away from exclusive single points of view. Mother Ireland falls in love with this new landscape, its fields, vegetation, and ordinary objects. It is in this alien setting where she achieves a sense of belonging as an Irish woman. As Kearney argues 'it is often by journeying beyond the frontiers of Ireland – either physically or imaginatively – that we find a new desire to return and discover what is most valuable in it. Ireland has nothing to fear from exposure to alien cultures. It is often the migrational detour through other intellectual landscapes which enables us to better appreciate our own traditions' (Kearney, 1988, p. 25).

Like Kearney, Boland implies that grounding oneself in a new place is both possible and positive, for it allows the subject to adopt a more critical attitude towards hegemonic ideals. By retaining this national icon, the woman poet does not ultimately reject nationalism, but establishes a dialogue with it. On the other hand, by recurring to exile, the woman poet enhances her intention to formulate a workable idea of nationalism, as a more inclusive and fluid ideology. In this sense, Boland lays claim to a new understanding of what it means to be Irish: for this poet, Irishness is a category that is beyond national boundaries. As Gray Martin points out, 'Boland's idea of nation accommodates difference and in so doing at once deconstructs, and some would say, feminises, previously held hegemonic and exclusionary ideas of nation' (Gray Martin, 2000, p. 288).

Nevertheless, not all critics are quite so positive about Boland's treatment of the idea of the nation. Edna Longley for instance, objects to the poet's use of the concept of nationalism, especially to her use of the image of the Achill woman (which Boland employs in both her poetry and prose), asserting that 'her alternative Muse turns out to be the twin sister of Dark Rosaleen ... Boland's new Muse, supposedly based on the varied historical experience of Irish women, looks remarkably like the Sean Bhean Bhocht. By not questioning the nation, Boland recycles the literary cliché from which she desires to escape' (Longley, 1994, p. 188). (Accusations such as this have been sharply repudiated by Ní Dhomhnaill (1992, pp. 27-28), who, raising her voice in Boland's defence, argues that this female poet 'is dead right to engage polemically' with the image of Mother Ireland). What Longley is really reacting against is Boland's reliance on certain traditional concepts. Whereas Boland wants to articulate a workable nationalism for women (as a poet she needs a sense of connection and belonging to a nation), Longley wants to replace nationalism 'with issues of culture and politics' (Gray Martin, 2000, p. 288). She suggests that the debate of what constitutes Irishness must be dropped from Ireland's cultural and political discourse: 'I think that "Irishness", with its totalitarian tinge, ought to be abandoned rather than made more inclusive' (Longley, 1994, p. 179). Nevertheless, as critical as Longley is of Boland's stance on nationalism, she seems to coincide with Boland when defending an open, fluid sense of Irish cultural identity, one that avoids binarism and exclusion. In June 1974, at the time of writing the poems in *The War Horse* (1975), Boland published an essay in the *Irish Times* entitled 'The Weasel's Tooth'. This essay expressed her belief in the fallacy of the Yeatsian vision of cultural unity, because, as she explains:

> There is, and at last I recognise it, no unity whatsoever in this culture of ours. And even more important, I recognise that there is no need whatsoever for such a unity. If we search for it we will, at a crucial moment, be mutilating with fantasy once again the very force we should be liberating with reality. (Boland, 1974, p. 56)

In her poetry, Boland suggests that cultural unity is not possible in an Irish culture characterised by fragmentation and disunity. Concluding her essay 'From Cathleen to Anorexia: the Breakdown of Irelands', Longley makes the following argument:

> It would be preferable to downgrade nationalism to the ignoble status traditionally enjoyed by Unionism …. The image of the web is female, feminist, connective – as constrasted with male polarisation. So is the ability to inhabit a range of relations rather than a single allegiance …. [Yet] to admit more varied, mixed, fluid, and relational kinds of identity would advance nobody's territorial claim. It would undermine cultural defences. It would subvert the male pride that keeps up the double frontier-siege. All this would be on the side of life. (Longley, 1994, p. 195)

Boland's poetry reflects Longley's sense of cultural identity. As we have seen in 'Mise Eire' and 'Mother Ireland', Boland rejects traditional exclusivism, for 'more varied, mixed, fluid, and relational kinds of identity'. She defends a complex Irish identity, one which encompasses the different experiences of women's lives. Thus, both women treat the idea of Irish culture as pluralistic. The difference lies in their approach to nationalism: whereas Longley sees nationalism as harmful, Boland wants to formulate a new understanding of it. As an Irish poet, she needs a sense of connection with her past, and this involves establishing a dialogue with the idea of the nation. In this sense, Boland's stance is in-between that 'post-nationalism' and 'post-colonialism' that Graham (1994) identifies. Her position is, to borrow Graham's terminology, one that still places 'ultimate importance on the nation as the cultural dynamic of colonialism/post-colonialism; but it stops celebrating the nation and seeks to demystify the "pathos of authenticity" which the nation demands' (Graham, 1995/6, p. 35).

Establishing a new relationship between women and nation is at the core of Eavan Boland's poetry. As we have observed in 'Mise Eire' and 'Mother Ireland', the traditional national icon breaks free of the conventional text and becomes the author of her own statements. In both cases, Boland does not ultimately reject nationalism; she looks instead for a different relationship with the past and with Irish identity. The conventional relation between gender and nation is not discarded, but reworked in order to open new perspectives for the Irish poem. Boland's search for cultural identity is, in this sense, in-between that 'post-nationalism' and 'post-colonialism'. Even though she attempts to construct a suitable and stable sense of national identity, she succeeds in moving away from defending her Irish identity in essentialist and exclusive terms.

In this sense, Boland's poetry exemplifies the modernist/postmodernist debate that pervades much postcolonial writing. On the one hand, her emancipatory force is grounded precisely in her reconceptualisation of nationality, and her desire to preserve, rather than reject, modernist categories such as 'Irishness'. On the other hand, she tries to transcend the essentialist constraints of a dogmatic nationalism by challenging the fixity of categories and envisaging new forms of resistance that overcome

Western binary thought. In this sense, Boland occupies a liminal stance, an interstitial location 'in-between' her need to find a stable 'sense of place' that counteracts her historical and cultural uprootedness, and her desire to celebrate a cross-cultural form of Irishness, one that surpasses all sorts of geographical boundaries. Her remarkable achievement as a poet lies in her ability to stretch, by constant negotiations and re-appropriations, the borderlines of inherited definitions of nationality and femininity.

Notes

[1] See Kearney's (1988, p. 17) call for a 'post-nationalist network of communities, where national identities may live on where they belong – in languages, sports, arts, customs, memories, and myths – while simultaneously fostering the expression of minority and regional cultures within each nation'.

[2] The stance that Boland adopts in her work can be categorised as 'anti-anti-essentialism', a term Aidan Arrowsmith (2000. p. 69) borrows from Paul Gilroy's (1993) study of black and Jewish diasporic identities. Arrowsmith (2000, p. 66) maintains that some contemporary Irish women writers are, nowadays, particularly interested in exploring the ways they can position themselves beyond the constraints of essentialism of a dogmatic nationalism, and 'the nihilism of anti-essentialism'" This critic gives the example of Anne Devlin's 1994 play *After Easter* See pp. 143-155 below, in which the protagonist Greta is ultimately unable to identify complacently with the opposing ideological positions of her two sisters ('the dogmatic certainty of Aoife's nationalism' and the postmodern uncertainty of Helen's internationalism').

[3] See, for instance, poems such as 'The Achill Woman', 'Outside History', and 'We are Always too Late', where Boland explores the movement from an apparent ability to connect with the Irish past to the ultimate impossibility of so doing (*Outside History*, 1990, pp. 27-28, 43-44, 45).

References

Arrowsmith, A. (2000), 'Inside-Out: Literature, Cultural Identity and Irish Migration to England', in *Comparing Postcolonial Literatures: Dislocations*, ed. A Bery and P. Murray, Macmillan Press, London, pp. 59-69.

Atfield, R. (1997), 'Postcolonialism in the Poetry and Essays of Eavan Boland', *Women: A Cultural Review*, 8 (2), pp. 168-182.

Bhabha, H. (1995), *The Location of Culture*, Routledge, London, New York.

Boehmer, E. (1995), *Colonial and Postcolonial Literature: Migrant Metaphors*, Oxford University Press, Oxford.

Boland, E. (1974), 'The Weasel's Tooth', *Irish Times*, 7 June, pp. 56-57.

Boland, E. (1975), *The War Horse*, Arlen House, Dublin.

Boland, E. (1987), *The Journey and Other Poems*, Carcanet Press, Manchester.

Boland, E. (1990), *Outside History*, Carcanet Press, Manchester.

Boland, E. (1996), *Object Lessons: The Life of the Woman and the Poet in Our Time*, Vintage, London.

Boland, E. (1998), *The Lost Land*, Carcanet Press, Manchester.

Boyce Davies, C. (1994), *Black Women, Writing and Identity: Migrations of the Subject*, Routledge, London and New York.

Fogarty, A. (1994), '"A Noise of Myth": Speaking (as) Woman in the Poetry of Eavan Boland and Medbh McGuckian', *Paragraph*, 15 (1), pp. 92-102.

Fogarty, A. (1999), '"The Influence of Absences": Eavan Boland and the Silenced History of Irish Women's Poetry', *Colby Quarterly*, 35, (4), pp. 256-274.

Fulford, S. (2002), 'Eavan Boland: Forging a Postcolonial Herstory', in *Irish and Postcolonial Writing: History, Theory, Practice*, ed. G. Hooper and C. Graham, Palgrave Macmillan, London, pp. 202-221.

Gilbert, S. M. and Gubar, S. (2000), *The Madwoman in the Attic: the Woman Writer and the Nineteenth-Century Literary Imagination*, Yale University Press, London.

Gilroy, P. (1993), 'The Black Atlantic: Modernity and Double Consciousness', Verso, London.

Graham, C. (1994), 'Post-Nationalism/Post-Colonialism: Reading Irish Culture', *Irish Studies Review*, 8, pp. 35-37.

Graham, C. (1995/1996), 'Rejoinder: the Irish "Post-"? A Reply to Gerry Smyth', *Irish Studies Review*, 13, pp. 33-36.

Gray Martin, K. (2000), 'The Attic LIPs: Feminist Pamphleteering for the New Ireland', in Kirkpatrick, K. (ed.), *Border Crossings: Irish Women Writers and National Identities*, Wolfhound Press, Dublin, pp. 269-298.

Hall, S. (1990), 'Cultural Identity and Diaspora', in *Identity: Community, Culture, Difference*, ed. J. Rutherford, Lawrence & Wishart, London, pp. 222-237.

Kearney, R. (1985), 'Myth and Motherland', in *Ireland's Field Day*, ed. S. Deane, Field Day Theatre Company, Derry, pp. 61-88.

Kearney, R. (1988), 'Thinking Otherwise', in *Across the Frontiers: Ireland in the 1990s*, ed. R. Kearney, Wolfhound Press, Dublin, pp. 7-29.

Kiberd, D. (1996), *Inventing Ireland: The Literature of the Modern Nation*, Vintage, London.

Longley, E. (1994), 'From Cathleen to Anorexia: The Breakdown of Irelands', in *The Living Stream: Literature and Revisionism in Ireland*, ed. E. Longley, Bloodaxe, Newcastle upon Tyne, pp. 173-195.

Meaney, G. (1993), 'Myth, History and the Politics of Subjectivity: Eavan Boland and Irish Women's Writing', *Women: A Cultural Review*, 4, (2), pp. 136-153.

Mohanty, C. T. (1991), 'Introduction: Cartographies of Struggle', in *Third World Women and the Politics of Feminism*, ed. C. T. Mohanty *et al*, Indiana University Press, Indianapolis IL. pp. 1-47.

Ní Dhomhnaill, N. (1992), 'What Foremothers?', *Poetry Ireland Review*, 36, pp. 18-31.

Said, E. (1994), *Culture and Imperialism*, Vintage, London.

Spivak, G. C. (1993), *Outside in the Teaching Machine*, Routledge, London, New York.

Villar Argáiz, P. (2006), '"The Text of It": A Conversation with Eavan Boland', *New Hibernia Review/ Irish Éireannach Nua: A Quarterly Record of Irish Studies*, 10 (2), pp. 52-67.

Wilson, R. E. (1990), 'Eavan Boland', in *Sleeping with Monsters: Conversations with Scottish and Irish Women Poets*, ed. G. Somerville-Arjat and E. Wilson, Polygon, Edinburgh, pp. 79-90.

Inimitable Ordinariness: Writing Ireland in John Banville's *The Newton Letter*

Monica Facchinello
University of York

I

John Banville's *The Newton Letter* (1982) is a strange kind of epistle, written in an unnamed arctic place by an anonymous Irish historian to a female recipient he ambiguously refers to as both 'Clio', the name of the Muse of History, and 'Cliona', a traditional name in Ireland. Echoing Hugo von Hofmannsthal's *Ein Brief* (1902), known in English as *The Lord Chandos Letter*, from which Banville directly quotes, *The Newton Letter* opens as an attempt to explain a recent state of disquiet and a crisis of writing: 'Words fail me, Clio' (Banville, 2002, p. 1). The historian tells his friend of how, after he moved down from Dublin to Ferns in County Wexford early the previous summer planning to complete his ongoing project – a historical biography of the scientist Isaac Newton – he found himself unable to pursue his work. Banville's protagonist, who, like the novelist, 'was born down there, in the south', rented a gate lodge owned by the Lawlesses, a curious family who live in the nearby big house called 'Fern House'. As triggers of his crisis, he indicates two main factors, a sudden 'morbid fascination' for Newton's own 'breakdown' in 1693 and the uncanny and enigmatic setting at Ferns. As the narrative unfolds, *The Newton Letter* is principally an account of the summer the protagonist spent in company with the Lawlesses.

Hofmannsthal scholars have generally treated *The Lord Chandos Letter* as a personal document and a statement of the writer's own crisis about language (Schultz, 1961). In his introduction to a recent edition of *The Lord Chandos Letter*, Banville also points out that the Viennese writer, 'after *Ein Brief*, abandoned poetry for the drama' (Banville, 2005, p. viii). More than one detail in *The Newton Letter*, the narrator's anonymity, his geographical origins and above all the closing signature 'Dublin-Iowa-Dublin/ Summer 1979 – Spring 1981', which is clearly not the historian's but Banville's, justify the temptation to read the novella in similar terms. Like Hofmannsthal's prose fiction, *The Newton Letter* was also written in a stage of transition in Banville's artistic life. It signals a deviation in the novelist's original project of four 'historical' fictions, which was to include a book on Newton and one on Einstein in addition to *Doctor Copernicus* (1976) and *Kepler* (1981). As the correspondence between the publishers and the writer suggests, the change of plan was partly dictated by the poor sales of *Doctor Copernicus* [1]. More importantly, the novella stages Banville's return 'home' especially after the partial historical and geographical 'exile' of *Doctor Copernicus* and *Kepler*. The contemporary Irish setting of the novella also takes the writer back to the question about writing Ireland, which had haunted his fiction since his parodic Big House novel *Birchwood* (1973). It is not my intention to suggest that *The Newton Letter* be read as the account of a personal experience; like Hofmannsthal, Banville would not approve of viewing a work of art mainly as a personal testimony of the artist. However, it is significant that the historian's personal struggle in many ways reflects the writer's own, and that it is born out of and conducted at a specific time when the urge was felt, especially among revisionist historians, to question and re-examine consolidated images and myths. I will suggest that *The Newton Letter*, which is also a story about crisis and re-birth, stages the start of a new aesthetics in Banville's fiction. The writer's response to the question of writing Ireland is not only to explode traditional narratives of the nation in Irish writing, as the narratives in *Birchwood*, *Doctor Copernicus* and *Kepler* do, but to avoid inadvertently replacing old myths with new ones. In the novella any attempt to reproduce a truthful picture of its contemporary Irish setting is doomed to fail. Failure, which determines the overall satirical tone of the book, constitutes a central ingredient of Banville's new aesthetics.

The terms of the narrator's crisis reach far, for he fails as historian, writer and man. Early in the text he thanks his friend Cliona for sending him a copy of the latest biography of Newton by the fictional stereotypical academic historian Popov; the gift was meant to encourage the narrator to finish and publish his book. In fact, for Banville's historian Popov's book only provides another example of a narrative mode he is no longer comfortable with. He points out that, although the biographer opens with the disclaimer, '*Before the phenomenon of Isaac Newton, the historian, like Freud when he came to contemplate Leonardo, can only shake his head and retire with as much good grace as he can master*', he then proceeds to forge yet another all-defining, coherent portrait of the scientist conforming to the mode of conventional historical biography. Even when the biographer is aware of the enigmatic nature of his subject, the fixed order of historical narrative ultimately prevails, as the narrator effectively puts it: 'Then out come the syringe and the formalin'. The narrator's dissatisfaction relates particularly to the heroic narrative of scientific discovery, 'this Popovian Newton-as-the-greatest-scientist-the-world-has-known', which 'now makes [him] feel slightly sick'. At the realisation that his book too is 'a celebration of action, of the scientist as hero, a gleeful acceptance of Pandora's fearful disclosures, wishy-washy medievalism kicked out and the age of reason restored', he feels compelled to abandon his project.

Banville's 2002 review of the recent biography of Newton by Patricia Fara, *Newton: The Making of the Genius* (Banville, 2002), published in the *Irish Times*, sheds more light on the nature of the historian's crisis. In the review, the novelist points to instances of idolisation of the scientist in past biographical accounts. Newton, for example, fulfilled the need of Enlightenment for 'earthly saints' with whom to replace 'heavenly agents' in human affairs. Fara herself reflects on the need of the Empire, Banville notices, 'to identify certain singular, great men who would be both imperial symbols and icons of the state'. Even the word 'science' commonly applied to Newton is inaccurate, as Banville writes: 'Before the 19th century and the development of industrial technology, what we call science was known as "natural philosophy," and was engaged in not by professionals but by gifted, frequently wealthy amateurs' (Banville, 2002). It is no coincidence that historians who had set out to forge the myth of the scientist often ignored Newton's biblical studies and practice of alchemy, activities which, as Banville's narrator points out, 'so [embarrass] his biographers (cf. Popov *et al.*)'. The narrator of *The Newton Letter* refers to the historical biographer as an embalmer, a category from which he is now eager to dissociate himself: 'only I *did* have the grace to pop off before the deathshead grin was properly fixed'; and later in the narrative we read: 'I'm not a historian anymore'.

The reaction of Banville's historian to the narrative mode of scientific mythography visibly bears upon the contemporary debate over Revisionism in Ireland. He is after all a historian based in Dublin, writing in the early 1980s, and shares with Irish revisionist historians a similar dissatisfaction with established historical narratives and idealisation of supposedly emblematic individuals. In his article '"The Great Enchantment": Uses and Abuses of Modern Irish History', Ronan Fanning identified as a chief characteristic of modern Irish historiography its 'continuous compulsion to confront myth and mythology' (Fanning, 1999). Roy Foster and others have argued that, since the early nineteenth century, side by side with the growth of Irish nationalism, Irish historiography developed the idea of the history of Ireland as a particular 'story', conforming to the narrative conventions of the story form, with heroes and villains, a recognisable plot and intended outcomes (Foster, 2001). Not only does Banville's protagonist share the uneasy accommodation of Irish revisionist historians within the house of traditional Irish historical narrative, but he also takes on a clear revisionist stance, which, significantly, informs not so much his Newton biography but his account of the contemporary Irish setting at Ferns. Over the period of his stay, as he comes closer to the people, objects and landscapes there, he finds himself questioning a number of accepted versions of Irish society.

II

Within the novella's intricate web of coincidences and intertextual allusions, the historian's loss of faith in historical narrative and temporary abandonment of his project is directly linked to Newton's crisis – 'Newton himself, I believe, saw something of the matter in that strange summer of 1693' – and indirectly to Lord Chandos's. According to Banville's narrator, Newton's breakdown after the disastrous conflagration in 1693 was not caused by the loss of his work but by the realisation of the limits of the scientific medium in the investigation of reality:

The joke is, it's not the loss of the precious papers that will drive him temporarily crazy, but the simple fact that *it doesn't matter*. It might be his life's work gone, the *Principia* itself, the *Opticks*, the whole bang lot, and still it wouldn't mean a thing. Tears springs from his eyes …. Someone beats out the flame. Someone asks what has been lost. Newton's mouth opens and a word like a stone falls out: *Nothing*. He notices details, early morning light through a window, his rescuer's one unshod foot and yellow toenails, the velvet blackness of burnt paper. He smiles.

…

It needed no candle flame, it was already ashes. Why else had he turned to deciphering Genesis and dabbling in alchemy? (Banville, 1982, p. 27)

Like Lord Chandos, [2] Banville's Newton finds an escape among commonplace things – 'He notices details'. The narrator's interest similarly moves from his scholarly project to the unknown but familiar surroundings in Ferns. From the beginning he is not indifferent to the landscape: 'Time is different in the country', he notices. Walking '[a]mid those sunlit scenes', he feels detached: 'Even the pages of my manuscript had an unfamiliar look'. With the help of a guidebook he sets out to identify local trees and birds, but the illustrations 'would not match up with the real specimen before [him]'. He is increasingly attracted by the small community in the nearby big house, Edward and Charlotte Lawless, her niece Ottilie and a young silent boy, Michael, and finds himself spying on them: 'I would see Charlotte herself, in wellingtons and an old cardigan, hauling out a bucket of feed to the henhouse. Next comes Ottilie, in a sleepy trance, with the child by the hand'. From being a passive, acute observer he gradually starts interacting with them; he meets Charlotte in the garden and is invited to join them for dinner by Edward. He also becomes involved in a lustful sexual relationship with Ottilie: 'It's strange to be offered, without conditions, a body you don't really want' (Banville, 1982, p. 30).

His venture among the living, however, is no more successful than his biographical study of the long-dead scientist or his attempts at naming the local fauna. Observations and conversations, he is keen to tell Cliona, repeatedly led him to make assumptions about the lives of the inhabitants of the big house which would later be proved wrong. Most of his assumptions are visibly informed by the narrative of Irish literary tradition, with which the historian appears strikingly familiar. The text of the letter is everywhere punctuated with emblems and echoes from the works of major Irish writers. The chestnut tree in the house yard is referred to as 'that great rooted blossomer' as in Yeats's poem 'Among School Children'. In 'the ruins of a tennis court' and 'I might have written to you last September', we hear direct allusions to Elizabeth Bowen. This is to name only a few examples. Banville's narrator is clearly a writer and his early assumptions show an inclination to impose on Fern House and its inhabitants the conventions of both pastoral literature and the Irish Big House novel. His comment at the spectacle of the Lawlesses' morning routine is one example: 'It all has the air of a pastoral mime, with the shepherd's wife and the shepherd, and

Cupid and the maid, and scribbling with a crystal cave, myself, a haggard-eyed Damon'. A paragraph later, he tells his friend of how he 'had them spotted for patricians from the start':

> The big house, Edward's tweeds, Charlotte's fine-boned slender grace that the dowdiest of clothes could not mask, even Ottilie's awkwardness, all seemed the unmistakable stamp of their class. Protestants, of course, landed, the land gone now to gombeen men, and compulsory purchase, the family fortune wasted by tax, death duties, inflation. (Banville, 1982, p. 14-15)

On his first visit to the house, he sees Charlotte as the long-suffering wife and Edward the stereotypical 'waster,' always searching for new alibis 'for his drinking'. He remembers feeling sympathetic towards Charlotte and wishing he could 'let her know [he] understood everything' (Banville, 1982, p. 22).

Another series of assumptions derive from the narrator's, or rather the novelist's personal myths. A product, like Banville, 'of a post-peasant Catholic upbringing', the narrator is attracted by the Lawlesses' enduring 'style' and 'pure refinement' despite the loss of their supposed past comfort. On more than one occasion Banville has recalled his juvenile attraction to southern Ascendancy families. In his review of *Independent Spirit* (Banville, 1997) by the 'quintessential European' as well as 'Anglo-Irish Nationalist', Hubert Butler, for example, Banville recalls the strict social divide in 1950s and 1960s Ireland between Protestants and Catholics and his secret fascination for his '"separated brethren:"' '[W]hat splendid specimens they seemed to me, these brisk, equine ladies in their flowered frocks, and kindly-eyed gentlemen in brogues and "good" but threadbare tweeds, languidly celebrating their annual *fête galante*'. He remembers 'imagin[ing] them, at day's end, bumping in their shooting-brakes up the long avenues to their ivy-covered, many-windowed mansions, where already the servants – kinsmen and kinswomen of my parents – were lighting the candles and setting out the canopied dishes for dinner'. Likewise, the narrator promptly imagines the Lawlesses on their way to 'church,' rather than 'Mass', and Charlotte's Sunday meal not as the 'dinner' of his childhood in a Catholic family, but a 'light lunch'.

Soon, however, he is confronted with the fact that the Lawlesses, as the name suggests, will not fit in the overall image he has conjured for them. He encounters Charlotte in the greenhouse and calls her 'an enthusiastic gardener', but is told that that is her job and the family's main source of financial sustenance: '"It's how we make our living," she said'. On his first visit to Fern House for dinner, he is surprised at discovering that the meal is consumed in a 'big whitewashed kitchen' instead of the 'gaunt dining room' he had expected. And in place of 'linen napkins with faded initial, a bit of old silver negligently laid', there is a plastic tablecloth. When he wrongly refers to Michael as Charlotte's son, he can no longer hide his embarrassment. He feels inadequate and out of place, and the heir of a literary tradition and traditional narrative mode which repeatedly prove inapt tools when applied to the present, ever elusive reality at Ferns: 'at my back that great rooted blossomer, before me the insistent enigma of other people'. Although his immediate reaction is to leave, it is the prospect of something for him to learn that holds him back: 'Some large lesson seemed laid out here for me'.

If *The Newton Letter* calls into question the validity of a number of literary stereotypes, it also exposes the distorting effects of personal feelings. The narrator's internal response to each individual in Fern House – sympathy or aversion, curiosity or indifference – has a bearing on his imaginary portraits of them. As he loses interest in Ottilie and falls in love with Charlotte, for example, the hard-of-hearing middle-aged woman is transformed into a Yeatsian 'gazelle': 'I stopped to watch her, the dark glossy head, the pale neck, and those hands … Light of evening, the tall windows – Oh, a gazelle!' Pondering the mysterious family relations between the Lawlesses, he becomes more suspicious toward Edward and pictures him as a Maturinian usurper – '[I] tried to imagine Edward here, younger, less besotted, watching the old man, Charlotte's father, waiting for him to die, planting his claim to Ferns by seducing the daughter'. He goes as far as to imagine him as a sexual predator, taking advantage of a sixteen-year-old Ottilie, and to picture Michael as Edward's illicit son. In fact, Ottilie finally tells him that Charlotte's silence and her attractive aloofness are the effects of the modern drugs she is treated with: 'Valium, seconal, I don't know, some dope like that'. And it is only on his train journey away from Ferns that the narrator discovers that Edward's poor physical condition is not caused by drinking but by a terminal cancer: 'He has it in the gut, I believe'. Until the end of his visit, Banville's narrator is blind to the commonplace tragedies in the lives of the Lawlesses, as he confesses:

> I wish I could have erected a better monument to him [Edward] than I have done, in these too many pages; but I had to show you how I thought of him *then*, how I behaved, so that you would see the cruelty of it, the wilful blindness. (Banville, 1982, p. 96)

In this confession we glimpse a new understanding of the potential destructive power of narrative, not only of historical or literary narrative, but of any narrative. The narrator's failure now is one with which anyone can feel somehow familiar.

Throughout the text of the novella Banville also challenges other sets of stereotypical representations of Irish society, such as the perceived intellectual divide between forward-looking, urban Dublin and retrograde, rural Ferns, often referred to in literary criticism as the opposition between the city and the country (Smyth, 1997). Banville's novella foregrounds prejudices on both sides. Edward, who ignores the narrator's crisis and rural origins, takes on an unnecessary defensive stance while discussing the ongoing debate over the country's neutrality: 'Yes, tell us now', he provocatively asks, 'tell us what you think, I'm very interested, we're all very interested, aren't we all very interested? A man like you knows all about these things … Down here of course we haven't a clue. Crowd of bog-trotters!' (Banville, 1982, p. 21) On the other hand, the representative of intellectual Dublin is a man who sees his knowledge repeatedly questioned by the ordinary people in Fern House: 'Know that word?';

'You don't know anything. You think you are so clever, but you don't know a thing'; and 'didn't you notice? …. You really didn't know … all this time, did you' (Banville, 1982, pp. 40, 68, 88). The Lawlesses, who leave the narrator's nostalgia for the pastoral myth unsatisfied, finally lead him to probe his own image of himself: 'What did I know?' he asks. The narrative registers a change in the attitude of Banville's protagonist, as he points out that he learned new and 'oddest things' in Ferns. Edward teaches him the word 'succubus', for example, and Ottilie tells him that terminal cancer patients are treated with 'morphine cocktail[s]'; from Charlotte he learns '[w]hy a ha-ha is so called' and that 'Finland was the first European country to give women the vote' (Banville, 1982, pp. 34, 40, 54). The Lawlesses are no idyllic family, or retrograde community, but ordinary, present-day people, with complex histories of modern kind.

References to real, contemporary social debates in Ireland, such as over the country's neutrality and the plan for a new power station in Carnsore, and recent episodes of violence further situate Ferns in the present and in relation to the country as a whole, while setting another trap for the discombobulated narrator. We are told of his presence at Michael's birthday party at the end of July and his encounter with the Mittlers, relatives of the family, named, like Edward, Charlotte and Ottilie, after the protagonists of Goethe's *Elective Affinities*. When Edward's sister Bunny suggests toasting 'August the twenty-seven', he immediately assumes it must be 'Mountbatten' she is referring to – the murder of Lord Louis Mountbatten alongside two young boys and a relative by an IRA bomb planted on his boat in County Sligo:

> 'Mountbatten?' I said. One of their dwindling band of heroes, cruelly murdered. I was charmed: only *they* would dare to make a memorial of a drawing-room tea party. 'Terrible thing, terrible'. (Banville, 1982, p. 44)

To the narrator's disbelief, Bunny points out that in fact she meant Warrenpoint, where eighteen British soldiers were killed by Provisional IRA land mines in County Down on the same day [3]. The oddly sinister woman whom he first could only see as a unionist, suddenly reveals herself a fierce nationalist, whom he quotes as proposing that a street should be named after 'the glorious twenty-seven'.

The narrator's account of his stay at Ferns is a comedy of misconceptions. Banville himself highlighted the novella's humorous potential: 'It is funny', he said in an interview, 'in that practically every sentence … has a misconception in it. The narrator has got something wrong in practically every remark that he makes. That seems to me comic' (Banville, 2000). Unlike the crude mishearings and mistaken identities of the traditional comedy of errors, in Banville's novella misconceptions are shown as arising for significant reasons. The narrator's erroneous interpretation of the ambiguous 'August the twenty-seven' leads to a manifestation of the grim reality of the violence often hidden behind the legitimating screen of the nationalist cause. 'It's dead men you are talking about', Edward reminds his sister, though to no avail. Banville's fierce nationalist character Bunny employs no euphemism: '"There is nothing wrong with this country … that a lot more corpses like that won't cure"', and '"Long live death!"' (Banville, 1982, p. 45) But most importantly, the narrator's repeated failing warns him against facile assumptions and compels him constantly to re-examine. His response at the discovery, eventually, that the Lawlesses are in fact Catholics certainly suggests so: 'Mass? They were *Catholics*? My entire conception of them had to be revised' (Banville, 1982, p. 64). He is urged to engage in constant revision in respect to each singular character in Fern House. As Ottilie recedes from him, for example, he realises that 'at first [he] had assumed that [he] understood her absolutely' and never considered asking questions that he now considers crucial, such as who Michael's parents are. He sets out to view the Lawlesses from new and different perspectives, yet without any better guarantee of success. He is keen to reveal to his friend Cliona, for example, that even at a late stage of his stay he was 'still misjudging' Ottilie. *The Newton Letter*, we may say, is a revisionist comedy, in which, for the Irish narrator who sets out to draw a picture of the new and familiar setting at Ferns, inevitable failure is a condition for success.

III

The Newton Letter stages the genesis of a new aesthetics in Banville's writing in which intense vividness figures side by side with inevitable epistemological failure. The narrator's loss of old certainties, which is registered in statements such as 'I am confused', 'I feel ridiculous and melodramatic, and comically exposed', and 'I am lost', is set alongside Newton's loss of scientific absolutes. According to Banville, although Newton was not a relativist, he knew well of the inexistence of the absolutes of time and space (Banville, 1981). Later in the novella the narrator returns to the scientist's crisis and more specifically to a second fictional epistle Newton addressed to John Locke in defence of the validity of the absolutes of space and time and motion, on which his system is founded. But Newton's letter, the narrator notices, betrays a hint of hesitation. The second Newton letter, which now lies 'at the centre of [the narrator's] work', is an adaptation of the section in Hofmannsthal's short prose in which Lord Chandos announces to Bacon his abandonment of writing:

> *My dear Doctor, expect no more philosophy from my pen. The language in which I might be able not only to write but to think is neither Latin nor English, but a language none of whose words is known to me; a language in which commonplace things speak to me; and wherein I may one day have to justify myself before an unknown judge.* Then comes that cold, that brave, that almost carven signature: *Newton.* (Banville, 1982, pp. 59-60)

As for Lord Chandos and the historian, Newton's intellectual crisis hinges on a crisis of language. If for Lord Chandos and Newton failure leads to renunciation, for the narrator of *The Newton Letter*, and for Banville, it paves the way to a new beginning.

In the novella failure is associated with achievement on more than one level. The narrator's loss of old certainties, for example, is made to coincide with the start of his deeply felt passion for Charlotte. In a scene in which six characters interact simultaneously in three groups of two and Charlotte and the narrator are temporarily isolated from the rest, the narrator's account to Charlotte of Newton's discovery of post-Einstein relativity leads to a climactic moment:

> 'Because [Newton] had to have certain absolutes', I said, look at me, keep looking at me, 'certain absolutes of of of, of space, time, motion, to found his theories on. But space and time and motion', beats, soft beats, soft heartbeats, 'can only be relative, for us, he knew that, had to admit it, had to let them go, and when they went', O my darling, 'everything else went with them'. Ah! (Banville, 1982, pp. 74-5)

Charlotte's intense looking as he tells her about Newton's crisis sexually arouses the besotted narrator – 'My lap was damp', he notices. This is probably the closest he can get sexually to her, as a married woman receiving psychological treatment.

In another sense failure becomes achievement in the way the narrator turns the loss of absolutes itself into the equivalent of an absolute in his narrative. Halfway through the novella, previous myth-loaded accounts of Charlotte are replaced by a series of failed pictures, which the narrator refers to as successful endeavours. The images of Charlotte in his memory, for example, are 'creased black-and-white snaps taken in a bad light, with a lop-sided horizon,' in the best of which 'Charlotte', he says, 'is not present at all, someone jogged my elbow, or the film was faulty'. And yet, he concludes, '[h]er absence throbs in these views more powerfully, more poignantly than any presence'. The only possible picture for the narrator, and for Banville, is one which vividly captures its subject while it exposes its failure to capture it in its singular essence. Such failure is determined by the limits of language and the distorting effects of the viewer's several lenses (inherited stereotypes and personal feelings) in equal measure, as the narrator experiences in his attempt to portray Charlotte in words:

> When I search for the words to describe her I can't find them. Such words don't exist. They would need to be no more than forms of intent, balanced on the brink of saying, another version of silence. Every mention I make of her is a failure. Even when I say just her name it sounds like an exaggeration. When I write it down it seems impossibly swollen, as if my pen had slipped eight or nine redundant letters into it. Her physical presence itself seemed overdone, a clumsy representation of the essential she. That essence was only to be glimpsed obliquely, on the outer edge of vision, an image always there and always fleeting, like the afterglow of a bright light on the retina. (Banville, 1982, p. 52)

Thus intended, imperfect representation in *The Newton Letter* is a success in that it excludes the assumption of a final picture of its subject, and fends off the risk of creating new stereotypes. In the place of the Newtonian universe of objective time-and-place, gravity and scientific laws, the narrator embraces a world which is at once subjective and evanescent, contingent, individual and concrete.

Significantly, it is at this stage that the narrator discovers a new creative power. After his repeated misconceiving, he diverts his focus from the general to the particular and concentrates, like Chandos, on 'mute things': 'Two little heart-shaped polished patches rubbed on the inner sides of those wellingtons by her slightly knock-kneed walk. The subtle web of light and shade that played over her face through the slack straw of the brim of her hat'. He is surprised at his ability to conjure vivid images of Charlotte even in her absence:

> If she was never entirely present for me in the flesh, how could I make her to be there for me in the lodge, at night, in the fields on my solitary rambles? I must concentrate on things impassioned by her passing. Anything would do, her sun hat, a pair of muddied wellingtons standing play-footed at the back door. (Banville, 1982, p. 52)

He compares his power of concentration to 'the concentration of the painter intent on drawing the living image out of the potential of mere paint'. He now sees himself as an artist who does not so much represent reality but re-invents it: 'By the force of my unwavering meticulous attention [Charlotte] would rise on her scallop shell through the waves and *be*'. The allusion to Botticelli's *Birth of Venus* strengthens the underlying sense of a new start, especially in aesthetic terms, in the novella.

The aesthetic evolution enacted in *The Newton Letter* merges Hofmannsthal's 'modern' view of art and the artist with Beckett's 'fidelity to failure'. In an overall picture of his summer in Ferns at the end of his letter, the narrator describes himself as 'a man living underground who, coming up for air, is dazzled by the light and cannot find the way back into his bolt-hole'. Hofmannsthal's view of the artist is eloquently described in a fictional dialogue between Balzac and Hammer-Purgstall in which he has the French novelist liken the artist to a stoker who only occasionally leaves the confinement of the boiler room and comes outside on deck (Schultz, 1961). And yet, the artist does not have less experience than other human beings, because his work is his fateful experience and his life. If as a young man, the artist is ready to sacrifice the external world for his work, as an old man he will no longer have an eye for it: 'Das Leben! Die Welt! Die Welt ist in seiner Arbeit, und seine Arbeit ist sein Leben!' ('Life! The world! The world is in his work and his work is his life'). As a man confined to his underground bolt-hole, Banville's narrator resembles Hofmannsthal's image of the artist, or even 'all those high cold heroes who renounced the world and human happiness to pursue the big game of the intellect', the narrator writes, among whom he mentions 'Koppernigk in Frauenburg', 'Nietzsche in the Engadine', and 'Newton himself'. But after his stay in Ferns, unlike Hofmannsthal's artist, the narrator of *The Newton Letter* is not only unable but also unwilling to return to his underground retreat: 'What shall I do? Find that fissure in the rocks, clamber down again into that roomy and commodious grave? I hope not. Begin afresh, then learn how to live up here, in the light?' (Banville, 1982, p. 96). For Banville's artist the return to the abundance of the external world is a starting point in his creative process.

The place 'up here, in the light' also indicates the unnamed arctic setting the narrator moves to shortly after he returns to Dublin at the end of the summer and where he is now writing his letter. Along with the narrator's literary and social background and personal feelings, the dislocated setting of the narrating is another aspect whereby Banville manifests the inevitable inadequacy of narrative reconstruction of reality and resists any assumption of mimesis. Away from Ferns, the narrator is compelled to rely on memory in his ongoing account of his time with the Lawlesses; and memory, for Banville, is an incorrigibly unreliable tool. The novelist's response to the inadequacy of representation visibly bears upon Beckett's, and more specifically Beckett's 'fidelity to failure'. In *Three Dialogues*, we read:

> All that should concern us is the acute and increasing anxiety of the relation itself, as though shadowed more and more darkly by a sense of invalidity, of inadequacy, of existence at the expense of all that it excludes, all that it blinds to. The history of painting … is the history of its attempts to escape from this sense of failure, by means of more authentic, more ample, less exclusive relations between representer and representee, in a kind of tropism towards a light … My case is that van Velde is the first to desist from this aestheticised automatism, the first to admit that to be an artist is to fail as no other dare fail, that failure is his world. (Beckett, 1984, p. 145)

The narrator's definition of his present setting as 'up here, in the light' makes a direct allusion to Beckett's later prose *How It Is* (1964), a text which particularly exemplifies the 'acute anxiety' of the relation between representation and what it represents. (Another allusion to Beckett's prose is audible in the narrator's comment on the text of Newton's second 'strange' letter: 'something *is* expressed, understood, forgiven even, if not in the lines themselves then in the spaces between, where an extraordinary tension throbs'. *How It Is* has been read in similar terms [4]). In *How It Is* Beckett writes: 'it's the place without knowledge … that is above in the light'. While it suggests a departure from the confined position of Hofmannsthal's artist and the act of coming 'outside', which in Banville's case is a recognisable, local contemporary Irish world, the expression 'up here, in the light' also designates a Beckettian place. It is the setting of the writing, a writing that captures its subject vividly, while it constantly reminds the narrator and the reader, through specific narrative strategies and stylistic effects, that no true and definite picture of it is possible.

The exposure of various deforming lenses through which the narrator views Fern House and its people is one of these narrative strategies. As I showed previously, emblems, myths and personal feelings act as one such lens. Pondering his newly-discovered power of concentration, the narrator himself refers to love as a lens: 'Who would notice such things, that did not fix on her with the close-up lens of love?' Another agent of distortion is memory in the way it gathers its material, 'beady-eyed and voracious', as the narrator notices. He associates his memory to 'a demented photographer' looking through the lens of a faulty camera. But the narrator alerts us to the fact that anything could cause a sudden change of perspective. He remembers, for example, an afternoon when he is unknowingly taken by Ottilie into Charlotte's bedroom. On finding out whose bed he is lying on, his immediate discomfort triggers a violent reaction: 'I slapped her face'. The unexpected event, he notices, brings about a drastic change in the way he views Ottilie and other people in general: 'That afternoon was to contaminate everything,' he writes, 'I looked at the others with a new surmise, full of suspicions. They were altered ...' (Banville, 1982, p. 68). Lenses as agents of distortion increasingly enter the narratives of Banville's later novels, especially *The Untouchable*, *Eclipse* and *The Sea*, and inform in particular the narrators' accounts of their original Irish settings. Lenses, of course, are also associated with the universe of Newtonian Optics, but in Banville's novels they represent the specific subjectivity of his narrators' viewpoints, as they observe the familiar world around them.

The text of *The Newton Letter* visibly defies conventional narrative formulas. Like Banville's narrators, the failed historian openly warns us against attributing too much truth to his account. He writes: 'I told you she went immediately to sleep, but I lied'. His letter exceeds the conventional narrative modes of the epistolary form, such as standard opening and closing formulas. It opens *in medias res* and closes with two open questions, followed by, instead of the narrator's signature, Banville's: 'Dublin-Iowa-Dublin/ Summer 79 – Spring 81' (Banville, 1982, p. 97). While it largely conforms to the main conventions of the 'story' form – the past tense, a precise setting, a beginning, a middle and the sense of an ending –, by foregrounding its rules, it also undercuts their validity. So, for example, he refers to the chance encounter with another Fern character on his train journey back to Dublin, who discloses the truth of Edward's poor physical condition, a final 'tying up of loose ends' and a joke that life insists on playing upon him. Similarly, the narrator anticipates the conclusion by saying 'There's not much left to tell'. He refers to the news of Ottilie's pregnancy, which concludes his account of the Lawlesses, as 'the most banal ending of all'. If the narrator of *The Newton Letter* is wary of traditional formal devices of internal coherence, Banville finds alternative sources of formal unity in patterns of parallelism and repetition. The obvious correspondence between the scientist's crisis and the narrator's, which in turn alludes to Lord Chandos's, is one of many. The text of the novella switches between two narrative voices, the narrating 'I' and the narrated 'I', and two settings and times, an unnamed place and Ferns, the present and the past. Botticelli's painting, which appears in the first half of the narrative – '[Ottilie] brought prints clipped from glossy magazines and pinned them over the bed, film stars, Kneller's portrait of Newton, the *Primavera*' (Banville, 1982, p. 32) – returns in the allusion to *Birth of Venus* in the second half. This is only to mention some examples of internal parallelism in the novella.

The presence of real geographic places in Ireland – Ferns, Dublin, Carnsore *et al* – and the mentions of real contemporary concerns and events in Irish society – the country's neutrality and the bloodshed in Warrenpoint and County Sligo – side by side with characters' names and sections of text openly borrowed from international literature – mainly Goethe and Hofmannsthal – effectively presents Banville's novella as the novelist's return to a familiar Irish setting and at the same time an act of artistic re-invention. *The Newton Letter* is a vivid picture of a modern, ordinary Irish setting as seen by a certain man at a specific period of time, one that is alert to detail but that manifests its inability to penetrate the inimitable ordinariness of its subject. What is enacted in the novella is the acute struggle of a contemporary Irish writer torn between the urge to return to Ireland in writing and the awareness that most of the tools at his disposal – traditional narrative modes and literary emblems – are, for many reasons, no longer valid. 'These private showings seem an invitation', he writes at the end: 'Go back to Ferns, move in, set up house, fulfil some grand design, with Ottilie, poor Charlotte, the two boys – for I feel it will be a boy, it must be – become a nurseryman and wear tweeds, talk about the weather, stand around chewing a straw? Impossible'. The novella stages a new starting point in Banville's fiction not because it solves this struggle but because it establishes it as almost a modus operandi in the novelist's later novels. 'All the same, I *shall* go back', he goes on to say,

> And in the end, it's come to me just this moment, in the end of course I shall take up the book and finish it: such renunciation is not of this world. Yet, I'm wary. Shall I have to go off again, leaving my research, my book and everything unfinished? Shall I awake in a few months, in a few years, broken and deceived, in the midst of new ruins? (Banville, 1982, p. 79)

After *The Newton Letter*, almost all Banville's fictions stage returns to familiar Irish settings recounted by narrators 'wary', like the anonymous historian, of the kind of relativist knowledge embodied in the aesthetics of fiction.

Notes

[1] For the texts of the correspondence between the publishers, David Farrer and Tom Rosenthal, Banville's agent, Anthony Shiel, and Banville see Kersti Tarien, 'The Textual and Thematic Evolution of John Banville's Fiction'.

[2] 'A watering can, a harrow left in a field, a dog in the sun, a shabby churchyard, a cripple, a small farmhouse – any of these can become the vessel of my revelation. Any of these things and the thousand similar ones past which the eye ordinarily glides with natural indifference can at any moment – which I am completely unable to elicit – suddenly take on for me a sublime and moving aura which words seem to weak to describe' (Hofmannsthal, *1902*, p. 123).

[3] In his 1990 review of Denis Donoghue's autobiography *Warrenpoint*, Banville comments: 'A memorable day, then, even by Ireland's savage standards'.

[4] In her post-structuralist reading of the text, Eva Ziarek makes a similar observation in relation to the text's investment on the heterogeneity of discourse and alterity, in her words: 'Beckett's peculiar stylistic invention preserves the significance of otherness not in what is said but in a blank between the words' (Ziareck, 1996, p. 174).

References

Banville, J. (2000), in *Reading the Future: Irish Writers in Conversation with Mike Murphy*, ed. C. Ní Anluain, Lilliput Press, Dublin, pp. 23-41.

Banville, J. (2005), 'Introduction', *The Lord Chandos Letter and Other Writings*, by H. Hofmannsthal, pp. vii-xii.

Banville, J. (1981), 'My Readers, That Small Band, Deserve a Rest', *Irish University Review*, 11 (1), pp. 5-12.

Banville, J. (1990), 'Portrait of a Critic as a Young Man', review of *Warrenpoint* by D. Donoghue, *New York Review of Books*, 25 Oct., pp. 48-50.

Banville, J. (1997), 'The European Irishman', review of *Independent Spirit* by H. Butler, *New York Review of Books*, 12 June, pp. 38-41.

Banville, J. (2002), 'The Last of the Magicians', review of *Newton: The Making of the Genius* by P. Fara, *Irish Times*, 1 June, p. 9.

Banville, J. (1982, 1999), *The Newton Letter*, Picador, London.

Beckett, S. (1964), *How It Is*, Calder, London.

Beckett, S. (1984), 'Three Dialogues', in *Disjecta: Miscellaneous Writings and a Dramatic Fragment*, ed. R. Cohn, Grove Press, New York, pp. 138-145.

Fanning, R. (1999), '"The Great Enchantment": Uses and Abuses of Modern Irish History', in *Interpreting Irish History: the Debate on Historical Revisionism*, ed. C. Brady, Irish Academy Press, Portland, pp. 146-160.

Foster, R. F. (2001), *The Irish Story: Telling Tales and Making It Up in Ireland*, Penguin, London.

Hofmannsthal, H. (1959), 'Über Charaktere im Roman und Drama: Gespräch zwischen Balzac und Hammer-Purgstall in einem Döbliger Garten im Jahre 1842', in *Prosa II. Gesammelte Werke in Einzelausgaben*, ed. H. Steiner, Fischer, Frankfurt, pp. 32-47.

Hofmannsthal, H. (1902, 2005), *The Lord Chandos Letter and Other Writings*, trans. Joel Rotenberg, *New York Review of Books*, New York.

Schultz, S. (1961), 'Hofmannstahl and Bacon: The Sources of the Chandos Letter', *Comparative Literature*, 13 (1), pp. 1-15.

Tarien, K. (2002), 'The Textual and Thematic Evolution of John Banville's Fiction', unpublished D. Phil. Dissertation, Oxford University, Oxford.

Yeats, W. B. (1989), *Collected Poems*, ed. A. Martin, Vintage, London.

Ziarek, E. (1996), *The Rhetoric of Failure: Deconstruction of Skepticism, Reinvention of Modernism*, State University of New York Press, Albany, NY.

Tom Paulin: Writing from the Edges

Gareth Reeves
University of Durham

'We make out of the quarrel with others, rhetoric, but of the quarrel with ourselves, poetry' – Yeats, of course (Yeats, 1994, p. 8). But of the quarrel with himself the poet makes rhetoric, is more the case with Tom Paulin, although not rhetoric in the way or to the effect critics such as Edna Longley maintain. She purports to take exception to the fact, not that Paulin's poetry can express anti-Ulster Protestant sentiments, but that it deals in stereotypes. His poetry, she claims, does not (as Derek Mahon's does) get inside, does not understand, the consciousness of those it would condemn; it lacks imaginative involvement (Longley, 1986, pp. 192-98, 201-206). However, Paulin makes no bones about his position as outsider: 'The question, at least for me, involves a recognition that the Irish writer who publishes in Britain has a neo-colonial identity'. This, in turn, raises the question of audience, which is particularly acute in Paulin's case as he sees it: 'And the central question which faces the neo-colonial and the post-colonial writer is – whom am I writing for?' The danger is that (like V. S. Naipal) 'he writes for nothing and nowhere' (Paulin, 1984, p. 18). Paulin's most engaged and engaging poetry attempts to get inside the outsider's perspective. It holds the rhetoric, the stereotypical and clichéd up for inspection and at arm's length: the quarrel with others is the quarrel with himself, and in the process he would explain himself to himself as well as to others. The fact that at times the rhetoric can be excessively rhetorical, or that the terms of the quarrel can change, from collection to collection, or from poem to poem, and in more recent poems even from line to line, does not alter the dynamic. Paulin could be describing himself when with evident, though qualified, admiration he claims of the loyalist historian Ian Adamson that 'he writes from the dangerous and intelligent edges of that consciousness' (Paulin, 1984, p. 188). Paulin writes intelligently, and often courting the dangerous, from the edges.

'Desertmartin', the third poem in Paulin's third collection *Liberty Tree*, has become a critical litmus test, if only because it pulls no rhetorical punches: it deals in dangerously angry stereotypes. 'Here the Word has withered to a few / Parched certainties', and if that is true of the Calvinist biblical Word, it is true also of the poet's diction, which scorches and parches:

> Masculine Islam, the rule of the Just,
> Egyptian sand dunes and geometry,
> A theology of rifle-butts and executions:
> These are the places where the spirit dies. (Paulin, 1983, p. 17)

As Michael O'Neill indicates, this is not mere name-calling: a diagnosis, beyond the present historical situation and context, is implied: 'Delineating the death of the spirit in theocratic, nationalistic terms, the writing ... reveals that use of the diagnostic phrase which makes Paulin so formidable a poet' (O'Neill, 1982, p. 68) [1]. It is a style partly indebted to Auden, though the diagnostic rhetoric has an asperity beyond anything in Auden. It is capable of bitter wit too, as when the 'Jock squaddy' turns into the ammunition of which he might be the firer or the target, 'happy and expendable, / Like a brass cartridge'; or when, with the sentence, 'It's a limed nest, this place', the poem plays around with its ornithological subtext ('The owl of Minerva'; 'Desertmartin', sand martin), most memorably at the end:

> And now, in Desertmartin's sandy light,
> I see a culture of twigs and bird-shit
> Waving a gaudy flag it loves and curses. (Paulin, 1983, p. 17)

Perhaps the wit rescues these lines from Peter McDonald's charge of 'breathtaking arrogance – how does the poet know that "the spirit dies" in places like these?' (McDonald, 1997, p. 86). But even if the charge is admitted, the arrogance belongs to the poem, not Paulin. And its speaker does not *know* that 'the spirit dies' here: this is what he imagines. What he 'sees' is transparently not what is in front of him. This is the rhetoric of the prophetic seer ('I see a plain / Presbyterian grace sour', 'I see a culture ...'), a jeremiad. It is also Paulin's version of the Romantic vision: if you cannot see something, then you imagine it, you bring it (ambitiously in Paulin's case) into visionary being.

However, McDonald is on to something when he also writes that this is 'finally a religious mode of denunciation' (McDonald, 1997, p. 86); and his reading of 'Desertmartin' is disconcerting, for at other moments his account of Paulin is sophisticated and attentive, especially when he writes that 'Paulin's relation to the identity he writes about is one which has to be inside and outside at once, trying to speak with the accent of the community he anatomizes, while also subjecting that community to a scrutiny complicit with the hostility felt towards it by its historic enemies. These contrary impulses can work as paradoxical forces in Paulin's writing .... ' (McDonald, 1997, pp. 102-3). McDonald overhears something of these forces when he writes parenthetically that 'Desertmartin' 'perhaps reveal[s] a deep Paisley influence on Paulin's way of thinking'; but, to repeat, the 'denunciation' is not by Paulin *in propria persona*. McDonald's would-be put-down reference here to Paisley, who earlier in the poem has had fired at him, with a fine rhetorical flourish, his soubriquet of 'the Big Man' ('it shouts / For the Big Man to lead his wee people'), throws some light. If 'Desertmartin' speaks in Paisley's idiom even as it denounces him, that is because the poem is a rhetorical battle. In spite of its insistent stating, it is not a statement of Paulin's beliefs or even political philosophy, although it goes without saying that much can be deduced from the poem about these things.

The speaker of 'Desertmartin' is very deliberately placed:

> Because this is the territory of the Law
> I drive across it with a powerless knowledge –
> The owl of Minerva in a hired car. (Paulin, 1983, p. 16)

The speaker is both inside and outside, a trespasser in the territory of the law, and consequently unable to act – except in his capacity as outsider, as 'hired' poet-rhetorician. Action and reaction: the power of the speaker's rhetoric is in proportion to the powerlessness of his knowledge. Hence the self-deprecating allusion to Hegel's 'owl of Minerva': 'The owl of Minerva spreads its wings only with the falling of the dusk' (Hegel, 1942, p. 13), meaning that philosophy understands reality only after the event and cannot prescribe how the world ought to be – 'powerless knowledge' indeed. Paulin begins the Introduction to his collection of essays, *Minotaur: Poetry and the Nation State*, with a brief discussion of Hegel's idea, in *The Philosophy of Right*, 'of the nation state as a version of the Greek *polis*' (Paulin, 1992, p. 3). Hegel evidently appeals to Paulin because he weighs the necessity of the body politic against the claims of art. Conceding with Hegel that the state is 'no ideal work of art', Paulin nevertheless welcomes the philosopher's notion that 'The state is more than the sum of its institutions; it exists through those institutions, but is also above and beyond them ... It inhabits our minds, shaping our beliefs and desires' (Paulin, 1992, p. 1). This may lead to 'powerless knowledge' in a poem such as 'Desertmartin', but it intimates something of those elsewheres which occupy Paulin ('he writes for nothing and nowhere'), and which in more assertively optimistic moments he has aligned with Field Day's 'fifth province' and located in the ideal of a revised eighteenth-century Protestant republicanism. This utopianism irritates Longley and McDonald. The latter in particular, again, is perceptive about this topic, writing that Paulin 'clings desperately to one date – 1798 [Wolf Tone's abortive 'United Irishmen' uprising] – and proposes a kind of Ulster dissociation of sensibility at the end of the eighteenth century.... [T]he questions that remain unsettled (and which Paulin's writing seems to take care not to address) are whether the poet is attempting to redeem or destroy his subject, and whether he is seriously addressing himself to this dissociated culture, or is holding it up to an outside audience for easy ridicule' (McDonald, 1997, p. 104).

However, Paulin's poetry does address itself to these questions, although not perhaps in McDonald's 'serious' way; and if anything is held up to ridicule, the 'audience' being addressed is the poet himself, an 'inside' audience as much as an 'outside' one. Another litmus test is 'The Book of Juniper', especially its final section, which invokes the 1798 rebellion:

> On this coast
> it is the only
> tree of freedom
> to be found,
> and I imagine
> that a swelling army is marching
> from Memory Harbour and Killala
> carrying branches
> of green juniper.
>
> Consider
> the gothic zigzags
> and brisk formations
> that square to meet
> the green tide rising
> through Mayo and Antrim,
>
> now dream
> of that sweet
> equal republic
> where the juniper
> talks to the oak,
> the thistle,
> the bandaged elm,
> and the jolly jolly chestnut. (Paulin, 1983, p. 27)

Edna Longley calls this one of Paulin's 'single-minded solutions' (Longley, 1986, p. 204); but single-minded is precisely what these lines are not. Even Alan Robinson, in what is still one of the most finely attuned accounts of Paulin's poetry, is too ready to hear 'The Book of Juniper' as a univocal performance, especially this 'symbolic reconciliation between England and a United Ireland', in which, he claims, Paulin is 'writing less as a propagandist than as a celebrant of the artistic imagination, whose visionary freedom is cognate with that of political liberty' (Robinson, 1988, p. 120). Wish-fulfillment rather than celebration: is there not something wryly comic about the rapprochement being intimated, especially with 'jolly jolly chestnut'? Or something too algebraic and gestural to carry conviction? 'Gothic zigzags' and 'brisk formations' sound like Paulinesque shorthand for things desirable and undesirable, reconciled in a phrase; similarly with 'square' (negative) and 'meet' (that is, in greeting, positive). The 'visionary freedom' teeters on the edge of disbelief even as it is uttered. The speaker's utopianism is for a future that the poetry reveals, or betrays, will never happen. 'I imagine', then 'Consider', then 'now dream': the progression is from personal testimony to something gesturing at the visionary, a would-be future. But who is being asked to 'consider', and what is the tone here? Knowing Paulin's early Audenesque apprenticeship, one can't help thinking of 'Consider this and in our time', although Paulin's 'consider' lacks Auden's panoptic authority (Auden, 1991,

p. 61). Or is there a biblical inflexion ('Consider the lilies of the field')? Or is this lecturese? 'Now dream' sounds not so much like visionary address as self-communing and self-persuasion.

We are approaching Yeatsian territory here, but with a marked difference. Yeats's poetic dreaming is typically magnificent conjuration, dependent on 'the affections of our heart' ('In Memory of Major Robert Gregory', Yeats, 1961, p. 148), but, whatever the occasion, dreaming which is deliberately self-generated, worked on and worked up, until it takes on an imagined life of its own – as the poet defiantly confesses in 'The Circus Animals' Desertion': 'And this brought forth a dream and soon enough // This dream itself had all my thought and love.... / It was the dream itself enchanted me' (Yeats, 1961, p. 392). Robert Gregory's talents are necessary for the place Yeats would find for him in the poet's pantheon and to fit the poet's artistic credo: 'We dreamed that a great painter had been born / ... / To that stern colour and that delicate line / That are our secret discipline' (Yeats, 1961, p. 150). Yeats's dream rhetoric is magisterial. By contrast the rhetoric of 'The Book of Juniper' is decidedly dreamy, vaguely oracular and undirected. Who, once more, is being commanded, or asked, to 'now dream'? A phantom question-mark hovers over the dream. Perhaps the dream itself enchants the poet, but its status is intriguingly uncertain. It is expressed in gestural telegraphese, and is mysteriously allegorical. (In my experience no two people arrive at the same decoding of the juniper, oak, thistle, and so on). And for whom does the poet 'imagine' his 'swelling army'? In Yeats's 'The Fisherman' the poet is certain for whom, or in spite of whom, he imagines his fisherman: 'I began / In scorn of this audience, / Imagining a man ... ' (Yeats, 1961, p. 167). Or again, at the end of 'Easter 1916' the poet, or rather his assumed readership, his 'we', reckons to 'know [the] dream' of the Irish Republican Brotherhood, and to know that in itself it is 'enough' (Yeats, 1961, p. 204). But does the poet of 'The Book of Juniper' have that sort of certainty? Is *his* 'dream' enough? Nor are these comparisons with Yeats fortuitous, for 'Memory Harbour' is there, in the final section of 'The Book of Juniper', not only because the phrase 'Memory Harbour and Killala' gestures at rapprochement in a dreamily euphonious collocation of the private 'good place' with a place in the public consciousness of horrific disaster, but also because it is the title of an early painting by Jack B. Yeats. The painting brings together many of the images the painter was to develop in later works, in a symbolic dreamscape of youthful memories (and incidentally many of the Yeatsian associations of the harbour, which is the village of Rosses Point, were highlighted in the writings of Jack's brother).

The poet of 'A Written Answer' would appear both to acknowledge and to defend himself against the sort of criticism made of 'The Book of Juniper' by those who, like Longley and (more sinuously) McDonald, accuse his poetry of ideological *parti-pris* [2]. The poem spells out the Audenesque lesson of parable art, that the poet 'designs a fictionary universe / which has its own laws and isn't quite / the same as this place that we call real', and goes on seemingly to confess that, though 'The Book of Juniper' invites decoding, it does not satisfy on this level, but that nevertheless its poetic 'fictionary universe' is pleasing: 'I like his image of the elm and chestnut' (Paulin,

1983, p. 40). But the poem is a joshing performance, its *mea culpa* hedged about by comic and tonal antics. The 'fictionary universe' lesson sounds a touch condescending; and the self-mockery of the 'fictionary' name Rupert Brookeborough is tricksy: Rupert Brooke, byword for the poet who idealises war, is evidently conflated with Lord Brookeborough, leader of the Ulster Unionist Party for twenty years (until 1963) – outmoded poet joining hands with outmoded politician seems to be the joke. '[T]his author is a fly man' not only because his poem 'A Written Answer' is, punningly, 'all about fishing', but also because Yeats's 'Fisherman' was a fly man too, the poet imagining:

> the down-turn of his wrist
> When the flies drop in the stream;
> A man who does not exist,
> A man who is but a dream. (Yeats, 1961, p. 167)

The poetry here makes Yeats's dream figure very present to the reader. Maybe Paulin, with foolish longing, is imagining his poetic *alter ego* as the non-existent creation of Yeats's imagination, the dreamer become the dream in an aesthete's impossible 'pure circle of itself' ('The Other Voice', Paulin, 1980, p. 45). If so, the poet of 'A Written Answer' is quick to puncture the idea, for the comic bathos of the last line, 'and the critics yonder say his work is alright', acknowledges what irritates critics such as Longley, that his audience is chiefly 'yonder' – in Britain, not Northern Ireland. In an essay on MacNeice, entitled 'The Man from No Part', Paulin writes 'The Irish sense of place is very exacting and intransigent, and many people can never forgive the man who goes, in that tantalizing phrase, "across the water"' (Paulin, 1984, p. 75). That man is as much Paulin as he is MacNeice.

One of those whom the poet of 'The Fisherman' scorns is 'The clever man who cries / The catch-cries of the clown' (Yeats, 1961, p. 166) – surely a proleptic reference to Paulin! In the essay on MacNeice, Paulin also writes, in relation to his theme of the deracinated Irishman, 'few Irish writers have totally resisted the temptation to export their Irishness. And in any case Irishness is a sometimes clownish commodity which depends on being transported elsewhere' (Paulin, 1984, p. 76). Even if some would regard this as yet another stereotype, it is clear from poems such as 'A Written Answer' that the 'clever' Paulin has decided to make a virtue, or at any rate poetry, of 'the catch-cries of the clown', as is even more evident, with disarming self-awareness, from his subsequent career, poetic as well as extra-poetic.

Notes

[1] O'Neill is commenting on 'Desertmartin' in a review of a pamphlet of poems by Paulin entitled *The Book of Juniper*. This pamphlet was published in 1981 (Bloodaxe, Newcastle), two years before the publication of *Liberty Tree*, the volume of poems which also contains 'Desertmartin' and from which I quote.

[2] I owe this suggestion to my student Clara Dawson.

References

Auden, W. H. (1991), *Collected Poems*, ed. E. Mendelson, Faber, London.

Hegel, G. W. F. (1942), *Hegel's Philosophy of Right*, trans. T. M. Knox, Oxford University Press, London.

Longley, E. (1986), *Poetry in the Wars*, Bloodaxe, Newcastle.

McDonald, P. (1997), *Mistaken Identities: Poetry and Northern Ireland*, Oxford University Press, Oxford.

O'Neill, M. (1982), 'Cultural Imaginings', review of T. Paulin, *The Book of Juniper* and D. Walcott, *The Fortunate Traveller*, *Poetry Introduction 5*, in *Poetry Review*, 72, (2), pp. 68-70.

Paulin, T. (1983), *Liberty Tree*, Faber, London.

Paulin, T. (1984), *Ireland and the English Crisis*, Bloodaxe, Newcastle.

Paulin, T. (1990), *The Strange Museum*, Faber, London.

Paulin, T. (1992), *Minotaur: Poetry and the Nation State*, Faber, London.

Robinson, A. (1988), *Instabilities in Contemporary British Poetry*, Macmillan, Basingstoke.

Yeats, W. B. (1961), *Collected Poems*, Macmillan, London.

Yeats, W. B. (1994), *Later Essays: The Collected Works of W. B. Yeats, vol. V*, ed. W. H. O'Donnell, Scribner's, New York.

The Healing of Trauma in Anne Devlin's *After Easter*: Female Experience and Nationalistic Historiography

Wei H. Kao
National Taiwan University

Many people, if asked to identify the reasons for learning history, would answer that history is our link to the past, allowing us to understand our present experiences in the context of earlier occurrences. This answer seems proper, though one may, if being wary of potential ideological fallacies, question 'whose' past gets to be recognised or legitimised. In the case of Ireland, a country born out of sectarian conflicts, different shades of republicans, loyalists, Catholics, Protestants, Presbyterians, nationalists, and unionists may hold dissimilar interpretations of their shared past, understanding their version of history as the true one in line with a preferred patriotic agenda. As Colm Tóibín (1996, p. 215) recalls, the historical stories he acquired at school in the South 'ha[d] no complications or ironies or half-truths', and usually comprised 'heroes and traitors and villains'. Understandably, those 'traitors and villains' would be the ones who expressed reservations about, or were clearly against, Catholic nationalism or Irish patriotism.

What is beyond question is that the antagonistic sentiments involved in a patriotic narrative render it almost impossible to maintain an objective angle to prove 'one particular interpretation [is] more true than another' (Saul Friedlander, 1997, p. 384). More specifically, history always has to be understood through chosen rhetoric which omits other crucial but politically inappropriate historical elements in the making of a historical narrative. Those excluded elements may include differences in gender, class and region, whereas political, militant, and religious conflicts are often given greater attention. As to the making of the history of Irish women, feminists have pointed out that, traditionally, Northern Irish women lack an equal footing with men in historical representations. Their political activism in the Troubles, for instance, due to the internment of husbands and sons, was mostly 'understood as an extension of their domestic role, [and] … widely acknowledged among women' (Persic, 2004, p. 170).

The polemics surrounding the neglect of certain historical elements in traditional historiography have been brought into focus by Irish revisionist historians' accounts of the nationalistic and unionist violence out of which the Free State was built. The revisionist examination of the given historiography in the 1970s, following the outbreak of the Northern Ireland conflict in 1969, coincided with the emergence of 'Second Wave' feminism in the international context [1]. As both the Northern Ireland conflict and Second Wave feminism arose out of the civil rights campaigns, and the latter was particularly engaged with an anti-war agenda, some women intellectuals were inspired to rethink the consequences of male-dominated Irish politics, and banded together to contend against discrimination. Anne Devlin, dramatist, and the subject of this essay, participates in an historical revisionary project in defending women's representation in literary texts.

Growing up in a socialist family in the Catholic West Belfast area during the 1950s and 1960s, Devlin is particularly interested in Irish women's dilemmas in a divided society from a working class perspective [2]. Her first play, *Ourselves Alone* (1985), which reflects the Troubles from the viewpoints of mothers, wives, and lovers, sought 'to test republicanism against feminism and feminism won', as she stated in an interview (Devlin, quoted in Foley, 2003, p. 73). *After Easter* (1994), her second drama, furthers the feminist exploration of identity issues and the psychological pain suffered by women caught up in the Troubles. Both plays are feminine narratives, tackling women's experiences in particular, and both are responses to feminism's punning call for the making of 'her-story' in opposition to the traditional male-led historical discourses, or historiography. In other words, the female-centered perspective in both plays offers an alternative interpretation of the Conflicts, which, to some extent, critiques the militant, masculine political discourses that have largely dismissed the presence of women. Although Devlin and revisionist historians do not exactly share the same agenda in demonstrating Irish experience - the former makes use of fictional elements; the latter re-assess historical material - their questioning of republican and loyalist ideologies is consonant to a certain degree. This article will therefore analyse Devlin's *After Easter*, a play less discussed than its predecessor but with similarly distinct feminist components, to observe how the playwright contextualises the plight of women as the result of political antagonism and patriarchal orthodoxies - due to which their lives are stringently under social and religious surveillance.

The titles Devlin chooses for her plays thoughtfully highlight her interrogation of the Irish tradition. She initially prompts the audience to conceive *Ourselves Alone* as a nationalistic play, given that the title is the English translation of Sinn Féin, the political wing of the outlawed Irish Republican Army. Nevertheless, the play features three women in one politically torn family, standing 'ourselves alone' against their male lovers' unyielding expectation of women to be loyal supporters of men in both private and public spheres. 'Ourselves Alone' then becomes a pun suggesting the questionable republican tradition in which women's subordinate role has been taken for granted. *After Easter* also works as a pun through which the audience, if not yet aware of the timeframe in which the story is set, may associate the play with the 1916 Easter Rising and expect to see what has happened 'after' Easter. It could be argued that this association is not simply a misunderstanding of the title, because it may also suggest Devlin's intention to address the far-reaching consequences of the Easter Rising on women.

More specifically, the tongues of fire that are manifested to the protagonist Greta as religious visions 'on Pentecost Sunday, seven weeks after Easter' may suggest that the liberty of women is always under fire (Devlin, 1994, p. 26). This 'liberty is very important to [Greta]', but she '[has] felt watched all [her] life' (Devlin, 1994, p. 25). What should be noted is that the liberation of Ireland from British domination - which was the agenda of the Easter Rising - did not secure the equality of the 'Irishmen and Irishwomen' whom the 1916 'Proclamation of the Irish Republic' had addressed (it begins by addressing 'Irishmen and lrishwomen … Ireland, through us, summons her children to her flag and strikes for her freedom'). Different shades of Irishwomen's voices, to a large degree, were either dismissed by or absorbed into the nationalistic propaganda [3]. For instance, Irish suffragists and women lobbyists for the anti-Home Rule campaign were not well received by republicans. The neglect of women dissenters' experiences, along with revisionist historians' concerns with the problematic nationalistic historiography, prompted Devlin to write *After Easter*. It is a play that not only depicts Greta's own distress during a restricted period of time but also illustrates why 'the whole of Ireland [i]s crying out' to Greta and Irishwomen in general (Devlin, 1994, p. 11). The play also examines women's positions in the nationalistic discourse, and in what way their individualities might have been erased - with the wholehearted approval of the nation - by the male republican mainstream.

In contrast to *Ourselves Alone*, in which the mother figure is absent and male republicans are dominant, *After Easter* has a father character who is ill, never appears on stage and later dies of heart failure. The father's critical illness brings the two middle-aged sisters, Greta and Helen, back to Belfast from England, reuniting them with other family members: their highly nationalistic sister, Aoife, their Catholic mother, Rose, and a young brother, Manus. The family reunion, however, does not unite this politically, culturally, and religiously split family, but exhibits the ways in which a Belfast family is subject to various social determinants. The subjugation compels working-class women, as in Greta's Catholic family, on to the silenced, social margin where gender and other social norms are still strictly applied to them. To escape from the antagonistic political climate, and being weary of the double marginalisation of Catholic working-class women at home in Belfast, Helen leaves for London, working as a commercial artist and talking with an intentionally neither Irish nor English but American accent. Her mimicry of an American accent 'gets [her] through the door' to commercial markets, whereas 'an Irish accent gets [her] followed round the store by a plainclothes security man' (Devlin, 1994, p. 9).

Helen's preference for an American accent suggests an identity issue that also troubles Greta, whose father was 'the first Communist on the Falls Road' to bring his children up 'like Protestants', so as not to become nationalistic 'rebels' (Devlin, 1994, p. 39, 46). With this ambiguous political background, Greta is forced to drop out of a convent school and later, without her family's approval, she marries an English Marxist from Oxford who refuses to baptize their children, and has an extramarital affair behind Greta's back. Greta's unfavourable childhood experience at school together with her frustration in marriage, failure to keep up with a political ideal, distress about living in a politically divided family, and deprivation of the custody of her children, drive her to madness. Being helpless and bored, she flees from a dinner party – held by her husband's mistress – and in desperation sits in the middle of the road, refusing to move. She is arrested by the police and hospitalised in a mental institute for her potential suicide attempt. Greta, however, argues that she is not mad; 'the difference between insanity and politics is only a matter of numbers'. She contends that if twenty people sit down together on the road and make a protest, they would be thought politically dangerous, whereas a lone woman cannot protest and stop the traffic on her own (Devlin, 1994, p. 3).

Helen's and Greta's exiles in London and Oxford can be interpreted as their reaction to being marginalised by Northern Irish politics and culture. In this respect it is notable that Helen's American accent underpins her 'highly successful' career as a commercial artist. Her survival strategy is based on a language and accent not her own but which, nevertheless, enables her entry as a marginalized subject into the mainstream cultural scene. What is also interesting is that she refuses to speak with a British accent – there are 'limits to [the] betrayal' she can take as an Irish Catholic (Devlin, 1994, p. 9). Her tactic does not erase her Irish identity, as she can still talk to her family with the 'right' Irish accent. Her hybrid identity with an imitated American accent, to borrow Jacques Lacan's description of the effects of mimicry, is 'the technique of camouflage practised in human warfare'; a technique not just to 'harmoniz[e] with the background, but against a mottled background, of becoming mottled' (Lacan, 1997, p. 99). Her mimicry of an American accent, rather than a standard British accent, creates a political and cultural ambivalence that challenges the colonial discourse, 'emerg[ing] as the representation of a difference that is itself a process of disavowal' (Bhabha, 1994, p. 86). It could therefore be claimed that Helen's insistence on speaking with an American accent in London – former capital of the colonial empire - negates the received relationship between the centre and the margin in the colonial administration.

Greta, however, is not as crafty as Helen in concealing her Irishness in Oxford. She feels most irritated when she is discovered to be Irish on any occasion. Feeling isolated, she does not 'go out looking for people who have the same or a similar accent', as most overseas Irish people might do to maintain a sense of Irish community (Devlin, 1994, p. 4). Her resentment of the 'Irish' label, understandably, results from the consequences of the ongoing Northern Ireland troubles, which led many contemporary English people to be wary of potential terrorists. Her resentment also suggests her reluctance to be identified with the republican violence or unionist ideology which simplistically labels the Irish as either Catholic/Protestant or

Nationalists/Unionists without acknowledging the existence of other dissidents or social minorities. What is noteworthy is that Greta's frustration over the identity issue lies partially in the fact that she cannot locate a ready-made discourse in which unreligious and apolitical women like her are sufficiently attended to, and nor can she make up a survival strategy as Helen does. Her difficulty over issues of identity, therefore, makes her a vulnerable person and unable to communicate intelligibly with others. Sitting in the road, her hallucinations, screams and giggles are speechless expressions against the pervasive ignorance of what women have to say in a male-dominated culture. Her major trouble is that few people listen to her with patience, including a male psychiatrist. Take her monologue at the beginning of the play: Greta is articulate, whereas her psychiatrist, Campbell, fails to understand her distress at being betrayed in her marriage, being a mother whose baby was taken away at two-and-a-half weeks, and of being an unwelcome daughter at home in Belfast. The doctor only makes his medical judgment by observing whether Greta can speak morally, which brings forth her cynical outburst to the doctor as follows: 'I don't know which is worse - your moral good health or your hypocrisy!' (Devlin, 1994, p. 3).

The male psychiatrist's negation of Greta's experiences is not an exceptional case, as most Catholic Irishwomen, particularly those on the working-class social margin, do not generally have a public forum in which they can achieve self-expression. On the other hand, the repressive family ideology has plotted a fixed role for women to take - that of a moral and domestic caretaker. Allegorical role models of women, for example, Kathleen Ni Houlihan, Dark Rosaleen, 'Mother Ireland' and other incarnations of Ireland-as-Woman, had all stood iconic and unarguable with nationalistic endorsement. To be heard, Irishwomen in this play are prompted to learn a republican form of speech, which Greta's younger sister, Aoife, has done eloquently. Those who are unable or unwilling to articulate such a speech are either silenced or forced to scream or giggle.

The fact that Greta suffers a 'double exclusion' for being a woman on the social margin may be, in the postcolonial perspective, in consonance with how Gayatri Chakravorty Spivak, in 'Can the Subaltern Speak?', describes the quandary of the Indian untouchable in light of the caste system. In this article, Spivak contends that the discourse of oppression, in the process of representing (and mastering) this social 'Other' deprives her of a voice. The act of representation is bound up with a variety of social, economic and colonial intellectual powers, desires and interests such that the subalterns are still unable to talk in their own voice but are subject to elitism [4]. While Spivak does not rule out the possibility that some subaltern men and women, thanks to being systematically studied and encouraged, are now more able to articulate their views and feelings, she points out that their utterances are unlikely, for a range of historical and social reasons, to be fully audible to the colonial power elite (Spivak, 1996, p. 291). Greta's experience of 'double exclusion' is the kind of psychobiography that Spivak refers to and may account for the reason why she is not properly understood by the English male psychiatrist. He assumes Greta is mad, and her words make no sense from his elitist medical perspective. He assumes a psychobiography based upon her responses to his queries in order to judge if she is fit enough to be discharged from hospital. As a doctor he feels justified in speaking for Greta, constructing her speech in - to borrow from Spivak once again – a kind of 'epistemic violence' (Spivak, 1996, p. 219). This is a kind of violence which 'constituted/effaced a subject that was obliged to cathect (occupy in response to a desire) the space of the Imperialists' self-consolidating other' (Spivak, 1996, p. 219). Whether Greta can be discharged or not, from the English doctor's point of view, depends on how 'dangerous' she might be were she to be sent back to Belfast (Devlin, 1994, p. 3). The 'logic' of epistemic violence dictates that the female object, represented by Greta cannot present her own voice without being misunderstood: she is to be treated as a passive object to be watched or attended to by the dominant classes. Observing Greta's and Helen's cases from the revisionist historians' perspective, we may reasonably comment that *After Easter* not only documents the possible experiences of the silenced 'Other' in Irish society, albeit fictionally, but also shows the playwright's efforts in challenging the nationalistic historiography, which has been, in Spivak's view, dominated by elite personalities, institutions, activities and ideas.

The rise of Irish revisionist historiography has long been seen as a counteraction to the Northern Ireland Troubles of the 1960s. These writers, witnessing the bloodshed of numerous civilians, started to re-appraise the nationalist violence out of which the Free State had emerged and their contribution facilitates the emergence of alternative readings of Irish culture, political events and religious ethics. Similarly, in *After Easter*, alongside the feminist reading described above, Devlin offers another outlook on the Troubles and their consequences from civilian, rather than passionately patriotic, viewpoints. Her focus on the former could be regarded as a creative approach to the revisionist historiography through which Northern Irish civilians - particularly those not appearing in the militant scenes - show how helplessly they are subject to the antagonistic ideologies. Take the scene in which Michael, the father, is hospitalised for heart surgery. The hospital is guarded by armed policemen with bullet-proof jackets due to the danger of shooting in the street. When the family is due to return home, their car, parked outside the hospital, is found to have been attacked and the windscreen broken. It is also reported that nine people were shot dead in a pub on the Donegal Road at almost the same time. This event most distresses Greta, who regards herself as the harbinger of death. To 'stop the killing,' and perhaps to redeem her sense of guilt, she steals a chalice full of communion wafers from Clonard Monastery, distributing them to people in the bus queues in the city centre (Devlin, 1994, p. 46). She is arrested by the police but soon released, because 'in England they lock her up if she's mad but let her go if she's political. In Ireland they lock her up if she's political and let her go if she's mad' (Devlin, 1994, p. 47). This incident irritates Greta's mother, Rose, as it may result in their being killed by extremist unionists - 'Catholics are being murdered in their beds in this area' (Devlin, 1994, p. 47). Rose is also concerned that Greta's criticism of religious education, if reported in the newspaper, would cause her school uniform shop to be closed and her family left penniless as a consequence.

The significance of the street shooting lies in the fact that Devlin presents its consequences from the viewpoint of a merchant class, rather than a unionist or republican one. The event is depicted not in a tone of praising heroes or expressing consolation for victims' families, but with some degree of cynicism. Take the scene when Manus, the only son in the family, is held by local policemen for attempting to defy their road block on his way home, and happening to hold a box which the police suspect might be a bomb. When opened, the box contains only three white veils which his mother has made for church activities. This scene is tragicomical given that Manus is almost mistaken for a terrorist and killed, but on the other hand, the incident shows that civilian life is so disturbed that Rose's shop could be closed down just because one of her family members does not follow the community's code of conduct. What is most ironic is that the policemen do not even apologise for giving Manus and his family such a fright, but only 'wish [them] a nice day' and depart. The violence they brought into the house, as well as that of the street shooting, seems to be justified by the political authorities; the civilians can only put up with, or suffer the consequences of violence. Nevertheless, the playwright does not idealise Catholic women on the social margin. Rose, the shop owner, lends money - with supposedly high interest - to those who cannot afford communion dresses for their children's First Communion. Disgusted by the way in which she makes money from raising children, Manus describes her business as 'grubby' and himself as a 'money-lender's son' who is unwelcome in the community (Devlin, 1994, p. 64). It can therefore be contended that Devlin intends to present the materialistic concerns of a Catholic family, rather than a holy family image as expected by the Church. The financial priorities that concern Rose are with the same as those of every working-class mother, whereas Manus sits, it seems, in religious judgment on his mother:

> ROSE: But I kept you. I educated you. We came up from the country with nothing and your father couldn't get work and I started knitting and then I did dressmaking and I made my money fairly and squarely. And when they couldn't pay I lent them the money. There's nothing wrong with that. I paid for your music lessons. Remember that.
>
> . . . . . .
>
> MANUS: [Dad] wasn't unrealistic; he was ashamed! I mean, you had a captive community here, didn't you. No communion dress, no First Communion. It was either a new communion dress or damnation and your interest rates stood between them and their souls. (Devlin, 1994, p. 64)

Manus is the most religious amongst his siblings. However, his piety is not associated with, or backed up by the unionist or republican ideologies which has turned Ireland into a highly troubled state. Instead, he dramatises the concerns of revisionist historians and the polemics of Irish historiography. Through Manus, the playwright demonstrates that what results in political antagonism is often because history is interpreted selectively and narrowly by political historians, so that some events become 'sacrosanct and immune to criticism or even to serious examination', and 'a model of pure heroism in a world of good and evil' (Laffan, 1991, p. 107). Feeling repulsed by the ways in which history is interpreted and its direct consequences on civilians, Manus 'paint[s] on the walls of all the police stations and army barracks: 'Forget 1690! Forget history! Remember – the pursuit of happiness is a Right of Man!' (Devlin, 1994, p. 53). His 'pursuit of happiness' as the basic right of an individual and 'forgetting history' show that he is, to borrow a phrase, attempting to awake from the historical nightmare that has troubled Irish people for centuries. The history he proposes to forget, as the play shows, includes Protestant and Catholic, unionist and republican, in that he paints these words on the walls not only of barracks but also of convents. Unlike successive revisionist historians Manus does not demonstrate how Irish history should be re-read; what is more noteworthy is that he does it by action; it is an action that calls forth a reading that is necessary to incur sectarian violence and the misuses of history as political and religious weapons. Manus's longing for peace in Ireland can be seen from his non-violent, continual painting of the same phrases everywhere in Belfast, '[e]ven if no one spoke them or they got painted over, it wouldn't matter, they'd come through again and again, they'd come through' (Devlin, 1994, p. 534). Manus's insistence on 'forgetting history' can also be considered as his awareness of the problems of constructing 'community history' for political purposes. That is, the words he paints on the walls, apart from being a proposed solution to the Troubles, correspond to Benedict Anderson's much cited proposition that the nation is an 'imagined community' (Anderson, 1991, *passim*). Anderson argues that such a community produces a shared cultural contract and a national identity through various cultural representations, traditions, histories and social practices. What is worth noting is that in Northern Ireland, the 'imagined community' is a much divided one that defines itself in relation to the Other without recognising differences within classes, genders and locations.

After Easter is a domestic drama which also shows how a family endures political agitation. Aoife, the elder sister of Manus, is the most enthusiastic supporter of the IRA. While Manus feels disillusioned about the given historiographies that antagonise Irish people of different communities, Aoife sees everything with political eyes. For instance, she assumes that the spirit that appears in Greta's hallucination is 'an English ghost', while Helen doubts if ghosts have a nationality (Devlin, 1994, p 11) The star constellation that Greta dreams about is in Aoife's view, '[t]he Plough! You saw the symbol of the Irish Citizen Army'; alternatively, according to Helen '[i]t could have been the Pleiades. The seven sisters' (Devlin, 1994, p. 15). Aoife's passion for the republican cause, it is implied, is maintained through political imagination, rather than detached observations. To tackle this issue, the playwright sets Helen, Aoife, Greta and Manus in contrast to each other in order to examine different political attitudes towards 'Irishness', on which the Irish nation has been built, promoted and imagined by romantic nationalists. As we have seen, Aoife is the most loyal to Irish patriotism with her categorical interpretations of nationalistic symbols. Manus, although he is disappointed about the ways in which history is mishandled by politicians, does not deny 'Irishness', viewing it as cultural learning which he wishes to acquire. Nevertheless, the kind of 'Irishness' he pursues is not overtly patriotic, but a mechanism to enable him to re-build a cultural identity which his communist father concealed from his children, wary that it would encourage rebellious thoughts in them. Consequently the adult Manus endeavours to learn 'the music, the language, the culture . . . spend[ing] all my time trying to get it back' (Devlin, 1994, p. 39). What is interesting is that Manus contends that he is happy to play both types of music, as 'it's Irish, it's [our] music' (Devlin, 1994, p. 38). This differs from other characters in the play who are apt to classify Irish music into Fenian and Orange. It can be argued that, through Manus, Devlin is suggesting that only when the Irish are able to appreciate the legacies of the different communities in Ireland can real peace be in view. That said, Manus's open attitude towards the Irish legacy is not the sole, unquestionable one that the playwright introduces to her audience in *After Easter*. Helen, who has lived in self-imposed exile in London, disguising her Irish accent and whose Irish cultural identity was nearly disregarded by her father, has a different opinion to Manus regarding the identity issue. As a commercial artist whose works are popular on the both sides of the Atlantic Ocean, she prefers to see herself as a citizen of the world, rather than as an insular, self-absorbed Irish citizen content with her Irishness. Hence, on hearing Manus playing an Irish fiddle she advises him not 'to stoop to other people's expectations. Don't descend to folk, compose something new' (Devlin, 1994, p. 39). In her opinion, good art does 'not rise above the tribe' necessarily, whereas Manus supposes, through having rejected the political labels of a shared cultural identity, 'all great art will have the tribe behind it' (Devlin, 1994, p. 39). In my opinion, Devlin presents extremist, moderate and apolitical viewpoints on the identity issue, not to uphold any one view but to explore possible ways of dealing with the issue.

What is also worth noting is that according to his sister Helen, Manus is 'really gay' (Devlin, 1994, p. 36). Although Aoife does not believe it, and prefers to think 'that's just a phase he's going through', suggested homosexuality is one of the multifarious layers of identity which make up Manus. It could then be argued that implies that personal identity or sexual orientation should not be less crucial than the cultural, ethnic, religious and national identities for which different Irish communities have been striving for centuries (Devlin, 1994, p. 36). The subplot concerning Manus' purported sexuality reveals the weakness of national discourses in which only the political is addressed, discussed, and respected. In such discourses sexual orientation, gender and class, are largely neglected. The themes of gender and identity are central to *After Easter;* equally so are death and rebirth. In the early scenes of the play we are made aware of the father's critical condition in hospital, and this is the catalyst which draws the family back to Belfast. However, this family reunion does not really help to effect a reconciliation due to their differing attitudes to religion, politics and sectarian violence. Helen for example left for England because she could no longer tolerate her father's socialism: 'I had my revenge on my socialist father. I became a capitalist in the most intimate sense: I only come if there's money' (Devlin, 1994, p. 73). Moreover, she cannot identify the political demands of nationalism and unionism in Ireland. Her reconciliation with her family and Ireland begins on the first night of her home visit, after her thumb is accidentally and agonizingly slammed in the car door. She then dreams about a banshee, the supernatural harbinger of death by which Greta had previously claimed to be haunted, the dream that supposedly presages the death of a family member. Helen interprets this dream as a sign that she has been negating her Irish roots, and she should have lived with them more creatively and freely. She therefore sells her apartment in London, deciding to return to Belfast and to be an Irish artist, after her father's funeral. Greta's longing for a rebirth can be seen in her series of hallucinations. One of the hallucinations takes place three days before her birthday: 'I became delirious enough to believe that the sleeping-bag which I insisted on sleeping in on the floor of my room was the womb and I had gone back into it to be born again' (Devlin, 1994, p. 24). Lying in the 'womb,' she dreams that an old priest in a long black soutane 'loomed over me and placed a pillow on my face' (Devlin, 1994, p. 25). Her struggle against the 'smothering blackness' makes her turn around and around in the 'womb', until finding 'a sphere lit up in space far below me ... So I knew I was born that night, or I was reliving my birth' (Devlin, 1994, p. 25). Greta's sense of rebirth can be judged as a woman's tenacity against the patriarchal burden placed on her, a burden which silences her and other working class women. The imagery of the old priest and the 'womb' combine notions of extreme patriarchy and maternalism while suggesting that Greta has subconsciously refused to accept a communally inscribed 'single' 'Irish Catholic' identity. Instead, she eschews prejudice, preferring instead to love whatever offspring are delivered of the symbolic 'womb'. This also explains why she would cry out that she can be 'a Catholic, a Protestant, a Hindu, a Moslem, a Jew' (Devlin, 1994, p. 7). Her screams, after she hears of her father's death, can also be seen to symbolise the birth cries of a new-born infant. However Greta is no longer as innocent as an infant; finally she is a woman who is moving towards healing herself. Her strong sense of maternalism emerges after she and Helen cast their father's ashes into the wind on Westminster Bridge, turning the imaginary and symbolic rebirth into practice. Most importantly, Greta and her mother are reconciled by going 'hunting' at the end of the play. As Greta recollects, they do not harm a stag that runs to them, but feed it gently. The face of the stag, remarkably, transforms by taking on human features, and it takes Greta to 'the place where the rivers come from, where you come from' (Devlin, 1994, p. 75). Herein we can see Greta effecting a break with religious and biblical dogma. She does not see the stag as a sacrifice as in biblical teachings, but as a companion. Greta rides the stag 'to the top of the world' (Devlin, 1994, p. 75); her dominant position suggests that in her rebirth she has discovered herself; she will no longer be a marginalised object in a patriarchal society.

It could be claimed that male experiences in *After Easter* rarely come to the surface. The limited presentation of positive male voices, however, is explicable inasmuch as Devlin writes the play to explore different possibilities of women's lives without male dominance. Helen's independence, Aoife's status as a single mother and her allegiance to the IRA, and Greta's determination to be herself at the end of the play, illustrate a fictional approach to the writing of feminine histories, in contrast to univocal male truth. The various presentations of women's lives also demonstrate Devlin's consistently inconsistent attitude towards writing: 'I often say that the reason I'm a dramatist is because of my chronic indecision. ... It's almost impossible for me to have a single point of view' (quoted in Bayley, 1995, p. 28). Interestingly, Devlin also raises the possibility that patriarchal voices negate the existence of homosexual identity. Her brief mention of Manus's possible homosexuality reinforces the play's wider message that unsettling or unfavourable perspectives have historically been marginalised in traditionalist Irish politics.

The play approaches human experience in and around the Troubles from a variety of perspectives, offering, albeit covertly and symbolically, possible solutions to domestic and sectarian conflicts. Moreover, Devlin avoids singular or monologic viewpoints, instead encouraging open-ended readings of the thoughts and experiences of her characters, both male and female. The rebirth of Irishwomen, as one of the major themes in the play, may suggest a process in which Irish society is transforming itself towards a more liberal and progressive state than hitherto experienced, a state where the rights of social minorities are respected and the lives of civilian people are not conditioned by sectarian prejudices. Finally, the alternative viewpoints of Irish life that Devlin brings out through theatrical performance corresponds to the revisionist historians' appeal for the questioning of a given, male-dominant historiography. The traumas that Irishwomen have suffered for centuries can, nevertheless, form a new keystone upon which Ireland is striving to be a fairer and better country.

Notes

[1]   Despite the activities of late eighteenth-century pioneers such as Mary Wollstonecraft, not until the 1850s did an organised feminist movement evolve in Britain. The 'second wave' of feminism was a phrase coined by Marsha Lear, and indicates the increasing pace of feminist activities which occurred in America, Britain and Europe from the late 1960s onwards. The objectives of this movement include: equal political influence, improved working conditions, equal pay, more occupational choices, child care, and abortion rights.

[2]   Her father, Paddy Devlin (1925-1999), was one of the founders of the Social Democratic and Labour Party (SDLP). The initial objectives of this party included binding together the various strands of non-militant nationalism in the six counties.

[3]   The promotion of Irish nationalism can be seen in *Shan Van Vocht* (Poor Old Woman), a monthly journal founded by Alice Milligan (1866-1953) and Anna Johnson (1866-1902) in Belfast in 1896. *Inghinidhe na hEireann* (Daughters of Ireland), a women's republican support group, was highly regarded by nationalists for their active contribution to Irish independence. Other female groups, such as the Irish Women's Franchise League and the Irish Women's Suffrage Federation, were not much mentioned in nationalist propaganda because of their equivocal stance on the Irish Question.

[4] Spivak quotes Ranajit Guha's naming of the elitist, dominant groups involved in the making of Subaltern Studies. Most of the elites in these studied groups had been schooled at, or worked for, colonial institutes, adopting an elitist speech that is not necessarily the subaltern's own. These groups include: dominant foreign groups, dominant indigenous groups at the all-India level and dominant indigenous groups at the regional and local levels. Moreover, 'the same class or element which was dominant in one area ... could be among the dominated in another' (Spivak, 1993, p. 291).

References

Anderson, B., *Imagined Communities: Reflections on the Origin and Spread of Nationalism*, Verso, London and New York, 1991.

Bayley, C. (1995), 'A Passion for the Theatre of Ecstasy', *The Independent*, 25 March, p. 28.

Bhabha, H. K. (1994), *The Location of Culture*, Routledge, London and New York.

Devlin, A. (1994), *After Easter*, Faber, London.

Foley, I. (2003), interview with Anne Devlin, *The Girls in the Big Picture: Gender in Contemporary Ulster Theatre*, Blackstaff, Belfast, pp. 71-4.

Friedlander, S., (1997), 'Probing the Limits of Representation: the Holocaust Debate', in *The Postmodern History Reader*, ed. K. Jenkins, Routledge, London and New York, pp. 384-6.

Lacan, J. (1997), *The Four Fundamental Concepts of Psychoanalysis*, trans. A. Sheridan, Hogarth, London.

Laffan, M. (1991), 'Insular Attitudes: The Revisionists and their Critics', in *Revising the Rising*, ed. M. N. Dhonnchadha and T. Dorgan, Field Day, Derry, pp. 106-21.

Luddy, M. (ed.) (1995), *Women in Ireland, 1800-1918: A Documentary History*, Cork University Press, Cork.

McWilliams, M. (1991), 'Women in Northern Ireland: an Overview'. in *Culture and Politics in Northern Ireland 1960-1990*, ed. E. Hughes, Open University Press, Milton Keynes, pp. 81-100.

Persic, C. (2004), 'The Emergence of a Gender Consciousness: Women and Community Work in West Belfast', in *Irish Women and Nationalism: Soldiers, New Women and Wicked Hags*, ed. L. Ryan and M. Ward, Irish Academic Press, Dublin, pp. 167-83.

Spivak, G. C. (1993), 'Can the Subaltern Speak?', in *Colonial Discourse and Post-colonial Theory: A Reader*, ed. P. Williams and L. Chrisman, Harvester Wheatsheaf, London, pp. 66-111.

Spivak, G. C. (1996), *The Spivak Reader*, ed. D. Landry and G. MacLean, Routledge, London and New York.

Tóibín, C. (1996), 'In Two Minds about Ireland', in *London Review of Books: An Anthology*, ed. J. Hindle, Verso, London, pp. 213-32.

Social and Cultural Change in Ireland as seen in Roddy Doyle's Paula Spencer Novels

Eamon Maher
Institute of Technology, Tallaght, Dublin

Much has been written about Roddy Doyle's emergence as a highly successful writer of urban fiction at the end of the 1980s and the beginning of the 1990s, a period that saw the publication of *The Barrytown Trilogy - The Commitments* (1987), *The Snapper* (1990) and *The Van* (1991). All three novels were made into successful films and *The Van* was shortlisted for the prestigious Booker Prize.

1993, however, was undoubtedly the high point of Doyle's career to date: it saw the publication of *Paddy Clarke Ha Ha Ha*, which won the Booker Prize for its author. The award was a sweet validation of Doyle's literary merits, given the degree to which he had suffered at the hands of some critics. His novels were not always seen as literary, generously spliced as they are with expletive-filled dialogues and with plots generally revolving around loveable beer-swilling north-side Dublin working class characters. Doyle himself, in a feisty interview with Caramine White, took up the cudgels on the subject of the 'literariness' of his work:

> One of the big issues about my books is whether they are literary or not. They were on the list for books to be taught in schools, but they're off the list now because the Minister for Education decided they weren't literary. ... But the idea that they are less literary because they use the vernacular – I don't agree. The decision to use the vernacular is a literary decision. The decision to use the work 'fuck' is a literary decision. It's a decision of rhythm. ... I've tried to surround the characters with their own world. So that's where the language, the images, the music and the rest come from – the same reasoning. I try to get down to the characters. (Doyle, cited in Caramine White, 2001, p. 182)

Gerry Smyth maintains that 'Doyle depicts a side of Irish life that had never found its voice in the nation's fiction' (Smyth, 1997, p. 67), namely the 'new' working class suburbs of Dublin. Dermot McCarthy argues that the writer refuses to buy into the myth according to which Ireland suddenly 'reinvented' itself in the 1990s, with its spectacular shift from being a colonial to a postcolonial, rural-agricultural to urban-industrial, Catholic and nationalist to secular and post-nationalist, society. He notes:

> If Doyle's narrative imagination articulates anything of an abstract nature, it is that any ambition to be 'central' to anything is suspect; that playing the nation-state game as that game has been played for the past three centuries is not worth the candle; that replacing the stereotypical 'stage Irishman' role with another on the 'world stage' is still 'performing' or 'acting' in a way that calls into question the authenticity of the agent concealed within the role. (McCarthy, 2003, p. 6)

One aspect on which most commentators are agreed is how easy Doyle's novels are to read. The trilogy is very amusing in places, but, contrary to what some critics would have you believe, it does not attempt to belittle the impact of unemployment and unplanned pregnancy, alcohol abuse and poor dietary habits, issues that are all touched on in the three novels. Michael Cronin argues that the backdrop to the trilogy was the arrested modernisation of the Republic of Ireland in the 1980s after 'the economic reforms of the 1960s and the tentative moves towards liberalisation of the society in the 1970s' (Cronin, 2006, pp. 4-5) These developments would fall foul of two negating influences in the 1980s:

> The first was the virtual collapse of the economy in the 1980s, with record levels of unemployment, high inflation and substantial outward migration. The second was the backlash against moves to liberalise social legislation with the 1983 and 1986 abortion and divorce referenda. The triumphant trajectory of modernisation appeared to have been brutally interrupted and once again poverty, joblessness and emigration seemed to be the inevitable fate of the Irish urban poor. (Cronin, 2006, p. 5)

There are certainly examples of the triumph of failure to be seen in the trilogy but that is because Doyle was intent on avoiding any facile sentimental portrayal of the north Dublin city working classes. He pointed this out in an interview in 1993: 'If you say that you have to be wracked with angst and that you have to write of your direct experience which essentially must be miserable, you're denying an awful lot of people and an awful lot of possibilities' (Doyle, quoted in Fay, 1993, p. 39).

While drawing occasionally on earlier work by Doyle, my concern in this essay will be to highlight the way in which the publication of *The Woman Who Walked into Doors* (1996) marks a significant new phase in Doyle's career. From this point onwards he comes to grips with societal change in Ireland in a more systematic and ultimately convincing manner. I do not argue that this novel and its sequel, *Paula Spencer* (2006), are better or worse novels than Doyle's other fiction. Rather, my aim is to demonstrate the extent to which they chart the move from the Ireland of the 1970s and 80s right through to the early twentieth-first century. We do not need to be told how seismic a period this has been for Ireland. The cultural, economic, political and religious landscape was completely transformed by tribunals investigating payments to politicians, the unveiling of the systemic abuse of children in industrial schools and orphanages, and the clerical child abuse scandal. Doyle stated in an interview with Gerry Smyth in September 1996: 'For anybody living in Ireland, particularly in the last five years, it's not just an economic thing. It's cultural, religious, social, every aspect. You should bring your passport to bed with you because you're going to wake up in a different place' (Doyle, cited in Smyth, 1997, p. 102). The moral authority of the former pillars of Irish society, Church and State, slowly crumbled. People were no longer prepared to be preached to by people or the institutions they represented, especially when serious flaws had been exposed in relation to the activities of some of their number. Change was everywhere visible: divorce was legalised, and homosexuality decriminalised. Contraceptives became widely available, emigration stopped as the economy showed signs of unprecedented growth, and generally a wave of consumer liberalism swept through the country. Roddy Doyle campaigned actively for divorce and found himself resentful of a certain Catholic mindset that was opposed to change:

> It basically was the Catholic Church against everyone else. It was the insistence that if you're Irish, you're white and you're Catholic as well, and if you're not both of those things then you're not fully Irish. Ultimately that is what it (divorce referendum) was all about ... I felt that it was a real fight, a fight for the future of my children and the future of the country. I was very, very emotionally involved. (Doyle, cited in Fay, 1996, p. 19)

A certain amount of this type of anger is palpable in *The Woman Who Walked into Doors*, which emerged out of the screenplay Doyle wrote for the RTÉ/BBC film drama, *Family*. It offers a snapshot of the life of Paula Spencer from childhood up to her marriage to the violent and criminal Charlo, who, we are informed in the opening pages of the novel, dies in a foiled kidnap attempt of the wife of a bank manager. Gone are the easy-going Rabbittes of the *Barrytown Trilogy* who never really became violent or threatening. Charlo is a self-serving, domineering man who can switch from charming to nasty in the blink of an eye. To Doyle's credit, he does show some of the attractive qualities his character possessed in the eyes of his future wife. He offered an escape from a home that was dominated by an abusive father whose attentions were more focused on Paula's sister Carmel than on her. He played horsey-horsey with Paula and her younger sister Denise (a dubious enough activity) while ordering Carmel to make tea. Looking back on her youth, Paula recalls that Carmel and her father were always fighting: 'I remember the screams and the punches. She remembers them as well but she refuses to remember anything else, the good things about home and my father' (Doyle, 1996, p. 46).

Paula blots out a lot of the unpleasant parts of her childhood and insists on trying to explain away her father's perversity: 'He loved her. That was why he did it. Fathers were different then. He'd meant it for the best, being cruel to be kind. Carmel hated him. She remembers nothing else' (Doyle, 1996, pp. 46-7). School was an unpleasant experience from start to finish. Teachers had no interest in the children and little enthusiasm for their profession, whereas boys, probably following on their fathers' example, saw girls as 'sluts':

> Where I grew up – and probably everywhere else – you were a slut or a tight bitch, one or the other, if you were a girl – and usually before you were thirteen. You didn't have to do anything to be a slut. If you were good-looking; if you grew up fast. If you had a sexy walk; if you had clean hair, if you had dirty hair. If you wore platform shoes, and if you didn't. Anything could get you called a slut. (Doyle, 1996, pp. 45-6)

Paula gains some revenge on the male race on one occasion when she violently masturbates 'a good-looking thick' at the back of the class. For once, she feels she can exert power over men. The victory is short-lived, though, and the account of Paula's life up until the moment she meets Charlo shows her to have been damaged by her experiences at home and in school. She says that what happened her in school was in no way unusual: 'I wasn't the only one. It happened to all of us. We went in children and we turned into animals' (Doyle, 1996, p. 36). With such low self-esteem, it was natural that Paula should seek out a man who exuded confidence and disdain for all about him. She doesn't over-romanticise Charlo or try to make him into some sort of demi-God. She maintains that he respected her and made her feel good about herself: 'I stopped being a slut the minute Charlo Spencer started dancing with me ... People looked at me and they saw someone different' (Doyle, 1996, p. 45). Brian Donnelly quotes in its entirety the description of the first visit Charlo made to Paula's house and how proud she was of his confidence in front of her parents and concludes: 'Paula's recollection dramatizes the vibrancy and nervous excitement of a young woman in love and reveals the vulnerability that Charlo would prey upon so relentlessly' (Donnelly, 2000, p. 26). Shortly after their marriage, she would discover that her husband was just another in a long line of men who couldn't, or wouldn't, give her the respect that she so craved. In keeping with the psychological battering she received at home and in school, Paula always believed there was something wrong with her that made men act in a violent manner towards her:

> There was something about me that drew them to me, that made them touch me. It was my tits that I was too young for; I'd no right to them. It was my hair. It was my legs and my arms and my neck. There were things about me that were wrong and dirty. (Doyle, 1996, p. 35)

For a short time, Charlo and she had been happy. There was employment available for people who wanted it – the papers were full of ads for skilled labourers and people to work on the building sites that were springing up all around Dublin – but Charlo didn't always desire legal employment. It wasn't the trauma of being unemployed that made him hit her for the first time either. The descriptions of the beatings are harrowing and their impact is summed up by Paula in the following manner: 'I have a theory about it. Being hit by Charlo the first time knocked everything else out of me' (Doyle, 1996, p. 168). She was pregnant at the time and so the beating seemed even more unjustified. Alcohol offered a temporary escape from the horror into which her life had slipped; it got an ever-increasing hold over her as the domestic situation worsened:

> He butted me with his head. He held me still and he butted me. I couldn't believe it. He dragged me around the house by my clothes and by my hair. He kicked me up and he kicked me down the stairs. Bruised me, scalded me, threatened me. For seventeen years. (Doyle, 1996, p. 176)

The matter-of-fact manner in which this litany of abuse is recounted shows how with the passing years resignation took the place of anger. Then of course there was the constant recourse to seeing herself as being somehow responsible for Charlo's behaviour:

> I kept blaming myself. After all the years and the broken bones and teeth and torture I still keep on blaming myself. I can't help it. What if? What if? He wouldn't have hit me if I hadn't…; none of the other fists and belts would have followed if I hadn't… He hit me, he hit his children, he hit other people, he killed a woman – and I keep blaming myself. For provoking him. For not loving him enough; for not showing it. (Doyle, 1996, p.170)

For seventeen years, Paula endures this barrage of violence and nobody steps in to cry halt. The doctors and the nurses in the hospital didn't ask the obvious question when she presented with more bruises and broken bones. They smelt the drink and assumed she had fallen down the stairs, or walked into a door. Her parents didn't intervene, neither did her sisters, or Charlo's family, even though they must have all suspected what was going on. There is a sense in which society was complicit in what happened, in much the same way as Irish people turned a blind eye to the plight of girls who were committed to the Magdalen Laundries or children who were sent to the industrial schools. Paula was left with no one to turn to, exposed to an infernal repetition of the same scenario. Even a female doctor at the hospital fails to ask the obvious question. Had she done so, it might have been possible to do something to save Paula. But silence was the order of the day:

> 'I fell down the stairs again', I told her. Sorry.
> No questions asked. What about the burn on my hand? The missing hair? The teeth? I wanted to be asked. Ask me. Ask me. Ask me. I'd tell her. I'd tell them everything. Look at the burn. Ask me about it. Ask. (Doyle, 1996, p. 164)

Doyle manages skilfully to convey the confused mental state of his heroine. After one severe beating, Paula sees her husband worriedly examining her face and body and thinks: 'He loved me again. He held my chin. He skipped over my eyes. He couldn't look straight at me. He felt guilty, dreadful. He loved me again. What happened? I provoked him. I was to blame' (Doyle, 1996, p. 27). Brian Donnelly notes the difficulty Doyle must have encountered in remaining faithful to 'the linguistic range of the character without resorting to a succession of short sentences … His achievement in this case is that, by and large, he creates an appropriate eloquence for Paula' (Donnelly, 2000, p. 27). Her eloquence comes from the consistency of her psyche as wounded victim and a woman who is intuitive and self-critical. The narrative is in some ways Paula's attempt to make some sense out of her life. She is not a well-educated woman with recourse to a supportive family or social network: she is alone in her struggle to surmount her awful plight. Her children are suitably dysfunctional: John-Paul is a heroin addict and Leanne appears destined to follow the path to addiction also. The youngest, Jack, seems to be the only one to escape serious damage – so far.

It doesn't naturally occur to Paula to seek protection from her husband's attacks. Recording her experiences is therapeutic for her. She recognises that her sister Carmel has difficulty with her slightly sanitised version of events: 'I'm not. What Carmel says. Rewriting history. I'm doing the opposite. I want to know the truth, not make it up' (Doyle, 1996, pp. 56-7). There are times when she is extremely lucid about herself: she feels terrible guilt for neglecting the kids, not protecting them from their father. She recognises that she cannot give up the booze: 'I am an alcoholic. I've never admitted it to anyone. (No one would want to know.) I've never done anything about it; I've never tried to stop. I think I could if I really wanted to, if I was ready' (Doyle, 1996, p. 88). The event that sparks a transformation in Paula is the day she sees her husband looking at their daughter Nicola in an inappropriate manner. Something snaps in her as the primeval maternal instinct to protect their young takes over. Whatever she felt about him abusing her, Paula wasn't going to allow him inflict himself on their daughter. She hits him on the head with a frying pan:

> He dropped like shite from a height. I could feel it through my arms. He fell like I used to fall. All the years, the stitches, all the cries, the baby I lost – I could feel them all in my arms going into the pan. They lifted it. They were with me. Down on his head. (Doyle, 1996, p. 213)

This is the moment Paula frees herself from Charlo's insidious grip. However, that naturally doesn't rid her of all the other problems: alcohol dependency, psychological scars, financial worries, bringing up a family on her own. That said, there is a definite sense of elation when she takes her destiny in her own hands and drives the bullying husband out of the house. The kids are happy to see the back of him as well. This is how *The Woman Who Walked into Doors* ends. In an interview with Gerry Smyth shortly after the publication of the novel, Doyle hinted that he and Paula had not finished their dialogue. Like the French novelist François Mauriac's fascination with Thérèse Desqueyroux, a character who continued to fascinate him long after her appearance in one of his most successful novels, Doyle sensed that he would return to his heroine at a subsequent date:

> I would be open to the idea of going back to characters. For example, I like the idea of somewhere along the line going back to Paula when she is six years older and I'm six years older, Ireland will have changed dramatically, and there'll be plenty of material there to wonder what has happened to her. It would inevitably be a very different book because she's already told her story up to 1993, although that story is deliberately left open. (Doyle, cited in Smyth, 1997, p. 108)

It took a bit longer than he had expected, but return to Paula he did, and with most felicitous results. We note from the outset of *Paula Spencer* that we are dealing with a more mature woman (in her late forties), but still someone who has to confront her demons. Primary among them is alcohol, which she has not touched for a year but whose soothing balm she still craves. She works as a cleaner in Celtic Tiger Ireland, one of the very few native Irish engaged in this activity. Of the four children, two, John-Paula and Nicola, have left home, while the other two, Leanne and Jack, are still living with Paula. John-Paul is clean of drugs and living with the mother of his two children and Nicola is married with kids. To judge from appearances, they could be deemed to be doing alright, especially considering the trauma that marked their childhood. Still, underneath the surface, some serious problems persist: 'Leanne scares Paula. The guilt. It's always there. Leanne is twenty-two. Leanne wets her bed. Leanne deals with it. It's terrible' (Doyle, 2006, p. 5). Doyle makes use of this type of telegraphic style throughout: it is an effective way of conveying Paula's thoughts as they impinge on her consciousness. He shows a remarkable capacity to climb inside her head and convey the misgivings she harbours about what is happening to her children: Will John-Paul go back on heroin? Is Nicola happy? What will she do if Leanne continues to show such an unhealthy liking for drink? And Jack, the youngest and her favourite, will he manage to realise his full potential? Caring for her offspring is what keeps Paula on the straight and narrow, but it's hard going: 'She has to know where Leanne is. All the time. She's on her own here, but she's never alone. And it's not just Leanne. Her children are all around her, all their different ages and faces. She has four divided into thousands. There are so many Leannes' (Doyle, 2006, p. 160).

Her struggle with alcoholism is painful and constant. On one occasion she scours Leanne's room in search of a can or a bottle. She finally comes across a can under the bed and feverishly puts it to her mouth, but it's completely empty. She had a lucky escape and she knows it. Her drinking has wreaked havoc in her life and that of her children and yet she's only ever one drink away from slipping back into the abyss. She marvels at how her sisters Carmel and Denise can drink like fish and still not go under. Paula thinks back to the time when she lay on the floor after one of Charlo's beatings. Being sober brings acuity to her evocation of the past, but it does not necessarily bring healing:

> Maybe it's age. And it's definitely the drink. She's not sure. Maybe it's the way the brain works to protect itself. It invents a new woman who can look back and wonder, instead of look back and howl. Maybe it happens

to everyone. But it's definitely the drink, or life without it. It's a different world. She's not sure she likes it that much. But she's a new-old woman, learning how to live. (Doyle, 2006, p. 136)

Passages like this are what give Doyle's Paula Spencer novels such force. Her ruminations on life ring true; she gives us access to her most intimate hopes and fears and her comments are always consistent with her personality and character. Doyle allows her the freedom to develop and to reach some sort of accommodation with a much-changed Ireland. She doesn't bemoan her lowly position on the social ladder or resent the fact that Carmel is buying property in Bulgaria or that Denise is having an affair with a man she met at a parent-teacher meeting. Change is omnipresent:

> The whole area has changed. She's been here since the beginning. It was a farm a few months before they moved in. It was all young families, kids all over the place. Out in the middle of nowhere. No bus of its own. Near the tracks, but no train station. No proper shops, no pub. No church or schools. Nothing but the houses and the people. (Doyle, 2006, p. 17)

Paula doesn't express an opinion as to whether things have changed for the better or the worse but the reader has the distinct impression that she and the other inhabitants of this estate are the forgotten people, the ones who are left to survive as best they can in this concrete jungle, this ghetto where there is little hope of advancement. Religion, education, social amenities are conspicuous by their absence. It would take a giant step for anyone to rise to the top from such a background: the more normal destiny would be to remain rooted at the bottom of the social scale. Paula has to work very hard indeed to make ends meet. Possessing no educational qualifications, she finds herself in middle age cleaning office blocks and tidying up after open-air concerts. Through sheer hard work, she manages to get Jack a computer for Christmas and feels huge pride as she watches him surfing the internet. When she is working, even though her bones ache, at least she is being kept busy. Paula's friend, Rita Kavanagh, dates the arrival of a prosperous Ireland back to the emergence of so many children's clothes shops: 'I noticed them before all the new cars. And the talk about house prices. Even all the cranes' (Doyle, 2006, p. 166).

References to significant events give some chronological order to the narrative: the tsunami in Asia, the death of Pope John-Paul II, Liverpool winning the Champions' League, the tragic death of five girls in the Meath school bus accident. Paula's Dublin is a vastly different place to what we encountered in *The Woman Who Walked into Doors*. Religion was never a big influence in her life, the scepticism possibly fuelled by a negative impression a local priest had on her: 'The looks he gave me when he was talking about faith and the Blessed Virgin, it wasn't my tea he was after or my biscuits. It isn't just the bishops who like to get their exercise' (Doyle, 2006, p. 90). This is an evident allusion to Bishop Eamonn Casey, who provoked great scandal when it was discovered in May 1992 that he had fathered a child with a distant American cousin, Annie Murphy, some years previously, an event that marked the beginning of a downward spiral for the Catholic Church in Ireland. Paula turns up her U2 CD, thinking that she will impress the Poles living next door. Then again, they probably won't be there, as they leave early every morning and return late: 'Sunday's the only day she really hears them. She sees them go out on the street, in their good clothes. They're the only ones heading off to Mass' (Doyle, 2006, p. 272). Ireland has become a multicultural society, one that boasts full employment and growth rates that are the envy of the developed world. Things have definitely progressed from the declaration by Jimmy Rabbitte who, in *The Commitments*, encourages his band to produce a new form of soul music, stating that soul is about sex and politics, but a different kind of politics, the politics of disenchantment:

> 'The Irish are the niggers of Europe, lads'.
> They nearly gasped: it was so true.
> 'An' Dubliners are the niggers of Ireland. The culchies have fuckin' everythin'. An' the northside Dubliners are the niggers o' Dublin.
> Say it loud, I'm black an' I'm proud'. (Doyle, 1987, pp. 7-8)

Already in the first instalment of the trilogy, there was a social message evident in Doyle's work. Religion was not satisfying the needs of Jimmy Rabbitte's generation and social background and so they needed to find some worthwhile alternative: be it music, alcohol or sex. The economic climate was bleak, unemployment spiralling out of control, the population of the north city working class suburbs demoralised. In *Paula Spencer*, the problems encountered seem to be more existential than financial. In fact, the economic prosperity, the huge retail outlets, the bigger cars, the property abroad, have pretty much passed Paula by. Even those close to her who have improved their economic status don't seem to be terribly happy: 'They're all cracking open. They all have to baste themselves' (Doyle, 2006, p. 188). Doyle's heroine can at least point to some significant improvements in her own life: she has enough money to get by, she is a reasonable success as a sober mother and she is no longer the victim of a vicious husband. The final pages of the novel show her making her way to the Mater hospital to see Carmel, who has had a mastectomy. Paula has met an older man, Joe, whose wife left him for another woman and with whom she may enjoy some companionship, although it is far too early to judge how the relationship will develop. What the future holds for her in the new Ireland is also left hanging in the air. Her greatest achievement is to have survived in light of the rotten hand she has been dealt. The last lines read: 'It's her birthday. She's forty-nine. She bought a cake earlier. It's in the fridge. They'll have it when she gets home' (Doyle, 2006, p. 277). There are no wild dreams here, just a quiet determination to take each day as it comes.

At times, in the *Barrytown Trilogy*, readers have the impression that for all that they live in a pretty disadvantaged milieu, Doyle's characters nevertheless maintain an amiable and appealing disposition. They are far from wallowing in self-pity and appear, in fact, to be making a reasonable fist of their lives. Michael Cronin remarks:

It is possible to see why politically informed critics can object to the conventional representation of lowlife characters as amiable clowns, it is equally necessary to avoid the tyranny of a kind of pedagogic earnestness which becomes a veiled form of class condescension in its insistence on viewing the working-class life in one way and one way only. (Cronin, 2006, pp. 5-6)

It would be equally wrong for Doyle to have given himself over completely to the tragic aspects of Paula Spencer's experiences and to have given her an eloquent voice to rail against the inequity of her situation. But, as we have seen, what is most impressive about the two Paula Spencer novels is precisely the degree to which the author refrains from putting expressions in Paula's mouth that don't fit her character and background. He stated once in an interview: 'You can't graft anger onto characters just because it suits certain reviewers'. And he continues: 'The reader can make his or her mind up about the characters and what happens to them. The reader doesn't need me to tell him or her how to think' (Doyle, cited in Fay, 1993, p. 40). It is this restraint that distinguishes Doyle from his talented contemporary, Dermot Bolger, who, in *The Journey Home* (1990) in particular, tends to allow social commentary too free a rein. Take the following example of how the main character in the novel, Hano, while looking from the window of a city centre pub, has a premonition of the ominous fate that awaits Irish society:

Far below, Dublin was moving towards the violent crescendo of its Friday night, taking to the twentieth century like an aborigine to whiskey. Glue sniffers stumbled into each other, coats over their arms as they tried to pick pockets. Stolen cars zigzagged through the distant grey estates where pensioners prayed anxiously behind bolted doors, listening for the smash of glass. In the new disco bars children were queuing, girls of fourteen shoving their way up for last drinks at the bar. (Bolger, 2003, p. 47)

It is highly unlikely that Hano would have been capable of such detailed analysis of the way cosmopolitan Dublin was heading down the slippery slope of substance abuse, car theft and the orgy of underage drinking. So the only conclusion one can reach is that the novelist is transposing his own view of the situation on to his character. Hano, and the other depictions in this novel, feel displaced and marginalised in the hostile city that is Dublin. They are in a state of perpetual dislocation throughout the novel and the image that is translated of their hapless lives is an extremely pessimistic one. The error Bolger makes is to allow the (justifiable) anger he felt about political corruption and social discrimination to come across in the novel; Doyle is careful not to fall into that particular trap. This is not to detract from the important role Bolger has played in highlighting the ineptitude of the leaders of both Church and State when it came to tackling the massive gap between rich and poor, between the haves and the have-nots in Irish society. This ineptitude may have been linked to the threat such a move would have posed to their own privileged status in Irish society, a status that has been eroded in more recent years by revelations of political corruption and the clerical sex abuse scandals. I make this brief parenthesis in order to show how two talented novelists can differ in their treatment of analogous social contexts. While they have a similar ideological position on many issues, the manner in which they explore these issues in their novels is very different.

Brian Donnelly argues that Roddy Doyle's novels 'attempt to articulate a part of late twentieth-century Irish experience that had largely remained outside the horizons of Irish literature, ways of life hidden from the concerns of people who typically buy and read literary fiction in Ireland' (Donnelly, 2000, p. 27). With the publication of *Paula Spencer*, we can now add the early part of the twenty-first century to this assessment, where the experience of the heroine would be even more foreign to the bulk of Irish people who buy and read fiction. Donnelly continues: 'Like (William) Carleton, Doyle's enterprise involved an imaginative reproduction of the world of his characters, articulated in their own words' (Donnelly, 2000, p. 27). There is a certain language which has the ring of a real hammer on a real nail, which is true to the experience it conveys. This explains the popularity of Doyle's portrayal: there is no discernibly false note in what Paula says or thinks. Her feelings are ones with which all humans can identify and are expressed in a wonderfully transparent language. By commenting on what she lives through, she is providing a kind of diary for the progression of Irish society in the past three decades. This is what prompts Sylvie Mikowski to compare Doyle's chronicle of Dublin with that of McGahern's rural Ireland, both of which expose contentious hidden aspects of Irish society, especially in the realm of domestic violence:

> But while McGahern suggests a link between this violence and the history of the nation, Doyle resituates the problem of domestic violence in a more social setting, attributing the causes of this phenomenon to poverty, a lack of education and all the handicaps afflicting the most marginalized sections of the population. (Mikowski, 2004, p. 121)

Doyle is also one of the few contemporary Irish novelists to tackle in a serious way the consequences of immigration in the establishment of a multicultural society, the prosperity of an elite that has been hugely enhanced by the past few decades of economic prosperity and the quiet desperation of others who, like Paula, continue to struggle with their demons at a remove from the public limelight. Paula's is the kind of story that doesn't make the front pages of newspapers because she stumbles through her life with a quiet dignity, seeking merely to survive from day to day and to be as good a mother as she can be in difficult circumstances. She is representative of a generation of Dublin working class women who have been failed by the political, religious and educational systems and yet who survive and even manage to achieve some control over their lives in spite of the odds stacked against them. Paula seems to be a glowing example of how the human spirit is indomitable and Roddy Doyle deserves credit for giving a voice to such a compelling and utterly convincing post-Celtic Tiger woman. In fact, with the publication of *Paula Spencer*, Doyle has grown into a novelist of substance and is rightly now placed among the finest living Irish prose writers. He has become one of those people who manage to change a country, not by arguing about it, but by describing it. This, in my view, is what will end up being his major contribution to Irish letters.

References

Bolger, D. (2003), *The Journey Home*, Flamingo, London.

Cronin, M. (2006), *The Barrytown Trilogy*, Cork University Press, Cork.

Donnelly, B. (2000), 'Roddy Doyle: From Barrytown to the GPO', *Irish University Review,* 30 (1), pp. 17-31.

Doyle, R. (1987), *The Commitments*, King Farouk, Dublin.

Doyle, R. (1993), *The Woman Who Walked into Doors*, Vintage, London.

Doyle, R. (2006), *Paula Spencer*, Jonathan Cape, London.

Fay, L. (1996), 'What's the Story?', in *Hot Press*, 3 April, p. 19.

Fay, L. (1993), 'Never Mind the Bollix!', *Hot Press*, 17 (10), pp. 39-40.

McCarthy, D. (2003), *Roddy Doyle: Raining on the Parade*, The Liffey Press, Dublin.

Mikowski, S. (2004), *Le Roman Irlandais Contemporain*, Presses Universitaires de Caen, Caen.

Smyth, G. (1997), *The Novel and the Nation*, Pluto Press, London.

White, C. (2001), *Reading Roddy Doyle*, Syracuse University Press, New York.

Terrorised Youths – Colum McCann's *Everything in this Country Must* and the Northern Irish Troubles

Eóin Flannery

Oxford Brookes University

The Northern Irish Troubles have been well narrated within the novel form. Indeed, Michael Storey has estimated that as many as five hundred novels deal with the cultural geography and the political history of the conflict (Storey, 2004, p. 10) and there has been a rich body of critical writing on this work. However, with a few exceptions, the representation of the Troubles in the short story form has received considerably less critical attention. There are some honourable exceptions. Ronan McDonald has published an accomplished essay, 'Strategies of Silence: Colonial Strains in Short Stories of the Troubles', while Michael Storey's *Representing the Troubles in Irish Short Fiction* is the sole book-length survey of this literary genre and the striven history of the Northern Troubles. Notwithstanding the relative merits, and limitations, of these two interventions, the shorter fictional works of Colum McCann have not been represented in critical accounts of the fictional heritage of Northern Ireland. It is, therefore, my intention to redress such neglect here in focusing on McCann's collection, *Everything in This Country Must* (2000). Each of the stories in this collection are refracted through the consciousness of a youthful, emergent narrator and in each story McCann deliberately focuses on the complex processes of emotional awakening attached to this period of life – a period made all the more trying in the debilitating shadow of the Northern Troubles. Likewise McCann draws attention to the role of the body within these narratives: the blossoming, problematic sexuality of the female body; the immobile body of the father figure; and finally the ravaged body of the hunger striker, and I will summarily deal with this thematic *leitmotif*. In tackling the embedded contradictory convictions of the Northern Troubles, then, McCann avails himself of the suggestive and localised form of the short story, allowing its compressed borders of revelation to illuminate basic human truths in fragmentary moments of crisis.

With the publication of *Everything in This Country Must* in 2000, Colum McCann returned to the literary province of short fiction, the genre that had initially launched him as a writer of considerable promise in 1994, when, at the age of twenty-nine, he debuted with the short-story collection *Fishing the Sloe-Black River*. The later collection, however, is not confined to the short-story mode; *Everything in This Country Must* contains two short stories, 'Everything in This Country Must' and 'Wood', and a novella, *Hunger Strike*. Yet it is not just at the level of form that McCann strikes a note of continuity between the two editions. The earlier collection ends with a story entitled 'Cathal's Lake', a story that concerns itself with the violence of the Northern Troubles. 'Cathal's Lake', like many interventions on the cultural politics of violence, probes the mechanics of individual and communal rituals; the basis of the story is drawn from an old Jewish myth, which tells of the existence of thirty-six hidden saints, who bury the world's sorrows so that it can continue to function, as well as bringing to mind the Irish myth of the Children of Lir. The story is narrated from the point of view of a middle-aged man, the eponymous Cathal, whose ritualised rural existence is tethered to the cyclical violence of urban civil unrest in the North. McCann's importation of such mythic structures, however, is not confined to this story – his use of magic realism is a recurrent feature in his first collection of stories. His employment of the magically real transfuses the characteristically pessimistic political and philosophical tenors of realist representation with the narrative contingency of myth, magic and folklore. These structural devices are, typically, exiled from the mainstream of naturalistic representation on the grounds of anachronicity and naiveté. Significantly, McCann's co-option of magic realism into the minor art form of the short story, specifically in 'Cathal's Lake', is, then, both politically and aesthetically enabling. It is a coupling, at the levels of form and content, that eschews the aridity of telling in favour of the fertility of imaginative suggestion.

The narrative begins with the ambiguous reflection by Cathal that 'It's a sad Sunday when a man has to find another swan in the soil' (McCann, 1994, p. 173) – a statement that only assumes its full meaning at the end of the story. Its magically real connotations are replaced for the majority of the narrative by an uncharacteristically realist approach from McCann, whose style is most often noted for its linguistic sensuality and its rich symbolism. However, in this story, McCann stylistically melds the magical, the real and the mythic within the limits of the short story form. The accommodation of marginal individuals and constituencies within the narrative codes of the short story is abetted here in the coupling of narrative realism with the non-realist register of the magically real. This stylistic turn to magic realism imports another literary register that is traditionally associated with narratives of oppression, exile, displacement or cultural resistance.

In a fashion reminiscent of the works of Michael McLaverty, McCann's story navigates both the urban and the rural in the Northern province. The urban is portrayed as an incendiary crucible of intercommunal aggression, while the rural, almost Arcadian, milieu in which the enigmatic figure of Cathal lives is a sanctuary of calm and renewal. In contrast to these regenerative surroundings, on hearing of the death of a teenage boy in sectarian disturbances in Derry, Cathal imagines the *mis-en-scène* of the youth's demise:

> Maybe a head of hair on him like a wheat field. Or eyes as blue as thrush eggs. Young, awkward and gangly, with perhaps a Liverpool scarf tied around his mouth and his tongue flickering into the wool with a vast obscenity carved from the bottom of his stomach. A bottle of petrol in his hands and a rag from his mother's kitchen lit in the top. His arms in the beginnings of a windmill hurl. (McCann, 1994, p. 173)

The boy's strained, physical posture, poised in the act of violence is, however, abruptly altered in the next line, 'Then a plastic bullet slamming in his chest, all six inches of it hurtling against his lung at 100 miles per hour. The bottle somersaulting from the boy's fingers. Smashing on the street beneath his back. Thrush eggs broken and rows of wheat going up in flames' (McCann, 1994, p. 173). The verbal intensity of McCann's language here, together with the report of the statistical specifics of the plastic bullet, enforces the brute physicality of this uneven suburban military exchange. The image drawn by McCann is clearly that projected time and again on news footage from any one of hundreds of civil riots across the North of Ireland since the late 1960s. But also, the description recapitulates Seamus Heaney's image of the random murder victim in 'Keeping Going', wherein the body-as-image is dismembered and fractioned: 'And then he saw an ordinary face/ For what it was and a gun in his own face./ His right leg was hooked back, his sole and heel/ Against the wall, his right knee propped up steady,/ So he never moved, just pushed with all his might/ Against himself, then fell past the tarred strip,/ Feeding the gutter with his copious blood' (Heaney, 1996, p. 12).

The boy in McCann's story soon assumes the role of victim and of waked corpse – the quasi-rituals of riotous street violence, in which the youth had been implicated, are succeeded in the narrative by the rituals of death and of burial. And while the boy may repose in death, the chafing dynamics of politics and religion continue in arguments regarding his funeral ceremony. Walking through the courtyard of his farm, Cathal wonders 'if they're singing right now, over the poor boy's body?' (McCann, 1994, p. 179). He imagines the visible scars etched on the young body: 'The burns lighted by cosmetics perhaps, the autumn-coloured hair combed back, the eyelids fixed in a way of peace, the mouth bitter and mysterious, the tattooed hand discreetly covered' (McCann, 1994, p. 179). But this physical death, as McCann alludes to in later stories, is not the limit of the boy's narrative resonance; the sacrificial nature of his unwarranted violent death reverberates with ideological and symbolic import throughout the community, extending beyond the confines of the body's biological life-time:

> A priest bickering because he doesn't want a flag draped on the coffin. A sly undertaker saying that the boy deserves the very best. Silk and golden braids. Teenage friends writing poems for him in symbolic candlelight.

> The wilting marigolds jettisoned for roses – fabulous roses with perfect petals. Kitchen rags this time to wipe whiskey from the counter. Butt ends choking up the ashtray. Milk bottles very popular amongst the ladies for cups of tea. (McCann, 1994, p. 179)

The later stories of *Everything in This Country Must* resume this thematic preoccupation; all three narratives are meditations on the physical, emotional and geographical stresses of the internecine conflict in the North of Ireland. In a manner similar to the structure of Eugene McCabe's *Christ in the Fields*, McCann's own Troubles' Trilogy explores, and articulates, entrenched intercommunal beliefs from both sides of the sectarian divide. Specifically, 'Everything in This Country Must' is told from the point of view of a Catholic teenage girl; 'Wood' is narrated by an adolescent Protestant boy, while in *Hunger Strike*, another adolescent boy relates the most ambitious, and also problematic, of the stories, this time a Catholic youth. In these stories McCann's youthful protagonists straddle the border between a mature comprehension of the deep-seated forces that nourish the respective sectarian convictions of their families and localities, and a childlike lack of apprehension of the severity of these naturalised passions. And again, in this sense McCann's narratives recollect the childhood and adolescent emotions and territories of McLaverty's short story, 'Pigeons', and the novel into which the earlier story developed, *Call My Brother Back* [1].

The titular story, 'Everything in This Country Must', opens the collection and establishes a frantic tone in its opening paragraph. McCann initiates the story with a panicked scene in which the young girl and her father are faltering in their combined efforts to save their old draft horse from drowning in the flood-expanded waters of a nearby river:

> A summer flood came and our draft horse got caught in the river. The river smashed against stones and the sound of it to me was like the turning of locks. It was silage time and the water smelled of grass. The draft horse, Father's favourite, had stepped in the river for a sniff maybe and she was caught, couldn't move, her foreleg trapped between rocks. Father found her and called *Katie!* above the wailing of the rain. (McCann, 2000, p. 3)

Besides the obvious idiom of entrapment deployed here, McCann also reprises the verbal intensity of 'Cathal's Lake' cited above; there is a sense of urgency and of violent movement to the beginning of the narrative. The horse itself is of limited practical use on the family farm, but the frenetic rescue is actually fomented by the animal's symbolic value to the girl's father.

As we learn subsequently, and as is a thematic constant in 'Troubles' fiction, the low intensity warfare of the conflict has invaded the domestic space. In this context the girl's mother and brother were killed in a collision with a British Army vehicle some years previously, an incident that was officially adjudicated to have been accidental. And this is a motif that McCann employs in each of the stories in the collection: in 'Wood' the family remains integrated, but the boy's father has suffered a stroke and is effectively paralysed from the neck down, and in the novella, the boy's biological father is also deceased and has been surrogated by his own brother, an imprisoned hunger striker whom the boy has never met [2]. In telescoping the fractured contours of these familial situations, McCann demonstrates how 'political and power structures infiltrate familial and sexual relations' (McDonald, 2005, p. 254). In a colonial context, a context in which the fundamental historical dispute is rooted in the division and occupation of territory, the politics of reproduction and the constitution of communities of ethnic, racial or confessional solidarity are foundational matters. Equally, from a formal perspective, the 'deep' representational horizons of the short story mode find suitable material within the domestic privacies of the family unit, rather than in the more social landscapes of the novel form. And as McDonald mentions, the insinuation of the political on to the topographies of the domestic can be either explicit ideological presences, or more non-political and practical in nature. For a heavily militarised and surveyed society like Northern Ireland, the domestic space, or the family space acts as a kind of 'sanctuary space'. Familial milieus, or local suburban community spaces become sacralised against the physical, and discursive, intrusions of the counter-insurgency state apparatus. The stability attached to such locales becomes a locus of community solidarity, a sign of an inviolable collective will and an assertion of historical continuity. But as McDonald outlines, and as is demonstrable in McCann's fictions, the sanctity and the anchorage of the integrated family unit – the microcosmic incarnation of the broader community's accepted value system – is insistently compromised by external violations.

The fulcrum of the dramatic tension in McCann's narrative is the unexpected arrival of a British Army patrol onto the aforementioned rescue site. As the headlights of their vehicle approach it is assumed by both father and daughter to be those of a neighbour's vehicle. But when they catch sight of the uniformed figures exiting the jeep in order to aid the rescue efforts, the father recoils from his attempt to save the animal. Essentially, the draft horse's affective worth to him is negated by its rescue by the British soldiers, accomplices, however obliquely, to his more acute familial loss several years before. In this sense, then, the father is representative of congealed forms of cultural memory – embedded in divisive simplicities, which foreclose any semblance of political rapprochement, even at the level of the practical and interpersonal. While his perceptions of the soldiers are coloured exclusively by the pained hatred of his own private loss, his fifteen-year-old daughter, the first person narrator of the story, is of a more inclusive disposition. As she observes the various military bodies disperse in their rescue strategy, she christens each of them according to their physical features: one becomes 'Hayknife' because he 'had a scar on his cheek like the bottom end of Father's barn hayknife'; another 'had a moustache that looked like long grasses' and, therefore is dubbed 'LongGrasses', and yet another, whose 'hair was the colour of winter ice', is 'Icehair' (McCann, 2000, pp. 6-7).

Rather than retreat to the distance of anonymity, a silent idiom that engenders only suspicion, the girl personalises each of the soldiers in a catholic language of her own. And again, this explains McCann's formal logic – he relates this incident within the abbreviated form of the short story, but tellingly does so through the narrative device of the first-person testimony of an adolescent. The language of the young girl, then, suggests the possibility of hope through its very playfulness, yet it is not entirely the language of childhood. Nested within her colloquial attribution of names are the murmurings of an autonomous adolescent female sexuality, an energy that has traditionally been diagnosed as politically, culturally and morally subversive. In her father's jaundiced view, Kate's sexuality is to be protected and fenced off from the contaminating advances of these British soldiers. In the apparently conciliatory gesture of offering her the warmth of a British army jacket, Kate's father divines an ulterior, transgressive intent, 'LongGrasses was standing beside me and he put Stevie's jacket on my shoulders to warm me, but then Father came over and he pushed LongGrasses away. Father pushed hard' (McCann, 2000, p. 8). Rather than permit his daughter to be shrouded in the protective garments of this illegitimate occupying force, the father is driven to exact violence. Clearly the episode has multiple ideological resonances; the girl's emergent womanly body is transformed into a political document onto which the competing ideological freights of the 'Troubles' are projected. Furthermore, the scene is an enactment of a prevailing patriarchal authority, under which the girl's body is subservient to the contestatory designs of two male figures.

The most significant aspect of the passage cited above is, however, the girl's referral to one of the soldiers as 'Stevie'; during the rescue operation she has learned his real Christian name and is suitably impressed with his strident efforts to save the draft horse. As a consequence, she invites the group of soldiers to return to her house for tea and in order to dry off, an invitation that understandably infuriates her already indignant father. The other soldiers either remain anonymous or retain their nicknames, but Stevie emerges from the ideological confines of his uniform, his rank and his accent and a brief, but effective, drama of coy flirtation ensues between Katie and him. The theatre for this furtive action is within the domestic geography of a rural Catholic family, a kitchen in which a half dozen British soldiers are sharing tea with an embittered widower and his daughter. What is striking is that the usual scenario in which such a group would be together in such circumstances is under a violently intrusive operation of counter-insurgency, a security search. Predictably, perhaps, the father's belligerent attitude and equivalent remarks provoke one of the soldiers and the scene does, in fact, conclude with a reversion to type. The episodic flirtation between Katie and Stevie is bracketed between two acts of ideological assertion. As we have seen it ends with a sectarian argument, but our first description of the interior of the house, as the men wait for their tea, is of Katie meticulously preparing her father's brew:

> Father likes his tea without bags like Mammy used to make and so there is a special way for me to make it – put cold cold water in the kettle and only cold then boil it then put a small boiling water in the teapot and swish it around until the bottom of the teapot is warm. Then put in tea leaves not bags and then the boiling water and stir it all very slowly and

put on the tea cosy and let it stew for five minutes making sure the flame is not too high so the tea cosy doesn't catch flame and burn. Then pour milk into the cups and then the tea followed at last by sugar all spooned around into a careful mix. (McCann, 2000, p. 10)

The simple act of making tea is elongated into an absurd ritual of domestic control; in effect the girl's past and future unite in this banal household chore. She has assumed the roles of mother, wife and daughter within the domestic economy, but none of these roles, in their current guises, offers her any opportunity of escape, or of change. In this respect, the story, in its delineation of an oppressed female sexuality has a clear historical precursor in Joyce's 'Eveline'. The protracted surgery of brewing tea could easily be re-imagined as a task set for Eveline, in her parallel world of clipped domestic horizons.

However, whereas Eveline's desires to flee the cramped social and moral conditions of Dublin are still-born, McCann's narrative allows the unsettling capacities of human desire to infiltrate the hardened arteries of political entrenchment. Immediately subsequent to the lengthy rendition of the tea-making, Katie describes the energising thrill of her flirtatious interaction with Stevie; one act of dull repetition is juxtaposed with an air of possibility: 'My tea fuss made the soldiers smile even Stevie who had a head full of blood pouring down from where the draft horse kicked him above his eye' (McCann, 2000, 10). But, his smile is, of course, an affront to her father, 'Father's face went white when Stevie smiled but Stevie was very polite. He took a towel from me because he said he didn't want to get blood on the chair. He smiled at me two times when I put my head around the kitchen door' (McCann, 2000, p. 10). This illicit, and previously uncharted, exchange of sexual tension permits Katie a level of physical and emotional autonomy that has previously been foreclosed under her father's domestic regime. She felt her 'belly sink way down until it was there like love in the barn, and he smiled at me number three' (McCann, 2000, p. 11). This brief emotional transaction between Katie and Stevie provides McCann with a moment of political hope. The privacy of Katie's desires, then, are demonstrative of a secret language of solidarity, and this is a consistent feature of the entire collection; each of the young protagonists retains secrets and privacies from the probing eyes of their parents. McCann is actually employing flirtation as a political device in the narrative, a contrastive mode of behaviour to the rooted, and ruthless, passions of mutual antipathy.

The psychoanalyst Adam Phillips alludes to just such trajectories in his study of flirtation and contingency. Flirtation inaugurates a process of re-scripting, in which previously naturalised commitments to relationships, to ideologies or to vocabularies, can be opened to alteration:

> In flirtation you never know whether the beginning of the story – the story of the relationship – will be the end; flirtation, that is to say, exploits the idea of surprise …from a pragmatic point of view one could say that a space is being created in which aims and ends can be worked out; the

assumed wish for the more or less obvious sexual combinations, or commitments, may be a way of pre-empting the elaboration of, making time for, less familiar possibilities. Flirtation, if it can be sustained, is a way of cultivating wishes, of playing for time. Deferral can make room. (Phillips, 1994, p. xix)

If, as Seamus Heaney maintains, creative art kindles hope as a political energy towards the future, in this context the flirtatious act sustains liberatory impulses in the form of desire. Rather than cementing the staid certainties of their respective cultural codes, these two young people transfuse such stasis with an ambiguous language of risk. By inserting this erotically charged passage, McCann multiplies the narrative possibilities that can ensue from these lives; nothing may come of the episode, an episode that has other self-evident predecessors in 'across the barricades' fictional love affairs, but it does invite the chance that something may transpire. Equally, in eschewing the cautious conservatism of stereotype, Katie and Stevie import an element of contingency into the narrative; likewise, in sharing this series of moments they display generosity towards each other in offering a spur to the other's desire. Under the strained atmosphere of the family's kitchen, which is suffused by traditional sectarian borders, the vigorous unpredictability of flirtation provides emotional sustenance for Katie: 'Father is good, he was just wanting to dry my hair because I was shivering even in Stevie's jacket. From under the curtain I could see the soldiers and I could see most of all Stevie. He sipped from his tea and smiled at me and Father coughed real loud' (McCann, 2000, p. 12). Phillips is keen to highlight, contrary to Freud, that flirtation is a legitimate idiom of possibility, it is not merely a frivolous gesture of indecision. 'Flirtation' he suggests, 'is more than a trivial nostalgia for a world before the war. Like all transitional performances it is an attempt to re-open, to rework, the plot; to find somewhere else, in the philosopher William James's words, "to go from"' (Phillips, 1994, p. xxv). In essence, the act of flirtation leavens the tyranny of certainty, it is consistent with a subjunctive mood – a mood of maybe, and, therein lies its political voltage for McCann [3].

In *Hunger: An Unnatural History* (2005), Sharman Apt Russell argues that the physiological experience of hunger is, in fact, a form of articulation – hunger is a mode of somatic speech. Hunger demands to be satiated. Likewise, the choice of hunger in the pursuit of hunger striking takes this communicative essence to an altogether different register. Under circumstances of perceived political and/or cultural disenfranchisement hunger striking is a route through which the always already political, and politicised, body is re-calibrated for terminal acts of resistance. In the Northern Irish context, the mobilisation of the body in such extreme forms of political protest belongs to a longer continuum of somatic negotiation. The genealogies of fictions, myths and histories of the Northern conflict are all indelibly marked by spatial relations; dispute over territories at the local, provincial and national levels. With the spatialisation of power, in repressive and counter-repressive guises, the body became a focal site of contestation. As Allen Feldman suggests:

> In Northern Ireland the body is not only the primary political instrument through which social transformation is effected but is also the primary site for visualizing the collective passage into historical alterity. The body's material deformation has become commensurate with the deformation, instrumentation and 'acceleration' of historical time. (Feldman, 1991, p. 9)

Both Tom Herron and Scott Brewster have recently explored the body as trope in contemporary Irish poetry – the body as a victim of state and of paramilitary violences (Herron (1999) and Brewster (2005)). In this section I will turn to McCann's novella, *Hunger Strike*, in order to discuss the degenerative recalcitrance of the incarcerated and hunger stricken body during the Northern Troubles.

In his study of political violence and Northern Ireland, cited above, Feldman charts the ideological consumption and production 'of the body as a political institution' (1991, p. 8). Part of Feldman's project is to explore the H-Block hunger strikes of 1981 as rituals of re-appropriation by the republican prisoners. What is important about his analysis is that Feldman positions the hunger strikes within the broader framework 'of the cultural construction of violence' in the North, and does not simply draw easy analogies with other, ostensibly, non-violent or pacifist protestation. The hunger strikes, then, were elements of a longer process of somatic resistance within the state governed institutional space of the prison. Prior to the strikes, Republican detainees had engaged in lengthy 'blanket' and 'dirty' protests, both of which symbolically and literally saw the prisoners commandeer bodily autonomy – retrieving such authority from the state. The hunger strikes represented the next, and terminal, step in this logic of somatic seizure; incarceration subjected the prisoner to the routines, violences and surveillance of the state's authority, but these three voluntary rituals of bodily self-sacrifice were resistant in their excess. Rather than protest in the hope of a cessation of violence, the prisoners assumed control of the violence inflicted on their own bodies, indeed the violence of the protests exceeded that which the state itself had imposed. Under the conditions of the hunger strike, in particular, the body of the starving prisoner is both biologically terminal in its organic decline, but is simultaneously ever edging towards a symbolic perpetuity. The violence of the hunger strike protests, as Feldman details, effects a re-alignment of the symbolic order of violence in the conflict. In other words, the protests involved a re-scripting of the narrative terms of the dispute – republican prisoners now transcend all previously known, and habituated, forms of violence, and in this way strive for a level of legitimacy that is unavailable within the prevailing narratives of intercommunal or counter-state violence. As Feldman concludes:

> Legitimation here is tied to the capacity to effect a structural, ethical and semiological break with all preceding and contemporary forms of violence in the performance sphere out of which the sacrificial rite will emerge. The central conundrum of sacrificial violence is predetermined by the necessity of posing a structural discontinuity with mimetic violence through a new form of violence. Violence still remains the founding

language of social representation ...The sacrificial act can only sublate other forms of violence and transgression by the ritual repetition of violence. (Feldman, 1991, p. 260)

In McCann's narrative, the progress of one man's hunger strike is filtered through the consciousness of his teenage nephew, and McCann records the gradual biological decay of the hunger striker together with the resonant symbolic import of his actions for his dislocated adolescent nephew. McCann interweaves the troubling bodily landmarks of pubescent development, with their attendant emotional strains, and the combined performances of protest of the youth and his imprisoned uncle. The boy's masturbation on the beach is matched by his illicit theft of his mother's cigarettes, and her money. His attentive curiosity concerning his uncle's bodily degeneration, likewise, is echoed in the detailed descriptions given of the age-ravaged bodies of the elderly Lithuanian couple. The narrative action of *Hunger Strike* unfolds in and around Galway, but the emotional focus of the novella is centred on the North of Ireland, specifically the penal space of the H-Blocks. Having recently left his home in the North with his mother, the anonymous protagonist struggles to adjust to life in the west of Ireland. His accent, his age and his diffident temperament are varying indices of estrangement for the boy. And this period of geographical and emotional teenage transition is amplified by the news that his paternal uncle has committed himself to the hunger strike protests. Although the boy has never met his uncle, in fact he has only ever seen a picture of him, the symbolic voltage of the uncle's sacrifice, as Feldman outlines, transcends the limits of biological time and historical time, and enters epochal time. The mythic aura of this resistant act becomes an obsessive concern of the boy and at one point he initiates his own, unsuccessful, attempt at a hunger strike. In a certain light, the boy's commitment to his uncle is mirrored in the uncle's devotion to his own stable of abstract political ideals. Again it is significant that McCann chooses to mediate the hunger strikes through the narrative device of a thirteen-year-old consciousness, and through the compressed exposition of the novella. The relative concision of the narrative does not elaborate on the loss of innocence that is at the core of the story (as a novel would), nor does it extensively abbreviate the circumstances of this loss (as a short story would), but offers a constellation of events in which the boy gradually demonstrates the frustrations and confusions that are attendant with all forms of emotional awakening.

The journey to the west of Ireland, which furnishes nostalgic consolations for the boy's mother, is less rewarding for the youth. His detachment from his social and physical surroundings is manifest in various, and frequent, acts of delinquency: theft, vandalism and deception. These trivial acts of adolescent immaturity and pubescent defiance are marginal in comparison to the symbolically-charged actions that transcend these shallow teenage gestures. Specifically, his imitative enactment of a hunger strike, the short-lived routine of rowing with his elderly Lithuanian neighbour which is actively fostered by his mother, and at the story's conclusion, his attempt to destroy the old man's kayak. The story signals the very real, but often suppressed, fact that the conflagration in the north of Ireland was not simply confined to the geopolitical limits of the six counties. As Joe Cleary has argued, both British and Irish governments preferred to represent the conflict as a localised dispute, thereby absolving themselves and their own political jurisdictions of any direct responsibility (Cleary, 2002), and, in effect, quarantining the sectarian warfare within the dysfunctional jurisdiction of the Northern polity.

As a prelude to his own brief hunger strike, the boy exhibits a fascination with his uncle's body; however, the only material reference point that he possesses is a recollection of previously seen photographs. He calls to mind an image of his uncle's distinctive facial profile, which was 'hard and angular with shocking blue eyes; the hair curled; the eyebrows tufted; a scar running a line of outrage across the bottom of his nose' – it is a face that has been indented with unexplained violence. But as the boy realises, this image almost certainly bears little or no resemblance to his uncle's current bodily state. The dissolving body is now scripted with the resistance of the man's political convictions, his communal obligations. And although the boy can draw on no specific image that will singularise his uncle's individual suffering, he imagines through the lens of a newspaper article, which graphically details the conditions of those who have progressed from blanket protest, to dirty protest and are now on hunger strike. In this sequence we see a confluence of the boy's imaginative creation of his uncle's present bodily condition and McCann's insertion of brutal realistic description of a stark historical reality:

> There had been a photo smuggled out of the H-blocks during the dirty protest – a prisoner in a cell, by a window, wrapped in a dark blanket, with shit in swirled patterns on the wall behind his head. The boy wondered how anyone could have lived like that, shit on the walls and a floor full of piss. The men had their cells sprayed down by prison guards once a week and sometimes their bedding was so soaked that they got pneumonia. When the protest failed they cleaned their cells and opted for hunger instead. (McCann, 2000, pp. 55-56)

McCann further documents the insistent decline of the hunger striker's body when he notes, in empirical fashion, the gradual loss of weight by the starving prisoner:

> Ranged in a notebook in opposite columns:
> Day One – 147 lb – 66.8 kg
> Day Two – 146 lb – 66.36 kg
> Day Three – 144.9 lb – 65.86 kg
> Day Four – 143.9 lb – 65.4 kg (McCann, 2000, p. 72)

While, at one level the prisoner's body, as Feldman maintains, outstrips the material and enters the mythical, McCann's stark, metrical record of the declining mass of the imprisoned body reminds the reader of its actual disintegration. The medical report of the dissolving physiology of the prisoner is continued throughout the narrative, bringing a disarming extra-diegetic feature to McCann's text. As the stricken prisoner's hunger strike continues beyond twenty days and closes in on its thirtieth, extra commentary is added to the textualised account of this resistant somatic act:

> Twenty-seven – 127.3 – 57.81 kg – 110/60
> Twenty-eight – 126.8 – 57.6 kg – 115/68
> Twenty-nine – 126.3 – 57.4 kg – 110/59. Tonight the fuckers put enough food out to feed an army.
> Thirty 125.9 – 57.22 – 105/65 (McCann, 2000, p. 97)

The blood pressure of the hunger striker has now been added to the report – a narrative that gradually begins to read like an ongoing biography, or morbid medical diary. The protesting prisoner is somewhat replaced by the statistics of his declining physical state; the unrelenting slide towards death is the shadow that is cast across this newly authored biological narrative. Time, weight and blood pressure become imbricated in the mechanics of political struggle – a struggle that is revealed as callous and vulgar by the insertion of a short discursive comment about the prison authorities. Indeed this insertion merely serves to underscore the absence of discourse in this protest; verbal discourse has been abandoned in favour of the fatal narrative of the hungering body's inevitable collapse.

Moving to the domestic terrain of a rural Presbyterian family, McCann's second short story, 'Wood', explores the pervasive secrecy of life in Northern Ireland. As before, the first-person narrator is a youth, an adolescent boy, who narrates the clandestine, nocturnal activities he engages in with his mother at the family wood-mill. The farm on which the drama unfolds also functioned as a wood-mill, until the father suffered a stroke that left him severely disabled, effectively paralysed – a condition that reverberates with symbolism throughout the story, and again gestures towards the endemic inertia of Joyce's earlier collection. Furthermore, McCann again focuses on the notion of intergenerational tension – in 'Everything in this Country Must' it was a simple binary friction between father and daughter, in 'Wood' the intergenerational dynamics are more complex and fundamentally traumatic for the young boy. 'Wood' imports the rituals and symbolism of loyalism into the familial sphere. Rather than explicate the divisive contours of the spatial command of loyalist marches and spectacular seizures of contested public space, McCann's story deals with the private, practical mechanics of preparation involved in organising these events. He examines how political and moral principles are compromised when stark economic choices are confronted, and even within the remote family unit, new secrecies and deceptions are fostered under the weight of straitened political and economic circumstances. Simply, the boy is compelled to deceive his paralysed father by his mother, who sees the deception as necessary for the economic well-being of the family.

The dramatic strain is centred on the fact that the local Orange lodge have requested forty wooden banner poles to be manufactured at the mill, a request the mother has agreed to meet. However, as the following exchange reveals, there are political implications within the household: 'Your husband'll be alright with that, then? he asked. He will, aye. He was never mad keen before, was he?' While the father may remain permanently physically immobile, his political sensibilities, indeed his political imagination, extend beyond the sectarian paralysis that he sees around him. The family's participation in the triumphalism of loyalism may only extend to the provision of banner poles, but the father is alert to the divisive symbolism of the most mundane of actions. From his perspective the performance of loyalist identity and the spatial commemoration of past sectarian victories merely service further intercommunal antagonisms. The boy recalls that his father was a proud Presbyterian, but eschewed the 'meanness' of such public commemorations and forbade his children to attend the Orange parades. Here, again we see a disjunction between the generations, the father's disavowal of triumphalism and the attraction of such theatricality to the boy:

> He doesn't allow us to go to the marches but I've seen photographs in the newspapers. My favourite was the two men in bowler hats and black suits and big thick ribbons across their chests. They were carrying a banner of the King on a white horse. The horse was stepping across a river with one hoof in the air and one hoof on the bank. The King wore fancy clothes and he had a kind face. (McCann, 2000, p. 24)

The boy's waking dreams are electrified by the imagined prospects of the communal carnivalesque of the Orange parades; in the youth's yearning reveries the drama of the spectacle is evacuated of its divisive political connotations and he assumes a role within the parade as the creator of the displayed banner poles: 'Lots of people cheering and blowing whistles and drums playing. Ice cream vans giving out free choc ices. All the crowd would stand up on the tips of their toes and say my oh my, look at that, aren't they wonderful poles, aren't they lovely' (McCann, 2000, p. 33).

In producing the banner poles for the upcoming Orange Order parade the boy and his mother forge a covert bond that sees their activities shielded from his father and also from his siblings. Born of material necessity, even economic desperation, the situation casts the boy into a moral dilemma in which he is bound to deceive one parent in his professed loyalty to the other. Thus the complex contradictions of economic urgency, political fealty and sectarian bigotry in the North of Ireland are mediated through the maturing adolescent experience of this youth. And the intimate subterfuge within the family reaches a dramatic climax in the final pages of the story. On the morning of collection by the Orange Order the boy is permitted to shave his prone father. Yet this ritual that seems to resurrect a feeling of guiltless intimacy between the two merely continues the deception. The boy has been instructed to turn on the radio and increase the usual volume so that his father will not hear the stealthy approach of the collection van or the transfer of the poles from the mill.

The central tension, then, of McCann's narrative revolves around the stark physical paralysis of the boy's father – confined to bed and a routine of utter dependence on his wife and children, and the political paralysis of his community's repertoire of annual rituals. In effect, the passive, paralytic body of the father houses the imaginative possibility of political progress and hope, while the resolutely mobile bodies of Orange

Order commemorative marches, and, of course, those of his wife and eldest son, are, to varying degrees, complicit in the sustenance of political stasis. The mobile bodies of the commemorative march are further inscribed by intercommunal history and are politico-cultural texts of popular remembrance. We note the performance of community identity through the reclamation of space – the politically inscribed corporeal enacting the accumulated historical identity of the imagined loyalist community. The banner-poles, while obvious symbols of a more lateral cultural group at one level, demand, at another level, the physical participation of the individual in the confessional community. This surfaces in the manufacture, and the laborious production of the object; subsequently, in its symbolic transformation through detailed decoration, and finally, in the somatic articulation of the banner-pole bearer during the Orange Order parade.

In his critical reflections on the nature of the short story, the American author, Raymond Carver, a contemporary master of the genre in his own right, consistently accented the necessity of menace to the dramatic success of short fiction. Most memorably in his revealing essay 'On Writing', Carver argued:

> I like it when there is some feeling of threat or sense of menace in short stories. I think a little menace is fine to have in a story. For one thing, it's good for the circulation. There has to be tension, a sense that something is imminent, that certain things are in relentless motion, or else, most often, there simply won't be a story. What creates tension in a piece of fiction is partly the way the concrete words are linked together to make up the visible action of the story. But it's also the things that are left out, that are implied, the landscape just under the smooth (but sometimes broken and unsettled) surface of things. (Carver, 1984, p. 17)

In this sense, it seems entirely apposite for McCann to operate within the abbreviated literary parameters of the genre. We are offered cursory glimpses of ordinary lives lived within or adjacent to the crucibles of the Northern conflict. Each of the youthful characters in *Everything in This Country Must* operates in an environment that is uncharted and enigmatic – each is confronted with an emotional and physical situation that harbours potential threat. Similarly the incendiary unpredictability of the Northern crisis, primarily evidenced in the seeming random nature of violence, is played out *in parvo* within the adolescent dramas of McCann's protagonists. Through the recurring motif of the body, initially the fractioned body of the victim, and subsequently, the emergent sexual, the prone paralytic, and the resistant starving bodies, McCann's narratives foreground the methods through which the political extremities of the Troubles were scripted onto the carceral. Nevertheless, it is possible, as I have outlined, to divine moments of hope or of imagination in the stories beyond the foreshortened mindscapes of sectarianism.

Notes

[1] On these two works by McLaverty see Sophia Hillan, (2005) 'Wintered Into Wisdom: Michael McLaverty and Seamus Heaney, and the Northern Word-Hoard', *New Hibernia Review*, (9) 3, pp. 86-106.

[2] The dysfunctional family unit is a feature that, again, is apparent in Joyce's *Dubliners*.

[3] Naturally, from a feminist viewpoint, it can be argued that this heterosexual flirtation is merely another device in the service of a further system of inter-sexual repression, which will incarcerate Katie's sexuality within new constraints. However, this line of questioning is not my concern in the current essay.

References

Brewster, S. (2005), 'Rites of Defilement: Abjection and the Body Politic in Northern Irish Poetry', *Irish University Review*, 35 (2), pp. 304-19.

Carver, R. (1984), *Fires: Essays, Poems, Stories,* Vintage Books, New York.

Cleary, J. (2002), *Literature, Partition and the Nation State: Culture and Conflict in Ireland, Israel and Palestine,* Cambridge University Press, Cambridge.

Feldman, A. (1991), *Formations of Violence: The Narrative of the Body and Political Terror in Northern Ireland,* University of Chicago Press, Chicago and London.

Franco, J. (1985), 'Killing Priests, Nuns, Women, Children', *On Signs,* ed. M. Blonsky, Johns Hopkins University Press, Baltimore, pp. 414-20.

Heaney, S. (1996), *The Spirit Level*, Faber & Faber, London.

Herron, T. (1999), '"The Body's in the Post": Contemporary Irish Poetry and the Dispersed Body', *Ireland and Cultural Theory: The Mechanics of Authenticity,* ed. C. Graham and R. Kirkland, Macmillan, Basingstoke, pp. 193-209.

Hillan, S. (2005), 'Wintered Into Wisdom: Michael McLaverty and Seamus Heaney, and the Northern Word-Hoard', *New Hibernia Review*, 9 (3), pp. 86-106.

McCann, C. (1994), *Fishing the Sloe-Black River,* Phoenix House, London.

McCann, C. (2000), *Everything in This Country Must*, Phoenix House, London.

McDonald, R. (2005), 'Strategies of Silence: Colonial Strains in Short Stories of the Troubles', *The Yearbook of English Studies* 35 (1), pp. 249-63.

Phillips, A. (1994) *On Flirtation*, Faber & Faber, London.

Russell, S. Apt. (2005), *Hunger: An Unnatural History* Basic Books, New York.

Storey, M. (2004), *Representing the Troubles in Irish Short Fiction,* Catholic University of America Press, Washington.

Notes on the Contributors

Pilar Villar Argáiz
Pilar Villar Argáiz is a Lecturer in English Philology at the University of Granada, Spain, where she obtained a European Doctorate in English Studies (Irish Literature). She is the author of *Eavan Boland's Evolution as an Irish Woman Poet: An Outsider within an Outsider's Culture* (2007) and *The Poetry of Eavan Boland: A Postcolonial Reading* (2007). She has also published extensively on the representation of femininity in contemporary Irish women's poetry, on cinematic representations of Ireland, and on the theoretical background and application of feminism and postcolonialism to the study of Irish literature. In addition, Dr Villar Argáiz has co-edited *Literature and Theatre in Crosscultural Encounters: A Festschrift for ISCLT at Thirty* (2006).

Brian Burton
Brian Burton is a Visiting Lecturer in English at the University of Sunderland and an Associate Lecturer at the Open University. He has previously taught at the University of Durham and in further education. His interests include twentieth-century British and Irish verse, poetry of the North East, and existentialist literature. He has published articles on Derek Mahon, Samuel Beckett, and Gérard de Nerval. Dr Burton is currently working on studies of Basil Bunting and A. C. Swinburne.

Ulf Dantanus
Ulf Dantanus is the Director of the Gothenburg Programme at the University of Sussex. His main area of research is contemporary Irish literature. He is the author of *Brian Friel: A Study* (1988) and a contributor to *The Oxford Companion to Irish Literature* (1996) and *A Companion to Brian Friel* (2002). He has also published many reviews and articles in the field of Irish Studies: on James Joyce, William Trevor, W. B. Yeats, Seamus Heaney, Brian Friel and others.

Peter Dempsey
Peter Dempsey is Senior Lecturer in English at the University of Sunderland. He teaches contemporary fiction and has published articles on US authors including William Gaddis, Sara Paretsky and David Markson. He has co-edited a collection of essays on the American novelist Richard Powers to be published in 2008.

Monica Facchinello

Monica Facchinello is a Visiting Research Fellow in the Italian Department at the University of Leeds, where she is working on a comparative project which explores the fraught notions of home and belonging in twentieth-century Irish and Sardinian novelists. She recently completed a PhD thesis on John Banville in the Department of English and Related Literature at the University of York, under the supervision of Hugh Haughton. Her article, 'John Banville's *Doctor Copernicus* and *Kepler*' appeared in *Global Ireland* (ed's Pilný and Wallace, 2005).

Eóin Flannery

Eóin Flannery is Lecturer in English at Oxford Brookes University. He is the author of two books: *Versions of Ireland: Empire, Modernity and Resistance in Irish Culture* (2006) and *Fanon's One Big Idea: Ireland and Postcolonial Studies* (2008), and he has also edited two books: *Enemies of Empire: New Perspectives on Imperialism, Literature and Historiography* (2007) and *Ireland in Focus: Film, Photography and Popular Culture* (2008).

Wei H. Kao

Wei H. Kao, after receiving his doctorate from the University of Kent, now lectures at National Taiwan University. His articles on Irish women novelists and dramatists have appeared in *Moving Worlds: A Journal of Transcultural Writings*, *Journal of Beckett Studies* and *Fu-Jen Studies*, amongst others. He is the author of a monograph, *The Formation of an Irish Literary Canon in the Mid-Twentieth Century* (2007). A comparative study of Irish and world literatures will be forthcoming.

Paddy Lyons

Paddy Lyons lectures in English literature at the University of Glasgow, where he is Irish Literature convenor, and he holds a personal chair in English Studies at the University of Warsaw. He has published on Restoration theatre and on the poet Rochester, on literary theory, on twentieth-century fiction, and on Irish literature. As well as editing several volumes of conference papers and various journals, his editorial work includes *Congreve's Comedies* (1982), *Female Playwrights of the Restoration* (1991), Rochester's *Complete Poems and Plays* (1993), and *Complete Poems* (1996), and the 1818 text of Mary Shelley's *Frankenstein* (1992). He has also written on the psycho-linguistics of mass literacy, and is a translator of Louis Althusser.

Eamon Maher

Eamon Maher is Director of the National Centre for Franco-Irish Studies at the Institute of Technology, Tallaght, Dublin. He is the General Editor, with Grace Neville and Eugene O'Brien, of the *Studies in Franco-Irish Relations* annual book series. He has published and edited several books, including *John McGahern: From the Local to the Universal* (2003); *Crosscurrents and Confluences: Echoes of Religion in 20th-Century Fiction* (2000); with Eugene O'Brien, *La France face à la mondialisation/France and the Struggle Against Globalization* (2007); with Louise Fuller and John Littleton, *Irish and Catholic? Towards an Understanding of Identity* (2006); with Grace Neville, *France-Ireland: Anatomy of a Relationship* (2004). He is currently working on a study dealing with Catholicism in the life and works of John McGahern.

Willy Maley

Willy Maley is Professor of Renaissance Studies at the University of Glasgow, Fellow of the English Association (FEA), and Visiting Professor at the University of Sunderland. He is the author of *A Spenser Chronology* (1994), *Salvaging Spenser: Colonialism, Culture and Identity* (1997), and *Nation, State and Empire in English Renaissance Literature: Shakespeare to Milton* (2003). He is editor, with Andrew Hadfield, of *A View of the Present State of Ireland: From the First Published Edition* (1997). He has also edited five collections of essays: with Brendan Bradshaw and Andrew Hadfield, *Representing Ireland: Literature and the Origins of Conflict, 1534-1660* (1993); with Bart Moore-Gilbert and Gareth Stanton, *Postcolonial Criticism* (1997); with David J. Baker, *British Identities and English Renaissance Literature* (2002); with Andrew Murphy, *Shakespeare and Scotland* (2004); and with Alex Benchimol, *Spheres of Influence: Intellectual and Cultural Publics from Shakespeare to Habermas* (2007).

Alison O'Malley-Younger

Alison O'Malley-Younger is Senior Lecturer in English and Drama at the University of Sunderland. With John Strachan, she founded the annual Irish Studies conferences at Sunderland in 2002 and she is the Director of the North East Irish Cultural Network. She is a Board member of the British Association of Irish Studies. She has published in the fields of contemporary critical theory, women's writing in Ireland and contemporary Irish Drama. She has recently completed a monograph entitled *Brian Friel's Liminal Drama* and her *Drama: Text and Performance* is forthcoming from Edinburgh University Press. Dr O'Malley-Younger has edited, with Frank Beardow, *Representing Ireland: Past, Present and Future* (2005). Her current research project is *Stage Irishness, Ireland and the Colonial Gaze*, a study of the Irish works of the playwright Dionysus Lantner Boucicault.

Gareth Reeves

Gareth Reeves is Reader in English at the University of Durham. He is the author of two books on Eliot, *T. S. Eliot: A Virgilian Poet* (1989) and *T. S. Eliot's 'The Waste Land'* (1994) for Harvester's Critical Studies of Key Texts series, and of *The Thirties Poetry: Auden, MacNeice, Spender*, with Michael O'Neill (1992). He is the author of two volumes of poetry, *Real Stories* (1984) and *Listening In* (1993), and of many essays on twentieth-century English and American poetry.

Daniel W. Ross

Daniel W. Ross is Professor of English at Columbus State University in Columbus, Georgia, where he teaches Victorian literature, modern British literature, and Irish literature. He is the editor of *The Critical Response to William Styron* (1995). He has published on a variety of authors in addition to Styron, including Shakespeare, Wordsworth, Conrad, and Alice Walker. In recent years his research has focused on Irish literature, resulting in articles in several journals and collections on Seamus Heaney and Seamus Deane.

John Strachan

John Strachan is Professor of English at the University of Sunderland. With Alison O'Malley-Younger, he established the annual Irish Studies conferences at Sunderland in 2002 and he is a founding member of the North East Irish Cultural Network. A Romanticist, his books and editions include *Parodies of the Romantic Age* (1999), *Poetry* (2000), *British Satire 1785-1840* (2003), Leigh Hunt's *Poetical Works* (2003), *The Routledge Complete Critical Guide to the Poems of John Keats* (2004), *Blackwood's Edinburgh Magazine: Selected Criticism 1820-1825* (2006) and *Advertising and Satirical Culture in the Romantic Period* (2007). Professor Strachan is the Associate Editor for Romanticism for the seventh edition of *The Oxford Companion to English Literature* (to be published in 2009).

Index

A
Achebe, Chinua 87
Adair, Gilbert 11
   The Act of Roger Murgatroyd 11
Adams, Robert N. 14
Adamson, Ian 135
'AE' *See* Russell, George
Althusser, Louis xiii, 61, 66, 68, 72
Anderson, Benedict 150
Andrews, Elmer 55, 98
   The Art of Brian Friel 82
Ariosto 97
Arnold, Matthew 50
Arrowsmith, Aidan 108
Atfield, Rose 107
Auden, W. H. 25, 136, 138-39
   'Consider this and in our time' 138

B
Badiou, Alain xiii, 61, 63
Banville, John xv, **121-33**
   Birchwood 122
   Doctor Copernicus 122
   Eclipse 132
   Kepler 122
   The Newton Letter 11, 121-33
   The Sea 132
   The Untouchable 132
Barclay, William 40
BBC 159
Beck, Warren 14
Beckett, Samuel xi, xiii, 20, 26, 88, 108, 130, 131, 133 n4
   'Dante and the Lobster' 20
   How It Is 131
   Krapp's Last Tape 60, 61
   'Three Dialogues' 131
   Waiting for Godot 84
Bellow, Saul 6

Bertha, Csilla 77, 84
   'Brian Friel as Postcolonial Playwright' 77
Bhabha, Homi K. xiv, 78, 82, 84, 107, 108, 115
Bible, The 40, 41
   see also Jesus Christ; parable
Big House 43, 122, 124
'Bloody Sunday' 86
Boehmer, Elleke xv, 107, 108
Boland, Eavan xv, **107-18**
   'The Achill Woman' 118 n2
   'Mise Eire' 111-14, 117
   'Mother Ireland' 111, 114-17
   Outside History 118 n2
   'Outside History' 118 n2
   The War Horse 116
   'We are Always too Late' 118 n2
   'The Weasel's Tooth' 116
Bolger, Dermot 57, 166
   The Journey Home 166
Booker Prize 157
   see also Man Booker Prize
Borges, Jorge Luis 20, 39
   'Partial Magic in the Quixote' 20
Botticelli 130
   Birth of Venus 130, 132
Bowen, Elizabeth 124
Brandabur, Edward 14, 19
Brecht, Bertolt 66, 83
   The Life of Galileo 66
Brewster, Scott 177
British Royal National Theatre 87
Broadway 87
Brooke, Rupert 140
Brookeborough, Lord 140
Brown, Terence 27
Brunsdale, Mitzi 14
Butler, Hubert 125
   Independent Spirit 125
Butler, Mary 50

C
Cailleach Bhéarra 113
Cairns, David 79
   see also Richards, Shaun; *Writing Ireland*
Calvino, Italo 8, 39
Cambridge Companion to Brian Friel 77, 84
Carleton, William 167
Carver, Raymond 182
   'On Writing' 182
Casey, Bishop Eamonn 164

Catholicism xvi, 2, 4, 6-7, 12-13, 14, 26-27, 49-50, 70, 88, 127, 128, 143, 144, 145-47, 148-49, 150, 152, 158, 159, 172, 174
    see also nationalism; republicanism
Catholic Nationalism 143
Celtic Revival 112
Celtic Tiger 163, 167
Celtic Twilight 35
censorship 18
Chekhov, Anton 18, 72
    'The Lady with the Lapdog' 72
Children of Lír 170
civil rights 86, 144
civil war 41
class consciousness 157-58, 165-66
Cleary, Joe 79, 81, 85, 178
Clinton, Bill 86
colonialism 31-32, 34, 44, 57, 80, 135, 147-48, 158, 173
    see also post-colonialism
Connolly, Claire xii
Corbett, Tony 82
    Brian Friel: Decoding the Language of the Tribe 82
Corcoran, Neil 95
Corrington, John William 18
Cronin, Michael 158, 165-66
cultural identity xii, 108, 109, 110-11, 114, 117, 145-46, 150-51, 153
    see also essentialism; Irishness

D

Dantanus, Ulf 57
Dante Alighieri xiv, 13, **93-99**
    Divina Commedia (*Divine Comedy*) 13, 18, 93-98
'Dark Rosaleen' 70, 71, 116, 147
    see also 'Mother Ireland'
Davies, Boyce 115
Davies, John 103
Davis, Thomas 56
Dawson, Clara 140 n2
Day-Lewis, C. 25
Deane, Seamus 50, 70, 96
Derrida, Jacques 1, 9, 16, 23
    Aporias 1
    Speech and Phenomena 16
    Writing and Difference 16
Devlin, Anne xi, xv, xvi, xvii, **143-53**
    After Easter xv, 144-53
    Ourselves Alone 144, 145
Devlin, Paddy 153 n2

Donne, John 18
    'Meditation 10' 18
Donnelly, Brian xvi, 160, 161-62, 167
Donoghue, Denis 133 n3
    Warrenpoint 133 n3
Doyle, Roddy xi, **157-68**
    Barrytown Trilogy, The 157, 159, 165
    Commitments, The 157, 165
    Family 159
    Paddy Clarke Ha Ha Ha 157
    Paula Spencer xvi, 158, 163-68
    Snapper, The 157
    Van, The 157
    The Woman Who Walked into Doors xv, 158-63, 164
duine uasal (noble peasant) xiii, 49-50, 54, 57
Duncan, Dawn 79, 80, 81
    Postcolonial Theory in Irish Drama from 1800-2000 79

E

Eagleton, Terry 82
Easter Rising 145
Edgeworth, Maria 44
    The Absentee 44
Einstein, Albert 122, 129
Eliot, T.S. xiv, 27, 94, 98
Ellmann, Richard 3, 12, 13
Empire Writes Back, The (Ashcroft, Griffiths and Tiffin) 79
essentialism 51, 56,107-8, 109, 113, 117
European Union 46

F

Fara, Patricia 122
    Newton: The Making of the Genius 122
Fanning, Ronan 123
    '"The Great Enchantment": Uses and Abuses of Modern Irish History' 123
Fanon, Frantz 109
    The Wretched of the Earth 109
Feldman, Allen 176-77, 179
feminism 144-45, 153 n1
Field Day 81
    Nationalism, Colonialism and Literature 81
fifth province 137
Fogarty, Anne 107, 112
Ford, Ford Madox 59, 61
    The Good Soldier 59
Foster, Roy 123
Frazer, Sir James 99
French Revolution 88

Freud, Sigmund xiii, 39, 176
Friel, Brian xi, xiii, xiv, **49-58, 59-75, 77-89**
  Crystal and Fox 64-66
  Dancing at Lughnasa 85
  Faith Healer 83, 85
  The Freedom of the City 86
  The Gentle Island xiii, 49-58, 66
  The Home Place 80
  Living Quarters 66-67
  Losers 63
  The Loves of Cass McGuire 83, 84
  Molly Sweeney 61, 85
  Translations 67-71, 75, 79-89
  Winners 62-63
  Wonderful Tennessee 83-84, 85, 87, 88, 89
  The Yalta Game 71-75
Frost, Robert 40
Fugard, Athol 81
  Boesman and Lena 81
Fulford, Sarah 107

G

Gaelic place names 83
Gellner, Ernest 49
gender identity xv, 25, 5, 108-11, 113-14, 115, 117, 143-53
Genette, Gerard 17, 21
Gilbert, Sandra M. 115
Girard, Rene 52
Gladstone, William Ewart 4, 8
Goethe, Johann Wolfgang von 4, 127, 132
  Elective Affinities 127
Graham, Colin 109, 110, 117
  'Post-Nationalism/Post-Colonialism: Reading Irish Culture' 109
Gray, Thomas 64
  'Elegy Written in a Country Churchyard' 64
Gregory, Lady Augusta 50
Gregory, Robert 139
Gubar, Susan 115
Guha, Ranajit 154 n4

H

H-Blocks 177, 179
  see also hunger striking
Hall, Stuart 108, 114
Harris, Susan Cannon 52, 54
Heaney, Seamus xi, xiii, xiv-xv, 36, 40, 50, 71, **93-104**, 176
  'An Afterwards' 94
  'Bann Valley Eclogue' 104
  'Crossings' 98-99
  Electric Light 104
  'Envies and Identifications: Dante and the Modern Poet' 94, 95
  Field Work 94, 100
  'The First Flight' 97
  'Follower' 101
  'The Golden Bough' 99-101
  'Keeping Going' 171
  'The Loaning' 96-97
  'Man and Boy' 101-2
  'Punishment' 70, 96
  'A Retrospect' 102-3, 104
  'Sandstone Keepsake' 96
  Seeing Things 98, 99, 100, 101, 102
  'Squarings' 98, 104
  Station Island 96, 100
  'Station Island' 93, 98, 99, 102
  'The Strand at Lough Beg' xiv, 93, 94
  'The Tollund Man' 101
  'Trail of Tears' xiv-xv, 103
  'Triptych' 100
  'Ugolino' 95-96
  'The Underground' 100
Hegel, Georg Wilhelm Friedrich 137
  The Philosophy of Right 137
Herron, Tom 1677
Hewitt, John 34
  'Once Alien Here' 34
Hillan, Sophia 183 n1
Hofmannsthal, Hugo von 121, 128, 130, 131, 132
  Ein Brief (a.k.a. *The Lord Chandos Letter*) 121, 133 n2
Homer 16
  The Iliad 16
Home Rule 4, 26, 145
homophobia 51
  see also homosexuality
homosexuality 53-54, 55, 66, 151, 153, 159
  see also sexuality
Hooper, Glenn 79
Hoyt-Fitzgerald, Mary 40, 44, 46-47
hunger striking 176
  see also H-Blocks

I

IASAIL 82
Icarus 29
imperialism 7, 8
Inghinidhe na hEireann (Daughters of Ireland) 153 n3
intertextuality xv, 123, 131

IRA (Irish Republican Army) 127, 144, 150, 152
Ireland and Postcolonial Theory 84
Irish Free State 86, 144, 148
Irish Homestead, The 12, 13
Irish intelligentsia 50
Irish language 67, 68, 70
Irish Literary Revival xi, 49
Irishness 49, 51, 108, 109, 116, 117, 140, 146, 150-51
   see also cultural identity; essentialism
Irish Press 79
Irish Republican Brotherhood 139
Irish Revolution 88
Irish Studies xiv, 77-79, 85, 86
Irish Times 116, 122
Irish Women's Franchise League 153 n3
Irish Women's Suffrage Federation 153 n3

J

James, William 176
Jameson, Frederic 82
Jane Eyre 41
Jesus Christ 4, 40, 43, 44, 47
Johnson, Anna 153 n3
Joyce, James xi, xii, xiii, 1-9, **11-22**, 26, 50, 98, 102
   'The Boarding House' 14, 18
   'Counterparts' 18
   'The Dead' xii, 5, 6, 18
   Dubliners xii, 5, 6, 12-22, 180, 183 n2
   'Eveline' 175
   Exiles 17
   Finnegans Wake 19
   'Grace' 13, 14
   'Ivy-Day in the Common Room' 5, 6, 7
   'A Little Cloud' 13, 18, 20
   'A Painful Case' 17, 20
   A Portrait of the Artist as a Young Man 2, 6, 7, 16, 20
   'The Death of Parnell' 5
   'The Shade of Parnell' 3
   'The Sisters' xii, 11-22
   'Two Gallants' 18
   Ulysses 2, 11, 12, 13, 16, 17
Joyce, Stanislaus 5

K

Kafka, Franz xiii, 39
Kavanagh, Patrick 25, 84
   The Great Hunger 50

Kearney, Richard 109, 110, 112, 115-16, 118 n1
   Across the Frontiers: Ireland in the 1990s 109
Kenneally, Michael 79
Kennedy, Liam 77
Kennelly, Brendan 30
Kershner, R.B. 14
Kiberd, Declan 11, 50, 70, 80, 81, 108
   Inventing Ireland 80, 81

L

Lacan, Jacques xiii, 61, 63, 64, 65, 70, 146
language 55, 60, 63, 65-66, 67, 68, 73, 75, 81, 87, 89, 93, 94, 95-96, 98, 99-100, 103, 114, 115, 128, 129, 136, 146, 147, 162, 166, 167, 170, 174, 176
   see also Irish language
Lanham, Richard 15
   Handlist of Rhetorical Terms 15
Lanters, Jose 54, 57
Lear, Marsha 153 n1
Leersen, Joep 49
Leonard, Garry M. 14
Liverpool F.C. 164
Locke, John 128
Longley, Edna xv, 8, 27, 116, 117, 135, 137, 138, 139, 140
   'From Cathleen to Anorexia: The Breakdown of Irelands' 117
Longley, Michael 25
loyalism 181
   see also Protestantism; unionism
Lyotard, Jean-François 9, 60

M

MacNeice, John Frederick 26
MacNeice, Louis 8, **25-36**, 39, 140
   Autumn Journal 27, 31
   'Belfast' 26-27, 28, 33, 34, 35, 36
   'Birmingham' 29
   'Carrickfergus' 25-27, 29, 30, 32
   'Museums' 29
   'Ode' 31
   The Strings are False 28
   'Sunday Morning' 30
   'Valediction' 31, 35
   'MacSpaunday' 25
McCabe, Patrick 172
   Christ in the Fields 172
McCann, Colum xi, xii, xvi, **169-83**
   'Cathal's Lake' 170-72
   Everything in This Country Must 169-83

'Everything in This Country Must' 172-77, 180
Fishing the Sloe-Black River 170
Hunger Strike 172, 177-80
'Wood' 173, 180
McCarthy, Dermot 158
McCartney, Colum 93
McDonald, Peter xv, 136, 137, 139
McDonald, Ronan 169, 173
    'Strategies of Silence: Colonial Strains in Short Stories of the Troubles' 169
McGahern, John 167
McGrath, F.C. 50, 82, 83
    Brian Friel's (Post)Colonial Drama: Language, Illusion and Politics 82
McHale, Brian 17, 20
McLaverty, Michael 170, 183 n1
    Call My Brother Back 172
    'Pigeons' 172
Mahon, Derek 8, **25-36**, 135
    'Glengormley' 30, 32
    'In Belfast' 28-30, 32-36
    Night-Crossing 32
Man Booker Prize xv
    see also Booker prize
Mandelstam, Osip 10, 94, 97
    'Conversation about Dante' 94
Marsack, Robyn 33
Martin, Gray 116
Martyn, Edward 50
Marx, Karl 6
Marxism 86, 146
materialism 27, 29, 31, 35, 46
Maturin, Charles Robert 126
Mauriac, François 162
Mazzini, Giuseppe 3
Meaney, Geraldine 107, 113
Melville, Herman 39
    'Bartleby the Scrivener' 39
metafiction 14, 17
Mikowski, Sylvie 167
Miller, J. Hillis 40
Milligan, Alice 153 n3
Milton, John 4
modernisation 51, 158, 165
modernism 14, 59, 60, 65, 70, 75, 109
Mohanty, C.T. 108
Moore, George 50
Morley, John 4
'Mother Ireland' 26, 47, 54, 107, 111-16, 147
    see also 'Dark Rosaleen'; Ní Houlihan, Kathleen

Mountbatten, Lord Louis 127
Mrs. Dalloway 41
Muldoon, Paul 25
    Faber Book of Contemporary Irish Poetry, The 25
multiculturalism 164-65, 167
Murphy, Annie 164

N

na gCopaleen, Myles. *See* O'Brien, Flann
Naipaul, V.S. 135
narrative 11, 42, 43-44, 45, 56, 169-82
narratology 11, 14-22
Nash, Catherine 83
Nation, The 49
nationalism viii, 3, 7, 8, 9, 31, 32, 49-50, 52, 56-57, 98, 107-18, 123, 125, 136, 144-45, 146-47, 151, 153 n2, 153 n3, 158
    see also post-nationalism; republicanism; Catholicism
Naveh, Gila Safran 42
Newton, Sir Isaac 121, 122, 123, 128, 129
Ní Dhomhnaill, Nuala 116
Ní Houlihan, Kathleen 147
    see also 'Mother Ireland'
Nietzsche, Friedrich 17
    The Gay Science 17
Norris, Margot 14
Northern Ireland xii, xvi, 25-36, 56, 57, 70, 81, 82, 83, 86, 88, 95, 135, 140, 143-53, 169-82
    see also Republic of Ireland

O

O'Brian, Eugene 50
O'Brien, Flann 50
    At Swim-Two-Birds 17
O'Connor, Frank 14, 82
O'Grady, Thomas 5
    'Ivy Day in the Common Room: The Use and Abuse of Parnell' 5
O'Leary, John 1
O'Neill, Michael 136, 140 n1
O'Shea, Captain 2, 4
O'Shea, Kitty 2
O'Toole, Fintan 56, 80-81
Ong, Walter J. 17
Orange Order 180-82

P

paedophilia 19
    see also sexuality
Paisley, Ian xv, 1, 136-37
parable xiii, 39-47, 139

paralysis 2, 12, 14, 16, 21, 39, 43, 47, 55, 56-57, 180, 181, 182
Parker, Michael 55
Parkin, Andrew 46
Parnell, Charles Stewart 7, **1-9**
partition xii, 1
pastoral xiii, 55, 104, 124-25
Paulin, Tom xii, xiv-xv, **135-40**
   The Book of Juniper 140 n1
   'The Book of Juniper' xv, 137-39
   'Desertmartin' xv, 135-37, 140 n1
   Liberty Tree 135, 140 n1
   'The Man from No Part' 140
   Minotaur: Poetry and the Nation State 137
   'A Written Answer' 139-40
Peacock, Alan 82
   The Achievement of Brian Friel 82
Pearse, Patrick 111, 113
   'I am Ireland' 111
Phillips, Adam 175-76
Pine, Richard 82, 83
   Brian Friel and Ireland's Drama 82
   The Diviner: The Art of Brian Friel 82
Poetry Review 101
Pope John-Paul II 164
post-colonialism xii, xiv-xv, 70-71, 77-89, 107-18, 158
   see also colonialism
Post-Colonial Studies Reader, The 79
Post-Colonial Studies: The Key Concepts 87, 88
Postcolonial Text 77
postmodernism xiii, 108-9
post-nationalism 107-18, 158
Protestantism xii, 25-26, 27, 33, 34, 35, 40, 44, 125, 145-46, 150, 172, 180-82
   see also loyalism; Orange Order; unionism
Protestant Republicanism 137
Proust, Marcel 20
   Remembrance of Things Past 20

Q
Quintilian 16

R
Rea, Stephen 81
Reeves, Gareth 27
Regan, Stephen 84, 93-94
   'W.B. Yeats, Irish Nationalism and Post-Colonial Theory' 84
relativism 128, 129
religion xv, 27, 94, 136-37, 143, 164-65, 171
   see also Catholicism; Protestantism

republicanism 143-45, 147, 149, 150, 177
   see also nationalism; Catholicism
Republic of Ireland xiii, 66, 83, 86, 132, 158-59, 164
   see also Northern Ireland
revisionism xv, 109, 123, 128, 144-45, 148, 150, 153
Richards, Shaun 79, 80, 81, 83, 84-87
   'Irish Studies and the Adequacy of Theory: The Case of Brian Friel' 83
   'Placed Identities for Placeless Times: Brian Friel and Post-Colonial Criticism' 85
   'Throwing Theory at Ireland' 84
   see also Cairns, David; *Writing Ireland*
Robartes, Michael 3
Robinson, Alan 97, 138
RTÉ 159
Rushdie, Salman 108
   The Satanic Verses 108
Russell, George (AE) 12
Russell, Sharman Apt 176
   Hunger: An Unnatural History 176

S
Said, Edward 70, 82, 84, 107, 108, 110, 115
Scaliger, Julius Caesar 16
SDLP (Social Democratic and Labour Party) 153 n2
Sean Bhean Bhocht 116
sectarianism 31, 32, 33, 34, 47, 176, 182
   see also religion
sexuality 13, 52, 53, 54, 129, 173, 174-76, 178, 182
   see also homosexuality; paedophilia
Shan Can Vocht (Poor Old Woman) 153 n3
Shakespeare, William 16, 21
   Hamlet 88
Sim, Stuart xiv
Sinclair, John D. 98
Sinn Féin 144
   see also IRA; nationalism; republicanism
Smyth, Gerry 157, 159, 162
Sonnino, Lee 16
Spender, Stephen 25
Spenser, Edmund 97
Spivak, Gayatri Chakravorty xiv, 82, 108, 147-48, 154 n4
   'Can the Subaltern Speak?' 147
Steiner, George 83
   After Babel 83
Storey, Michael 169

Representing the Troubles in Irish Short Fiction 169
Subaltern Studies Group 109, 154 n4
Swift, Jonathan 1, 3, 8
Synge, John Millington 50
   The Playboy of the Western World 9, 55

T

Tarien, Kirsti 133 n1
   'The Textual and Thematic Evolution of John Banville's Fiction' 133 n1
Tasso 97
Thelma and Louise 103
Times, The 87
Tindall, William York 14, 19
Tóibín, Colm 143
Tone, Theobald Wolfe 7, 137
Torchiana, Donald 14
Tormey, Michael 49
   'The Ancient Race' 49
translation 95, 96, 99-100, 101
Trevor, William xiii, xv, **39-47**
   The Story of Lucy Gault xiii, 39-47
Troubles xv, xvi, 32, 143, 144, 146, 148, 150, 153, 169, 171, 172, 174, 182

U

U2 164
Ulster Protestantism 135
Ulster Unionist Party 140
unionism 143, 147, 148, 149, 150
   see also loyalism; Protestantism
United Ireland 138
United Irishmen 50-51
United Irishmen 137

V

van Velde, Bram 131
'verfremdungseffekt' 67-68, 69, 70-72, 83, 84
Vickers, Brian 16, 21
   In Defence of Rhetoric 16
Virgil xiv-xv, **93-104**
   The Aeneid 96, 97, 99, 100-4
   Eclogues xv, 104

W

War of Independence 42, 43, 47
Watt, R.J.C. 95
Weaver, Richard 18
Whitaker, T.K. 85
   Report on Economic Development 85
White, Caramine 157
Wilson, Rebecca 109, 110-11

Wittgenstein, Ludwig 19
Wollstonecraft, Mary 153 n1
Wordsworth, William xiii
   'Michael' 39
Writing Ireland: Colonialism, Nationalism and Culture 79
   see also Cairns, David; Richards, Shaun

Y

Yeats, Jack B. 139
   Memory Harbour 139
Yeats, W.B. xi, xii, xiii, 1, 2, 3, 7, 8, 9, 25, 35, 50, 84, 116, 126, 135, 139-40
   'Among School Children' 124
   Autobiographies 4
   'The Circus Animals' Desertion' 139
   'Come Gather Round me Parnellites' 8-9
   'Easter 1916' 7, 100, 139
   Explorations 3
   'The Fisherman' 139, 140
   'In Memory of Major Robert Gregory' 139
   Last Poems 8
   'News for the Delphic Oracle' 59-60, 61
   'Parnell' 9
   'Parnell's Funeral' 7-8
   Plays and Controversies xi
   'The Second Coming' 89
   'To A Shade' 4
   The Wind Among the Reeds 2

Z

Ziarek, Eva 133 n4